A FATHER'S APPEAL

A figure loomed in front of my car. The passenger door was jerked open. Daddy climbed into the passenger seat and brushed the rain from his face and hair.

"Thank God you came. We need to talk." His words tumbled out. "Have you heard from the police yet?"

"Yes, they came by last night. Daddy, will you tell me what's happening?"

"I killed him, baby. I plugged him right through the heart."

I stared at him in shock.

"Don't look at me like that," he said sharply. "I did it for you."

"For me?"

"Well, who else would I have done it for? I don't want the insurance money, believe me, every penny of it is yours. I don't expect anything out of this except your loyalty and your help."

I swallowed, found my voice. "Why do you need my help?"

His face was inches from mine. The car now smelled of Old S̶ ̶ ̶ ̶ ̶ ̶ ̶ ̶ ̶ ̶ ̶ ̶ ̶ ̶ ̶ ̶ ̶ ̶ cause I screw̶ ̶ ̶ ̶ ̶ ̶ ̶

DEADLY RELATIONS

CAROL DONAHUE AND SHIRLEY HALL

BANTAM BOOKS
NEW YORK · TORONTO · LONDON · SYDNEY · AUCKLAND

DEADLY RELATIONS

A Bantam Nonfiction Book/March 1991

*Cover photos: (top) Courtesy of
Jefferson Parish Sheriff's Office/Joseph Passalaqua,
(bottom) Courtesy of the authors.*

*BANTAM NONFICTION and the portrayal of a boxed "b" are
trademarks of Bantam Books, a division of Bantam Doubleday
Dell Publishing Group, Inc.*

ISBN 0-553-28920-9

Published simultaneously in the United States and Canada

Bantam Books are published by Bantam Books, a division of Bantam
Doubleday Dell Publishing Group, Inc. Its trademark, consisting of the
words "Bantam Books" and the portrayal of a rooster, is Registered in U.S.
Patent and Trademark Office and in other countries, Marca Registrada.
Bantam Books, 666 Fifth Avenue, New York, New York 10103

PRINTED IN THE UNITED STATES OF AMERICA

RAD   0 9 8 7 6 5 4 3 2 1

*For our husbands, Steve and Rodney,
whose love and encouragement made
it all possible.*

Acknowledgments

Special Thanks to:
Mama, Joanne, and Nancy, for helping to piece together events that took place over the course of many years, and for their courage in allowing us to tell our story;

Lt. Walter Gorman, (Maj.) Joseph Passalaqua, and Bob Broussard, for their invaluable input;

Our editors, Tom Dyja and Kate Miciak, for helping to shape the book;

Our agent, Irene Goodman, for believing in diamonds in the rough.

CHAPTER 1

CAROL

Paradise. That was Daddy's pet name for one and one-half acres of land in an unincorporated area ten miles west of New Orleans. In 1961 our street, Citrus Road, was just a gravel lane bordered by wooded acreage and a few sprawling rustic homes. In his typical fashion Daddy informed my sisters and me that we would all be pitching in to clear the overgrown tangle of woods he called the lot, our future homesite. It seemed a formidable project to us, the three older sisters out of four—only fourteen, twelve, and ten years old—but he assured us Mama would be helping, too. With everyone pitching in, he was convinced, we could knock this out in no time flat. After all, we were talking about paradise, and what could be more satisfying than to know that we had done every bit of the work ourselves? We believed him, but then Daddy could always talk people into doing things they wouldn't ordinarily do.

For the next three years, weather permitting, Daddy devoted his every spare moment to the fulfillment of his dream. He attacked it with all the gusto that had propelled him through war in the Pacific, years of financial struggle to earn a law degree, and his decision to go into the private practice of law. He was a powerhouse, exhausting to behold. He wielded a chain saw, felling trees—a handsome, blond Paul Bunyan in his late thirties, pausing every so often to mop his brow with a handkerchief and to survey what he, Leonard John Fagot, had accomplished.

Our job was to haul the fallen logs, branches, and bunches of thicket into piles for burning. If we performed our chores at times with a lack of spirit for the cause, it wasn't only because we did not share our father's vision. He worked us relentlessly, and his determination to complete the job was almost frightening. Simply said, Daddy scared us and always had. Oh, we loved him—loved him as we did no one else in the world—but many nights he'd come home in a bad mood, and we girls would hide away in our rooms to escape his temper. We didn't have a choice in the matter of clearing the land, and none of us dared to risk crossing him.

Mama acted as a buffer between Daddy's sometimes angry zeal and his cowed working crew. She packed hot dogs and marshmallows to roast over the piles of burning debris, which she called bonfires. She administered first aid to the endless stream of scrapes and abrasions, bug bites, and outbreaks of poison oak, one of which was so severe that it required the care of a doctor and disqualified my lucky sister Joanne from further torment, at least for a short time. Mama also kept track of the baby—Shirley, named for her—in the midst of all this activity, as the toddler climbed, fell, hid, and took off on little jaunts in the woods whenever the whim overcame her. Daddy, unaware that we were considering mutiny, was undaunted by our noticeably unhappy approach to the work at hand. When the heat and humidity of the southeast Louisiana summer caused us to grumble, he paced out the twenty-by-forty outline of the proposed swimming pool, conjuring images of cool blue water and days spent splashing and sunning at poolside. "Come on, girls. Remember, no pain, no gain," he said merrily. This was also his way, to be happy and eager and funny, and it worked like a charm in those days. Still, Mama was the one who really kept us going.

Three years later, in April 1964, he had accomplished everything he'd said he would. True to his word he had created a paradise. The house was contemporary—

forty-eight hundred square feet of brick and glass. The living room rose two stories with an exposed beam ceiling; floor-to-ceiling windows overlooked the crescent driveway and a beautifully manicured lawn that curved gracefully to the street. The rest of the ground floor was spacious, containing a large dining area, a kitchen with all the amenities, a library, a carpeted bath with a lighted-mirror vanity and shower. Sliding glass doors opened to a glass-enclosed area that ran the length of the house and included Daddy's card room, complete with poker table; mirrored dressing room and bath; and separate changing rooms for male and female swimmers. The combination game room and lounge area was furnished with rattan sofas, chairs, and tables, and a Wurlitzer jukebox that held a wide variety of tunes. Mama's favorite artists were Frank Sinatra and Tom Jones. Daddy loved country and western music—especially the great Marty Robbins—but he was equally fond of classical music. We were typical teenagers and were crazy about the Beatles, the Doors, and the Rolling Stones. Though Daddy referred to our music as "racket," on more than one occasion I caught him snapping his fingers and singing along to the Beatles. Sometimes he'd grab one of us by the hand and do a little dance, a modified version of the jitterbug. His dancing was terrible, but he was hilarious; I'd laugh so hard, tears would come to my eyes.

Upstairs were four bedrooms, a sewing room, and two more baths. At the top of the open stairway, a balcony with built-in cushioned benches looked down over the sunny living room. The effect was airy, spacious, and elegant. Outside, the pool was surrounded by a large patio area dotted with umbrellas, tables and chairs, and cement walkways bordered by lush foliage and tall, stately palm trees. At the rear of the grounds were the stables, painted barn red with white trim, and bordered by a colorful tangle of azalea, bridal wreath, and camellia bushes that all but hid them from view. A gravel driveway ran down the side of the property, affording easy access to the stables.

By this time Citrus Road had been paved, and the small, newly incorporated area was called River Ridge. Gentility and the serenity of the wooded area attracted those looking for a touch of country solitude—an oasis from city life. Charming, exclusive homes sprang up as new streets were developed, ending in culs-de-sac that afforded the ultimate in privacy for the nouveau rich— physicians, lawyers, and other well-to-do professionals, like Daddy.

My father's law practice had grown in the prior twelve years. He specialized in personal injury cases and had a tastefully furnished office in the impressive National Bank of Commerce Building in the downtown business district of New Orleans. He was held in high esteem by his clients and respected by friends and colleagues. Active in the Marine Corps reserve, he spent the required weekends and two weeks on active duty in the summer, and also volunteered his services for related projects, such as Toys for Tots each Christmas, showing films and lecturing on communism to students at local high schools, and staging military exhibits from time to time. During the war years his military record was outstanding, and I always derived a tremendous amount of pride in his accomplishments on the battle-field. He'd been highly decorated, and among his many awards and commendations were the Silver Star, the Bronze Star, and the Purple Heart. As a young child I was enthralled by his stories of the war. Impressionable and idealistic, I perceived his wartime actions as incredible acts of bravery. I was very smug in my belief that Daddy was one of a kind, a truly brave man of unbelievable daring and unflagging courage. Larger than life. He became my own personal hero, worthy of my complete devotion, deserving of my undying love.

He was also a generous father then, tending to over-indulgence. Daddy always displayed a great delight in lavishing gifts upon us. The gifts were often costly, and on more than one occasion they were given as the result of nothing more than a passing whim on our part. At the age of twelve I decided that I simply had to have a guitar. Daddy bought me one, a beautiful six-string Ovation. After plucking at it for several days, I realized that I hadn't the slightest bit of musical talent; I grew bored with the guitar and stuck it in the back of my closet. Another time I got a beautiful English riding saddle after badgering Daddy for weeks, insisting that I could ride no other way. I used the saddle for a while before deciding that it was really much more comfortable riding bareback. The saddle went the way of the guitar, gathering dust in a corner. Mama felt that we were spoiled, and she was right. Daddy's answer to her was always the same—"My kids deserve the best. I'm going to see to it that they get just that."

His generosity extended to his parents, as well. He purchased a small home for them in Kenner, Louisiana, a few miles from our home in River Ridge. He was a devoted son, intent on seeing that his parents wanted for nothing. Daddy maintained their home, made repairs when necessary, and beautifully landscaped the yard. It was obvious that Daddy was the apple of his mother's eye. Nanaine was very naive and utterly dependent on him because Daddy's father, Paw-Paw, fell victim to early senility in his mid-fifties. Paw-Paw was moody and irritable, full of piss and vinegar. As a small child I was terrified of him, and I trod very lightly in his presence, just as I did sometimes around Daddy and his temper. The disease progressed quickly, and Paw-Paw soon became too much for Nanaine to handle. He mumbled incoherently and roamed the streets at all hours of the night. Poor Nanaine would call our house, beside herself with worry, and Daddy would have to go round Paw-Paw up. Finally Paw-Paw had to be committed to a home.

Daddy's care of his parents was a sign of his outspoken philosophy of life. Though we were raised Catholic and received formal education in our faith, my parents were not deeply entrenched in church doctrine, nor did they try to impose it upon us. Their shared philosophy was simple. Right was right, wrong was wrong. Belief in God was not as important as belief in oneself. Telling the truth was essential, and integrity was the most important virtue one could possess. There was one crucial difference between my parents, though. While Mama often said, "Peace of mind comes from knowledge of oneself," Daddy would say, "Peace of mind comes from achievement." He often told us, "Achievement is the most satisfying feeling in the world. You are what you make of yourself. If you make nothing of yourself, then you are nothing. Reach for the stars. They're closer than you think." There was no such thing as defeat in Daddy's eyes. He felt defeat was for losers, success for winners. He believed deeply in the "impossible dream." To Daddy nothing was impossible, because he had reached all his goals.

Now a success, Daddy wanted to enjoy what he had earned and created, especially his four daughters and Paradise—his home. Though they weren't keen on going out on the town, both of my parents were charming and gracious hosts, so we entertained frequently. Mama was in charge of entertaining. She had an uncanny knack for making others feel at home, and I cannot think of a person who did not adore her. Daddy basked in the compliments freely given by guests, about how attractive his home was, how good the food, and, especially, how lucky he was to have such lovely, personable daughters. Physically, we girls were a combination of Mama's small frame and delicate features and Daddy's blond hair. Daddy accepted such compliments as his due, asserting often that while his girls had gotten their looks from his wife, they'd inherited his intelligence.

Mama loved to travel, and we visited Hawaii with the Pearl Harbor Survivors group for the twenty-fifth anniversary of the Japanese attack. My parents were so taken with the islands, they gave a luau upon their return home. It was the kind of party people dream of having. Fragrant wreaths of flowers floated on the surface of the pool, blazing tiki torches lighted the area, a fountain of rum and punch serviced the guests, who were dressed in brilliantly colored shirts. Hired dancers in long grass skirts performed the hula, their honey brown skin gleaming in the soft glow of the torches. Daddy meandered among the guests, chatting good-naturedly. Late in the night a hula dancer grabbed him and dragged him, half-protesting, into the midst of the dancers. At first he smiled sheepishly, but he quickly got into the spirit of things, wiggling his hips and giving his own comic rendition of the hula. The dance ended, and the guests applauded. Daddy gave an exaggerated bow. He loved the attention. The party was a marvelous success and was talked about for some time. Never since then have I had the pleasure of experiencing such a feeling of family closeness and warmth, and such camaraderie between generations.

My friends often told me how lucky I was. My best friend, Becky, once said to me, "I'd give anything to be you, Carol. You've got such great parents! You live like a princess in a fairy tale. I'd trade places with you in a heartbeat." Now, when I look back on those days filled with promise, it seems there should have been some foreboding of what the future would hold, that the dream was fast coming to an end.

We seemed a perfect family, close-knit and comfortable, with the ideal father. But something lurked under the surface, under Daddy's calm appearance. Daddy had always been impatient, and his temperament seemed to grow more abrasive as we got older. The currents of tension and anger that had always run through him and the house began to rise. It became harder to please Daddy, and pleasing Daddy was one of the things I lived for.

As we girls became teenagers, our parents laid down ground rules that we were expected to observe. The rules were fair, and at first we had no quarrel with them. But it seemed that as time went by, the rules became stricter. Joanne, Nancy, and I were not allowed to use the telephone after eight o'clock at night, and dinner and homework had to be done first. That didn't leave much time for three teenage girls to call their friends. Twice when telephone rules were broken, Daddy ripped the cord out of the wall, saying, "Since none of you want to obey the phone rules, this eliminates the problem." We filed complaint after complaint with Mama, insisting that the telephone rules were both unreasonable and unfair. Mama, who was wont to avoid stirring up a hornet's nest, confronted Daddy. I greatly admired her for it. We three older girls stood with our ears pressed to the closed library doors trying to overhear their conversation.

"Now, Len," she began, "it's a fact of life that teenage girls and telephones go hand in hand. The way things are, the girls only have about ten minutes each to talk to their friends. I see no reason not to extend their telephone time until nine o'clock."

Unswayed, Daddy said, "There are more important things in life than talking on the phone. Telephone curfew is eight o'clock, and that's *final!*"

The three of us crept back to our rooms. We knew the issue was dead. Daddy's rules were always final, and he didn't like them to be challenged. When we rebelled in typical teenage fashion, the punishment was swift and always seemed to be out of proportion to the "crime." Weekend curfew was ten o'clock even though most of our friends were allowed to stay out much later. Coming home a half-hour late resulted in a month's suspension of dating privileges. Mama argued in vain that his punishments were too strict. Her arguments, as usual, fell on deaf ears. Out of sheer defiance we broke the rules occasionally. Often I felt that punishment was preferable to facing the embarrassment of being treated as a child in front of my peers.

Daddy criticized our makeup, hairdos, and choice of clothing. "Wash that crap off!" he'd order. "That dress is entirely too short! And that hair looks like a rat's nest—

do something about it!" He threatened more than once to stick Joanne's teased and sprayed hair under the kitchen faucet. His criticism extended to our dates, as well. He'd make comments such as, "Tuck your shirt in, son. You look like a slob." Or, "Did it ever cross your mind that you should wear a belt when wearing pants?"

One night he thoroughly humiliated both Nancy and her date, in front of Mama and me. The young man wore penny loafers without socks, as was the fashion then. Daddy stared incredulously at the hapless boy's sockless feet, as if unable to believe his eyes. "I can't believe that your parents let you out of the house without socks. If you expect to take *my* daughter out, I suggest you go home and not come back here until you're properly attired, young man." Nancy's friend turned an embarrassed red, but he did leave, returning thirty minutes later with socks on.

I was a tenderhearted kid and distressed to know that he would be so impossibly unforgiving, so completely devoid of empathy. I romanticized his shortcomings, convinced that something in life had hurt him deeply. Surely, I thought, there must be some way for me to help him overcome that hurt.

"When a human being dies, Carol," he once told me, "he dies just like a dog, buried in a hole somewhere, with only maggots for company, and soon is long forgotten." His words were clearly those of a tortured man. My mission became very clear. I vowed that I would never abandon him.

During our teenage years, Shirley was just a young child, seven years younger than Nancy, nine years younger than me, and eleven years younger than Joanne. Shirley was a reticent child. She reminded me a lot of myself at her age, content to amuse herself for hours. We shared a love of animals, and just as I'd once done, Shirley brought home stray dogs and cats, and mothered wounded birds that often fell from the trees on our property. I'd gone through the typical horse-crazy stage, but Shirley's love of horses went beyond that. She developed a passion for them, learning to ride at the age of six. We owned two horses, and Shirley spent endless hours in the stables, braiding their manes and taking care of their needs.

One summer, when she was seven, she dug out my abandoned guitar from the recesses of my closet and taught herself to play by ear. Impressed, Daddy would listen to her play and applaud loudly. When Shirley said she wanted to learn to play the piano, Daddy surprised her by buying a Steinway baby grand and hiring a reputable teacher to tutor her. Shirley took to the piano with a natural flair, just as she'd taken to the guitar, and much to Daddy's delight.

He wanted each of us to excel. He felt that he had the financial means to ensure our success and that we would be less than grateful not to take advantage of that. As he often said, "I've worked hard to give you all that you have. Take advantage, and make something of yourselves." He elaborately mapped out our fortunes, on the basis only of his idea of what was best for us. It was his dream that we all graduate from college, marry professional men who were worthy of his lovely daughters, and live happily ever after right there at 279 Citrus Road. We would live in a compound, and he would build us each a house. One big happy family. It was a neat and tidy package, a generous idea, but one that gave no thought to the fact that we, or his future sons-in-law, might have other plans for our lives. Though his intentions were well meant, it seemed clear that he planned to exert his control over our destinies indefinitely.

At eighteen Joanne was the first to chip away at his dream by taking a job instead of enrolling in college. When she announced her decision one night at dinner, Daddy blew up.

"No daughter of mine is working as a damned clerk!" he raged. His face grew red with fury, the veins in his neck distended. "You know I've planned for you to go to college, and believe me, young lady, that's exactly what you're going to do."

Joanne's face took on a stubborn look, and her hazel eyes flashed in anger. "I don't mean to be unappreciative, but in the first place, I'm not a clerk, I'm a bookkeeper. And in the second place, this is what I want to do," she said, rising from her seat at the dining room table.

"Sit down, young lady!" he roared. "This discussion is by no means over!"

"It is for me," she tossed over her shoulder on her way out the door.

For weeks afterward we listened to an endless diatribe from Daddy. How could she do this to him, her own father, who wanted only the best for her? Where did he go wrong? She was spoiled, stubborn, and hardheaded, determined to do her own thing. Was that any way to show gratitude to a father who had given her the best of opportunities in life?

According to Joanne, she was not doing anything to him, not being stubborn, not showing ingratitude—she just wanted to be her own person. She remained unabashed by Daddy's determined efforts to make her feel guilty and continued to do just as she pleased. For a few months she had been dating a young man by the name of George Westerfield, who had just finished a stint in the navy as an enlisted man in the Submarine Service. The times I'd met him, he seemed likable and sunny-natured. A short, slender, blond-haired boy, he was always smiling and pleasant.

Daddy had barely recovered from Joanne's mutinous decision to forgo college when she dropped her next bombshell a few months later. We were gathered in the living room watching *The Ed Sullivan Show* when she bounded through the front door with George in tow. Smiling radiantly, she announced their plan to marry and proudly displayed her diamond engagement ring to all. Although clearly shocked, Mama recovered gracefully, hugged them both, and admired the ring.

Daddy was silent as we girls chattered happily, excited by the prospect of our first wedding. If the groom-to-be didn't notice the less-than-happy expression on his future father-in-law's face, everyone else did.

In spite of my happiness for Joanne, I felt sorry for Daddy. His brusque anger, I knew, was simply his way of expressing the disappointment he felt at her decision to marry. He seemed truly bewildered by her lack of concern for her future and no doubt thought that all he had strived to do for his firstborn had been in vain.

I was a junior in high school then, and one day Daddy said to me, "Promise me you'll go to college, baby. Don't waste your life the way Joanne has. If you do, the sacrifices your mother and I have made will have been for nothing. I want only the best for you." It was then I began to understand that behind his impatience, his unreasonable restrictions, and his talk of building a compound lay the knowledge and the fear that one day his girls would leave him.

As the months passed, Daddy reconciled himself to the marriage, and by the time the wedding day arrived the next year, in August 1966, he had put forth every effort in its preparation. He was determined that it be perfect. As always, he was eager to show off his beautiful home, and he drove us crazy preparing for the two hundred invited guests. He oversaw everything, from the invitations to the food. As usual, nothing we did pleased him, and he was beside himself, impatiently issuing orders until we were ready to drop from exhaustion. At nine o'clock on the morning of the wedding a van pulled into the side driveway, and a delivery man— a boy, really—dressed in jeans and sandals got out. His arrival was the first of many things destined to set my father off that day.

He met the boy at the door. "I distinctly told them not to deliver the flowers until after eleven o'clock," he told him, his voice like a razor's edge. "You'll have to take them back."

I could hear the frustration in Mama's voice as she tried to calm him down. "The flowers are already here, Len. What would be the point in his taking them back?"

Daddy's jaw tightened, and he turned to her. "The point is, Shirley, that if they stay outside in the heat for too long, they'll wilt. And I didn't pay all that money for wilted flowers, goddammit!"

The delivery boy shifted uneasily from foot to foot. "Sir," he explained, "the flowers have been kept in a refrigerated truck. I don't think they'll wilt."

Daddy persisted. "What happens if they do? Are you going to be responsible?" His face was dangerously white.

"Len, please," interrupted Mama, "let's just put them inside in the air-conditioning."

"Do it, then. But I'm warning you, if so much as one flower wilts, someone's going to be damned sorry!" He strode angrily away, leaving Mama to direct the young man as to where to place the vast array of floral arrangements.

The band set up in the glass-enclosed sunroom overlooking the pool and patio area. A backdrop of colorful summer flowers was placed on the far side of the room to create a small stage for the ceremony. As the caterers assembled the large variety of food in the dining room, the bartenders set up business on the wet bar in the sunroom. Daddy wandered about, checking the final details with a critical eye. He chatted with the bartenders for a moment, then picked up the glasses, holding them to the light to make sure they were clean and free of smudges. No paper cups for him. It was crystal all the way.

He gathered the band members together and insisted that the music be soft and not played too loudly, and absolutely no rock and roll. After making a quick inspection of the remaining rooms on the first floor, he stood in front of the massive brick fireplace in the living room, brooding with satisfaction over the colorful Oriental rugs spread out on the floor. His eyes swept over his collection of paintings. Spotting one slightly off center, he adjusted it with a sigh of exasperation. I stood in the foyer and watched as he glanced up at the high beams on the two-story cathedral ceiling that Ida Mae, our housekeeper, had dusted to his instruction. From the determined look on his face it was obvious that he was going to allow nothing to ruin what he considered *his* day.

Somehow, in spite of his theatrics, we were able to prepare for the wedding and help Joanne maintain her high spirits. I watched her turn slowly with a rustle of silk in front of the full-length mirror in her bedroom and study herself. Her ivory wedding gown was beautifully made and a perfect fit for her petite figure. Leaning closer, she examined her face; an olive complexion, a small, slightly upturned nose, and wide hazel eyes just like our father's stared back at her.

Mama entered the room, beautiful in a cream-colored silk shantung knee-length dress and matching jacket. Her face lit up with pleasure as she saw Joanne standing before the mirror in her wedding gown. Looking at Mama's wistful expression, I thought of the wedding picture of my parents that hung on a wall in the living room—Daddy, handsome in his dress blues, his eyes proudly on his new bride, and Mama, in white satin, her sleek chestnut hair in soft waves about her face and her radiant blue-green eyes.

"Joanne, honey, you're lovely." Her eyes misted as she kissed my sister on the cheek.

"Thanks, Mama." Joanne smiled at her, then frowned. "What's going on downstairs? I heard Daddy shouting."

"Oh, you know Daddy," Mama answered lightly.

"I knew he was going to be in one of his moods today, griping and driving everyone crazy."

"Well," said Mama cheerfully, "it's all been taken care of, honey, so don't worry."

"But I do worry," said Joanne unhappily. "I want this day to be special; I don't want him to ruin it."

"Relax, honey." Mama smiled, then hugged Joanne. "It's going to be a beautiful day."

The guests began arriving shortly before two o'clock. Daddy, tall and slim in his formal wear, was at the door to greet them and act the perfect host. The bridal party assembled on the balcony. Shirley, aged seven, adorable in blue organdy with a matching band of blue ribbons in her coppery blond hair, stood by as the rest of us— Nancy and I; the groom's only sister, Margaret; and Joanne's good friend Barbara—took our places in line. Our gowns were peach chiffon, and we carried bouquets of mixed summer flowers with ribbons of peach and lavender. In our hair we wore bandeaux of matching flowers. Joanne, looking more beautiful than I had ever seen her, carried the same small, white satin prayer book that Mama had carried at her wedding. The little book was covered by an arrangement of white orchids, with several long, white streamers, and at the end of each was a tiny lily of the valley. The effect was exquisite and simple.

My heartbeat quickened as the pianist from the band sat down at the baby grand and began to play the "Wedding March." One by one we slowly descended the stairs, met Daddy and the groomsmen at the foot, and proceeded to the sunroom for the ceremony.

As I walked past the assembled guests, I noticed George's parents, Delores and George Westerfield, Sr. He was beaming, and she was wiping a tear from her eye. Deeply religious, the Westerfields took great pride in their only son, and I could tell that although they didn't know our family well, they were pleased by George's choice.

George was already in place when Joanne arrived, nervous but happy. With obvious pride Daddy turned her over to the groom, then seated himself next to Mama. Standing amid beautiful flowers, surrounded by loved ones, facing a bright and rosy future, the couple exchanged vows, and I thought it was the most romantic wedding possible.

I was an incurable romantic and hoped with all my heart that my wedding day would be every bit as lovely as Joanne's. I could see myself in a breathtaking gown of satin and lace, my long blond hair swept up from my shoulders, my arms laden with a bouquet of gorgeous flowers. My husband would be dashing, handsome, and charming, and he would gaze adoringly at me as I took my place at his side. It was a wonderful fantasy, and I was thoroughly convinced that it would one day come true.

When George leaned down to kiss the bride, Daddy watched him, his face impassive. I wondered what he was thinking. Was it possible that he was jealous of George?

The reception was in full swing as Mama and I circled through the crowd, laughing and chatting with the guests. Family members mingled with close friends, prominent local professionals, and business associates of Daddy's. Suddenly I noticed Joanne and Daddy in a heated conversation. Daddy wore his "I'm the boss and you do what you're told or else" look, and Joanne was on the verge of tears.

I looked at Mama, who hesitated. We both knew that if she went over and interceded, it might only make matters worse. Daddy could get belligerent at times, often causing an unwarranted scene in front of others. Whenever this happened, friends or guests usually pretended not to notice. It was a constant source of embarrassment to us.

We decided Joanne deserved our support and made our way over to them, smiling and nodding at guests along the way. As we got closer, I could hear him demanding, "I'm paying for the pictures, aren't I? He can damn well take whatever pictures I tell him to take!"

"But it's my wedding!" Joanne's voice faltered. "George and I want some pictures taken with our friends in them."

"Friends my ass! You take traditional pictures at weddings—pictures of the family, the cake, and the decorations."

Several of the guests were staring in our direction, as was George. Mama put her arm around Joanne's shoulder. "What's wrong, honey?" she asked.

"It's Daddy! He's been dragging me all over the place posing for these awful pictures. I want some pictures with George and me and some of our friends."

Mama turned to Daddy, still trying desperately to defuse the situation. "Can't you let her have her way, Len?" she asked. "You have enough formal pictures for now, and besides, it's rude of you to act this way. You're embarrassing her."

"Embarrassing *her!*"

Mama's face flushed. "Len, please lower your voice. People are listening."

"I don't have to lower my voice. This is my house, and I'll talk any way I want to in it. She'll take the pictures I tell her to take, and that's it!"

George walked up to Joanne and asked if anything was wrong. Joanne didn't answer, so he directed the question to Daddy, who walked away without a word.

"What's going on, Joanne?" George's troubled eyes followed Daddy, who stood beside the bar, glowering in our direction.

Joanne was very pale, and she was twisting a flower in her bouquet. "It's Daddy, George. I hate him sometimes. He doesn't care about anybody but himself. He's the most selfish person I know."

George looked at her in disbelief. I knew what he was thinking. Selfish? The man had just spent thousands of dollars on their wedding; he'd even bought them a new car for a wedding present. How could he be selfish? "Joanne, don't say things like that."

"It's true, George. Just wait until you get to know him. He's got to run the whole show; he's always been like that."

From across the room Daddy watched them, his eyes

dark and unreadable. Unbeknownst to the rest of us, he was planning to insure the life of George Safely Wester-field, Jr., before the ink even dried on the marriage certificate.

CHAPTER 2

CAROL

On August 7, 1967, Joanne gave birth to a beautiful baby girl at Touro Infirmary. The proud parents named her Kelly Lynn.

A few days later the whole family waited eagerly at the hospital to catch a glimpse of the new addition. Finally a nurse held a fat-faced, pink-cheeked baby girl up to the nursery window. The baby waved her tiny fists in protest.

"Look, George, she's waving at me," said Daddy, slapping him on the back.

"She's waving at me," George said, laughing. "She knows her Daddy when she sees him." He shook his head in exasperation. "What are you trying to do now, take the credit for my kid?"

"Well, she may be your daughter, but she looks just like me, lucky girl."

"While you're patting yourself on the back, Len," my mother interrupted, "remember this: Her last name is Westerfield."

George turned to Daddy, looking embarrassed. "I'd like to thank you for paying the hospital bills."

"Don't worry about it," Daddy replied, walking away. We followed him down the corridor in the direction of the maternity ward.

George struggled to keep up with Daddy's long strides down the hallway. "But I do worry about it. You've paid so many bills already."

Daddy stopped abruptly. "Look, George, I'm not going to say this again. I know you kids have had some problems, and I don't mind helping you out. And I certainly don't mind paying for the birth of my first grandchild."

When we entered Joanne's room she looked happy, though she still appeared to be a little groggy from the medication. George leaned over to kiss her on the cheek. "Look," she said. "Did you see the gorgeous roses Daddy sent?"

She pointed to the other side of the room. A large bouquet of red roses covered a table by the window. George stared at the extravagant arrangement in disbelief. The flowers must have cost hundreds of dollars. His own flowers to Joanne were all but dwarfed by Daddy's roses. It was hard not to feel sorry for him.

George said, "Where will we put them? They're never going to fit in our apartment."

Joanne hesitated a moment before answering. "Well, Daddy thinks it would be a good idea for us to spend a week or two at his house. That way Mama will be there to help me."

"I thought we were bringing the baby home with us. Your mother's offered to come stay at our apartment." He glanced in Mama's direction and then at the rest of us, seeking support. Finally his eyes came to rest on Daddy and the challenge there. I watched as George began to understand. They would stay with Daddy because Daddy wanted it that way. It was called playing the game. Daddy played a tough game, and George was beginning to learn the rules.

Not long after this I went into the library to talk to Daddy. The library was in the front part of the house, adjacent to the kitchen and dining room. It was the only room in the house not surrounded by glass; instead, it had several small windows. This was Daddy's retreat, his inner sanctum. One wall was given over to his law books, and the others were lined with books of every kind, including his collection on mind control and self-hypnosis. He was a firm believer in mind over matter.

Mama had had his World War II medals and citations mounted on a black velvet background and hung inside a beautiful gold frame, a present from his children one Father's Day. This hung along with several other war mementos on the one decorated wall.

Daddy had just tried a long and difficult case. He'd used every resource available to him in the three years it had taken to bring the case to trial. As the result of a tragic accident his young client was a paraplegic and had lost the use of her peripheral vision. Daddy had refused to strike a deal out of court, unwilling to accept less compensation than the injuries warranted. The gamble had paid off, and the court had awarded his client a fantastic judgment. Daddy's refusal to compromise had won him a hard-earned victory, and we were enormously proud of him.

When I entered he was sitting in semidarkness, leafing through a stack of photographs. I had seen those pictures before. Daddy referred to them as his "prize trophies." Some were of the SS *Nevada,* the battleship on which he'd served at Pearl Harbor that fateful day in December 1941, others of the SS *Arizona,* crippled by torpedoes, smoke billowing from her deck. Among snapshots of himself and his buddies in typical service poses were more disturbing images, photos of atrocities, reflecting the horrors of war. To this day I remember one particular picture. It was of a Japanese soldier with his chest torn open and his arms blown off. In the upper righthand corner Daddy had written "Bull's Eye!"

I was there to discuss college with him, but he seemed lost in thought, and it was several moments before he acknowledged me. When I mentioned that I had decided to go to Southeastern Louisiana University he seemed pleased and said that he would buy me a new car to get around in. I would also have a liberal allowance and the use of credit cards while in school. He seemed to be in a subdued mood, and since I didn't want to intrude further on his privacy, I left him to his own thoughts.

Several hours later Mama knocked on the library door, Daddy's dinner tray balanced in one hand. Getting no response, she cracked open the door and peered inside. The room was in deep shadow, and the heavy curtains obscured the last rays of sunlight filtering through the narrow windows. She saw his body slumped in the easy chair, but it was difficult to make out his features because her eyes were adjusting to the gloom after the brightness of the kitchen. Mama flipped on the lamp, then walked over and shook him gently. He was pale and seemed to have difficulty breathing. Panic crept up on her. She screamed so loud that I heard her from my bedroom upstairs. I was planning to run over to Lakeside Shopping Mall for a new pair of tennis shoes, and I was busy applying mascara to my eyelashes when I heard her. I dropped the tube of mascara and rushed downstairs to the library.

The look on Mama's face confused and frightened me. I could see Daddy's inert form in the chair. "Oh, my God! What's wrong with Daddy?"

"Is he dead?" sobbed my sister Shirley, rushing to his side.

Mama grabbed the phone to call an ambulance, but her hands were shaking so badly, she had difficulty dialing the number for East Jefferson General Hospital. When she'd finally placed the call, she gave our address and begged for an ambulance to be sent immediately.

Daddy remained unconscious. Mama undid the top buttons of his shirt and gently wiped his forehead with a cool washcloth. His eyes did not open. Shirley began to cry. The sight of him so completely helpless unnerved us deeply. We huddled by his side, not daring to move him for fear we might cause more harm. Within minutes, we heard the wail of the arriving ambulance. Two emergency technicians whipped a stretcher into the library. One slipped an oxygen mask over Daddy's face while the other checked his vital signs.

"Carol, I want you to stay here with Shirley," Mama ordered, as in one swift motion they lifted Daddy from the chair and placed him on the stretcher. "Get in touch with Joanne and Nancy. You can all meet me at the hospital in a little while."

An hour later we gathered in the hospital corridor, waiting for news of Daddy's condition. "What's taking so long?" I asked, my eyes on the large clock on the wall.

"I don't know," Mama answered. Lines of worry etched her face. "But I'm sure we'll hear something soon."

Joanne and George arrived, standing quiet and dejected, his arm around her shoulder. We were all in shock; none of us had ever given any thought to losing Daddy, the man who had always been there for us, a solid rock we had taken for granted. Although he was a difficult person to live with and we had all had our disagreements with him, he was the driving force in our lives. None of us knew what we would do without him.

The emergency room doors swung open, and the doctor, a man in his late forties with a kind, intelligent face, appeared. "Mrs. Fagot?" he asked. Mama nodded. "I'm Dr. Welsh; I've examined your husband. His preliminary tests indicate a heart attack. We're running more tests on him now, and he appears to be out of any immediate danger. We're doing everything we can to keep him comfortable."

Dr. Welsh's words stirred panic in me. People died all the time from heart attacks. I felt certain at that moment that Daddy would not live. I'd never thought of the day when Daddy might die. How could I possibly go on living without him? The thought was more than I could bear, and I burst into tears.

Mama's face reflected the shock I was feeling. "A heart attack?" she asked softly. "How serious is it?"

"We'll know more when all of the test results come in. For now we just want to keep him calm and his condition stable. His vital signs are very good, and we have every reason to believe he'll be just fine."

Dr. Welsh had not reassured me. No one else looked reassured, either. Both Nancy and Shirley slumped against the cool green walls of the hospital corridor as if suddenly unable to support their own weight. They seemed as dazed as I was.

Joanne turned to George and buried her face in his shoulder. George stroked her hair, his green eyes shiny with unshed tears.

Sensing our anguish, Dr. Welsh smiled kindly. "I promise you that he's receiving the best of care. I'm going to arrange for each of you to see him briefly. But remember, he needs rest more than anything else right now."

By then Daddy had been removed from the emergency room and placed in the intensive care unit. Visits were strictly limited to five minutes every two hours. We waited in a tiny room that offered a dismal view of Interstate 10. Gloomy silence hung over us as we sat for what seemed an eternity. Finally a nurse bustled in and announced that Dr. Welsh had arranged for us all to see Daddy together, since he'd been placed in a private room.

We followed the nurse down the corridor and to Daddy's room. The sight of Daddy lying in the hospital bed brought a fresh round of tears to my eyes. He appeared terribly pale and weak, and there were wires attached to his chest. On the wall to the left of his bed a monitor blipped as a green line of peaks rolled steadily across its screen. I quickly averted my eyes from the heart monitor, frightened that the green peaks might suddenly turn into the straight, flat line that means the heart has stopped beating.

Mama leaned over and kissed Daddy on the cheek as the rest of us stood huddled at the foot of his bed, studying him closely.

"How are you feeling, Len?" she asked.

He nodded his head, but did not speak. Tears formed in the corners of his eyes.

"I know how you must feel," she said, "but the doctor tells me you'll be just fine. We're pulling for you. We love you."

His hand lay limply on the top sheet, and she covered it with her own. She squeezed it, wanting him to know that she was there for him, as he'd always been there for her.

Daddy stayed in the hospital for five days. On the day of his discharge, Joanne, Nancy, and I accompanied Mama to the hospital. While waiting for the discharge papers to be processed, Dr. Welsh took us aside and explained that Daddy would be able to resume his law practice and most other activities after a reasonable period of time for recovery at home. It was important for us not to treat him as though he were an invalid. We were to help him get on his feet and return to a normal life. When the test results showed only a very slight narrowing of the arteries and no indication of any blockage, Dr. Welsh asked Mama about Daddy's health habits. She explained that Daddy didn't drink, didn't smoke, and was physically active, so the doctor decided his problem was probably stress-related. If that was the cause, Daddy could suffer angina, a constriction in the chest, whenever he became overly excited or upset. Mama was advised to purchase a small portable oxygen unit to have on hand in case of such an event.

Dr. Welsh prescribed nitroglycerin tablets to be taken if needed and a mild tranquilizer. For several weeks Daddy stayed in bed at home, despite our protests that he move about in order to recover more quickly. He was a difficult patient, complaining about petty things, restless, and unable to concentrate on anything. We waited on him hand and foot, but our ministrations were not enough to satisfy him. He seemed to play up his illness, basking in all the attention it brought him. His attitude frustrated and bewildered me. I didn't know how to respond to it. It was disturbing to feel that I had to walk on eggshells around Daddy. For the first time in my life, I found myself devising means to avoid being in his presence. I was ashamed of my feelings, but I simply could not cope with his constant pettiness and ill temper.

On the afternoon I left for college, just two weeks after his release from the hospital, he began to complain about the linen and pillowcases. Mama hovered over the bed, smoothing the covers.

"Why do I have these stupid flowered pillowcases? What's wrong with simple white pillowcases?"

Mama rolled her eyes at me in exasperation, but said nothing.

"And I have asked you over and over again to bring me a drinking straw. Without the straw I have to bend over and pick up the glass. I'm a sick man, dammit. Is that asking too much?"

"Relax, Len," Mama told him patiently. "Don't you think you'd better calm down?"

I felt sorry for Mama, who seemed thinner than usual, her face pale and drawn. Caring for Daddy was beginning to take its toll on her, and I wished there were more I could do to help.

"Calm down?" he shouted. "How can I calm down when I can't get even the simplest thing done around here? What am I supposed to do, get up and do it myself?"

It was an unfair charge, but Mama answered him soothingly. "Now, everyone in this house has bent over backward for you."

He yanked the sheet up around his chest. "I don't see it that way. They don't care about me. Don't they realize that I'm a heart patient?"

Reluctantly I came forward and kissed him on the cheek. Mama gave me a grateful look and slipped from the room. "How are you feeling?" I asked.

"Fine, honey," he answered. His voice was still weak, disturbingly different from the forceful, take-charge one I knew so well. "Everything's packed; I'll be leaving for school in a little while. I hate leaving you this way. Maybe I should postpone classes for a semester."

"No." He shook his head. "I don't want to stand in the way of your studies. Go and do your best for me; I'll be fine without you."

"You know I'm going to miss you, Daddy."

"I'll miss you, too. But you'll be coming home every weekend, won't you?"

"I'll try to, Daddy, but this is my first semester at school, and I'll be awfully busy . . ."

His face grew even paler, and he laid his head back on the pillow. For several seconds he said nothing.

"Daddy, are you alright?"

"Maybe just a little more water . . ." he said feebly. Feeling guilty about having upset him, I grabbed the glass and held it to his lips. In the back of my mind was the image of him, white-faced and unconscious in the easy chair.

"Don't worry, Daddy," I promised hastily. "I'll be home on the weekends."

College was a ball. I dated several guys at once, though I wasn't seriously involved with anyone special. It was midway through my first semester that I began dating Bruce Applegarth. Bruce attended Louisiana State University in Baton Rouge, and I met him on campus at a football game. I liked him instantly. He was very fun-loving and popular; only five feet six but stocky, with blond hair and devilish blue eyes. He drove a vintage 1956 Jaguar painted candy-apple red, and his fraternity brothers, a rowdy crew, jokingly called him the "party animal." He had a very lighthearted approach to life that only thinly disguised a deeper sensitivity. While he was not exactly the tall, dark, and handsome man of my dreams, Bruce was very easy to love. He asked me to go steady, and I agreed, proudly wearing his fraternity pin on the collar of my blouses.

I was barely eighteen and very naive. I fell for the oldest line in the world from Bruce: "If you love me, you'll sleep with me." One morning in early March, during my second semester at school, I woke up feeling deathly ill—so ill that I couldn't get out of bed. My roommate and dear friend, Ann, told the house mother of my dorm that I was very sick. Mrs. Alford took one look at me and called the campus ambulance. I was rushed to the medical clinic on campus, where I remained for two days, sick and delirious with fever. Mama was notified of my illness by school authorities. She came to my bedside immediately. The campus doctor determined that I was suffering from a severe bladder infection. Mama bundled me up in the car and drove me home. The following morning she took me to see her gynecologist, Dr. Samuels. I was miserable during his examination, still terribly nauseated, weak, and extremely embarrassed by his poking and prying at my insides. Much to my relief the exam didn't take long.

My relief was short-lived. Dr. Samuels's handsome, middle-aged face grew solemn. "Carol," he told me, "you have a severe bladder infection. You're also pregnant. About six weeks along."

I left his office in a daze, with a fistful of prescriptions in my hand. I had no idea what the prescriptions were for, but when Mama offered to stop on the way home to get them filled, I spoke up. "Just take me home, Mama. I feel too bad right now." There was no way I was going to allow her to find out the bad news that way. Once home, in the privacy of my room, I cried like a baby. I looked around at my familiar blue bedroom, still filled with my personal possessions, and I wished that I could go back to being a child again. I wallowed in self-pity, blaming Bruce. It was *his* fault, I thought bitterly. *He'd* been the one who'd pressured me into having sex when I wasn't ready for the responsibility. I hated him, I hated myself, and I hated the predicament I found myself in.

I had myself a good cry, and when my crying jag ended, I began to approach the problem more sensibly. Having a baby isn't the end of the world, I told myself. And you have no one but yourself to blame. Having resolved that much, I began to wonder how best to approach my parents with the news. While I knew in my heart that they would stand by me, I also knew that they would be crushed and disappointed by the news. I worried, too, about the effect my announcement would have on Daddy so soon after his heart attack.

I knew that I could confide in Mama. We'd always had a close relationship. I loved and trusted her, and I knew from experience that no matter how hurt she might be, she would never condemn or criticize me. I desperately needed her support, and it was a great comfort to me to know that I could count on her.

I decided to tell her right away. I called her to my room, and she sat at the foot of my bed Indian-style, her legs curled up beneath her.

"How are you feeling, sweetie?" she asked, smoothing my hair back from my forehead.

"Not so good, Mom." I looked at her sweet face and felt a rush of sadness inside. "I'm pregnant, Mom. Dr. Samuels told me so today."

Mama inhaled deeply, her blue-green eyes deepening with some inner emotion.

I stared down at the blue satin comforter, unwilling to meet her eyes. "I'm so ashamed, I don't know what to say."

"There's no need to feel ashamed, honey. I wish with all my heart that this hadn't happened, but every once in a while things seem to spin out of our control."

I nodded. Mama reached over and held my hand. "Don't come down on yourself too hard. We'll get through this together. I promise you."

"How will I ever tell Daddy?" The thought alone brought tears to my eyes.

Mama sighed. "It won't be easy, I'll grant you that. But he'll adjust in time. I think you'd do better to worry about how you're going to tell the father of this baby. I assume it's Bruce—am I right?"

"Yes," I admitted. I had told Mama about Bruce when we'd first started dating. "I guess I'd better call him and ask him to come over."

I phoned Bruce, and he arrived an hour later. Mama ushered him into my bedroom, then turned to leave the room, blowing a kiss in my direction before closing the door behind her. Bruce settled himself beside my bed.

Oddly, the thought of telling Bruce that I was pregnant didn't disturb me nearly as much as telling Mama had. I wasn't worried about letting Bruce down or destroying his faith and trust in me.

I didn't waste any time. "I went to the doctor today and found out that I'm about six weeks pregnant."

Bruce's blue eyes widened in surprise. "Are you sure?"

"Of course I'm sure. Now I know why I've been so nauseated."

"Have you told your parents?" Bruce shifted his weight in the wicker chair beside my bed.

"I've told Mama."

Bruce glanced nervously in the direction of my bedroom door. "Don't worry," I said. "She took the news pretty well, considering how much I've hurt her."

Bruce gazed at me with concern and embarrassment. "This is my fault, Carol. I . . . *we* should have been more careful."

"What we should have been was less stupid, Bruce. It never crossed my mind that this might happen. How's that for stupid?"

Bruce looked uncomfortable. "Look, it will be alright. We'll get married."

Married! Another thought that hadn't occurred to me. "That's just what I've always dreamed of, Bruce, a shotgun wedding!" I couldn't keep the sarcasm from my voice.

"Well, why not? We love each other, don't we?" Bruce answered, hurt.

I softened. "Yes, we love each other, but marriage is a very serious step to take. I don't know if I'm ready to get married."

Bruce was helpless. "What else can we do, Carol? You're not thinking about having an abortion, are you?"

"Of course not," I answered testily. "I would never do that to a helpless baby."

"Well then, what's left? Do you plan to raise this baby on your own? I mean, this is my kid, too. Don't I have some say in this?"

Actually, raising the baby on my own was exactly what I'd been thinking of doing. But this was the late sixties. Single motherhood was simply not fashionable, to say the least. Besides, I wasn't about to saddle my parents with an unwed mother for a daughter and the prospect of raising an illegitimate grandchild. Bruce was right. Marriage was the only choice.

"We'll get married, Bruce. It's the only right thing to do."

He smiled at me. "I do love you, Carol."

I made myself smile back. "I know you do. Go on home now and try to think of the best way to tell your parents. Meanwhile, I'll tell Mama what we decided and try to think of a way to tell Daddy."

After he left, I had another talk with Mama.

"If you think that's best, Carol. But I want you to think about this carefully. If you choose not to marry him, I want you to know that you and the baby will always have a home here."

I hugged her. "I'm lucky to have you, Mama. But I've decided to marry Bruce, for better or for worse, I guess."

There was only one serious obstacle left to get over— telling Daddy. There was still the problem of how to approach him and face the explosion that this would bring and its fallout. We decided that the news would be better received if the marriage were a fait accompli, so Mr. and Mrs. Applegarth, Mama, and Joanne accompanied Bruce and me to a justice of the peace. On May 9, 1968, a beautiful cloudless day, we drove across the state line to Mississippi. Bruce and I were wed in a civil ceremony that lasted all of three minutes. As he slipped the plain gold wedding band on my finger, I could not help being sad. I'd closed the final chapter of my childhood. I was a wife now, soon to be a mother, and life seemed very bleak.

After spending our wedding night at Joanne's house, Bruce and I went to Daddy's. Despite my carefully rehearsed speech, I simply blurted out the words and braced myself for the inevitable theatrical tirade. But it didn't come. Wearing a pained, martyred expression, Daddy congratulated us, wishing us well. Though he seemed to handle the news well, I couldn't shake the feeling that one day I'd pay for this defection.

The first weeks following our marriage we lived in Hammond, Louisiana, in a small white frame house on Cherry Street. Bruce transferred to Southeastern University so that we could resume our studies together. He enrolled in the summer session, but I was too ill with morning sickness to even consider going back to classes. I couldn't imagine why morning sickness had ever been so entitled. Nausea plagued me round the clock for the entire pregnancy.

True to his generous nature, Daddy offered to pay our living expenses. The agreement between Bruce and Daddy, who got along famously, was that Daddy would pay our bills as long as Bruce stayed in college. The arrangement might have worked out well had Uncle Sam not intervened. Out of the blue, Bruce received notification that he was to be drafted into the army.

The sudden turn of events disappointed and frightened us. The Vietnam War loomed. Several of our good friends had already been sent to Vietnam. In a calculated effort to avoid going there, Bruce joined the army for three years. Enlisting for a three-year stint all but guaranteed that the army would teach a man a productive trade, because it had to invest more time and money in him. And most important, men who signed up were less likely than draftees to be sent to Vietnam.

After spending eight weeks of basic training at Fort Polk in Louisiana, Bruce received orders transferring him to Fort Rucker, Dothan, Alabama. Daddy took the news of our relocation reasonably well. I was still marveling at the ease with which he'd accepted the whole affair when Bruce's orders for Germany came.

Bruce and I agreed that I would return home for a short while until he could settle and find living quarters for us. When Daddy heard that I would be joining Bruce in Germany, he sank back into his easy chair, grim-faced.

"Carol, are you out of your mind?" he asked. "Do you think for one minute I'm going to allow you to trek off to Europe when you're expecting a baby?" He shook his head. "I won't even consider it. It's totally out of the question."

"I appreciate your concern, Daddy, but I really think my place is with my husband."

He looked at me as though I had just dropped in from another planet. "Your place is right here, young lady, at home where you and that baby belong. If your husband had a grain of sense, he'd know that as well as I do."

Anytime Daddy sensed that others might have gained a little ground in presenting their side in an argument, he instantly reverted to strong-arm tactics. His already booming voice became louder, until it shut out everything else around him. In self-defense, I usually conceded the issue, though at times I gave him back nearly as good as he gave me.

"You're not being fair," I said, fighting to keep my voice level.

"Fair? I'll tell you what isn't fair. I gave you everything, and what have you done for me in return but blow it all?"

His words hurt, but they also made me very angry. "I knew it would come down to this sooner or later—that you'd throw it all up in my face!" I yelled.

He stared at me a moment, open-mouthed. Then, without warning, he slumped forward in his seat, clutching his chest.

"Daddy! What's wrong?" I asked, alarmed.

He stayed motionless, curled up in pain. Our argument was forgotten.

"I don't feel well, honey. I think I'd better lie down."

I helped to support him as he made his way over to the sofa. "You'd better get my pills."

I grabbed the bottle of nitroglycerin tablets from the bookcase, shook out one of the tiny white pills, and placed it under his tongue. His face twisted; he began to gasp for air. I ran for the oxygen tank that he kept on hand and placed the mask over his face, fingers fumbling, frantically twisting the valve, unable to free the flow of oxygen. I yelled for Mama, and she rushed in to start the oxygen. His breathing became less labored. After a few moments he pushed the mask away from his face and motioned for me to come closer. When I did, he clasped my hand in his. His grip was surprisingly strong for a sick man. He pulled me even closer. "What will I do without you?" he asked brokenly.

One week later Bruce received the news that I would not be joining him in Germany after all.

Meanwhile, Joanne was having problems of her own. She was pregnant with her second child, and her marriage was having its ups and downs. George just couldn't seem to stick with a job for any length of time, and she was besieged by bill collectors, the discomfort of pregnancy, and the demands of a young baby. Compounding her misery was the added burden of Daddy's constant interference in her marriage. Joanne couldn't afford a washer and dryer, so she washed her clothes at a Laundromat or at Mama's. Daddy, amazed that George would allow his wife to cart around heavy baskets of laundry while pregnant, ordered a washing machine and dryer for Joanne. The Sears truck pulled up at her apartment, and the appliances were installed. At first Joanne was delighted with them. George was not. He pouted for days, jealous and resentful that Daddy could afford to buy Joanne what he could not. Upset by George's attitude, Joanne begged Daddy to take the washer and dryer back. Daddy refused. He continued paying for the things Joanne needed, including Kelly's first pair of hard-top baby shoes. He paid Joanne's rent, medical bills, and utility bills. He paid for her groceries and dental care. However well intended Daddy's motives were, they wreaked havoc. Joanne felt that if Daddy wouldn't insist on giving them handouts, George would be forced to make more of an effort to support his own family. She was also fed up with Daddy's derisive comments about George. It was bad enough that he made them to her and to other people, but it was unnecessarily cruel to make them to George's face. She was the first to admit that her husband had his faults, but he also had his good qualities. He was a tender, loving father and a devoted husband, and was possessed of a happy, sunny disposition—an endearing, childlike naivete. There seemed no hope of change in either of the two men, and she was at a loss as to how to deal with the situation as it stood.

On September 27, 1968, Mama's birthday, Joanne gave birth to a second daughter, Lori Ann. The baby was a perfect tiny replica of George, with huge dark eyes, small features, and blond hair. Once again Joanne and George spent the first ten days after the birth at my parents' home.

As Joanne was packing her bags to return to their apartment, Mama said, "You look unhappy. Is anything wrong, Joanne?"

"No, Mama, I was just thinking about our lives."

I'd never seen Joanne look so sad.

"I think you're just a little depressed, honey," Mama said. "After all, you've just had a baby, and sometimes it takes a little while to feel normal again."

"I guess you're right. It's just that sometimes I get scared."

I studied her, resting my hand on my own unborn child. Something in her voice scared me, too.

"Scared? Of what?" asked Mama, her eyes troubled.

Joanne's hazel eyes darkened. She drew in a deep breath, then exhaled slowly. "Daddy."

There were so many frightening things about Daddy that I wasn't sure what to make of her answer.

CHAPTER 3

CAROL

"Pat-a-cake, pat-a-cake baker's man."

I giggled as I watched my dad try to clap together the two chubby little hands of my six-week-old son, Bruce Ryan Applegarth, Jr., born on December 16, 1968.

"Daddy, he's way too little for that. He doesn't know what you're doing."

"Sure he does. This little guy's smarter than you think." Cradling the infant's head with one hand while holding the small diapered rear with the other, he tenderly hugged little Bruce to his shoulder.

"How does it feel to finally have a boy in the family?" I teased.

Daddy grinned. "I never thought this would happen," he admitted. "He's such a good-looking boy, too."

I smiled with pride. My son was a beautiful baby. His eyes were a deep blue, fringed by thick dark lashes. He had a tiny little button nose and rosy cheeks. His honey blond hair, already thick for a newborn's, curled in adorable waves around his neckline. He'd been the center of attention while in the nursery at Lakeside Hospital, where he'd been delivered by cesarean section. The pediatric nurses oohed and aahed over him, claiming he was the most beautiful baby they'd ever seen. When I took the baby out with me, complete strangers would comment on his beauty, often mistaking Bruce for a girl. I was very proud of my son.

Mama had converted the upstairs sewing room into a nursery. She furnished it with a white crib, dresser, and changing table. Mr. and Mrs. Applegarth had given me a rocking chair when Bruce was born, so I put that in the nursery, too. In spite of the circumstances of our marriage, Bruce's parents seemed delighted by their new grandson and very happy for Bruce and me.

I was happy, too—at least for the most part. The only thing that kept my happiness from being complete was that Bruce had missed out on the last few months of my pregnancy. Other than during his five-day leave at the time of the baby's birth, I'd not seen Bruce since he'd left for Germany three months before. I often had the feeling that I was married to a shadow husband, a man with no real substance. Bruce and I stayed in close contact. We wrote each other often, and my parents' phone bill was outrageously high because of the weekly calls I placed to Germany. Still, while talking to Bruce over a long-distance wire and writing to him kept a semblance of closeness between us, it was not enough. It seemed to me that our first year of marriage should have been an important one, a time for us to grow together. That Bruce was missing out on the first months of his son's life bothered me.

One day, when the baby was three months old, I was sitting on the sofa in the library feeding him a bottle. Daddy sat across the room from me at his desk, diligently immersed in paperwork.

"Dad, don't you think the first year of marriage is the most important one?" I asked him.

He looked up from his work. "Sure."

I needed guidance and consolation from him, and I thought he might be able to make me feel a little better. "You know, this army life is the pits, Dad. I've seen so little of Bruce in the last six months, and I know this probably sounds terrible to say, but sometimes I have a hard time remembering his face. It's so unfair that he's missing out on seeing the baby grow. Bruce has been trying to find us someplace to live in Germany so the baby and I can join him there. I think we should live together as a family. It's the only sensible thing to do."

Daddy gazed at me solemnly. "Considering that you

had a cesarean section, it's a good thing you were here at home and not on some army base in Germany."

"I guess you're right, Daddy, but little Bruce is three months old now."

"I understand that," he began patiently. "But he's still much too young to travel that distance. Besides, you young people have no conception of what marriage is all about. So what if you don't see Bruce for several months? You two have a lifetime to spend together."

"I know that. But I think we should be together now."

He sighed. "Look, honey, in a few months, when I think you're ready to go, I'll buy you a ticket to Germany." He said the last words very matter-of-factly. End of conversation.

I stayed in the library, continuing to feed my son his bottle. I observed Daddy while he worked, wondering what he was so engrossed in. I watched as he clipped items from various newspapers and magazines. He stacked them into neat piles, totally absorbed in his work.

"Dad, what are you doing?" I asked curiously.

He answered me without looking up from his work. "I'm filling out some coupons for insurance. These types of policies are easy to get. You don't need a medical examination, and as long as I send in the premium payments, I'm guaranteed continuous coverage."

"Are you going to apply for *all* of those you just cut out?"

"Sure. I'm a firm believer in insurance. One never knows what will happen. A man can't have enough insurance. The day I go, my family's going to be sitting on top of the world."

I didn't like hearing him talk that way. I didn't want to think about the day he died, any more than I wanted to think about the day Mama died. It seemed gruesome to me, somehow, to be concerned with money and dying.

He went back to work, filling out the coupons, writing

checks for each one, inserting them into individual envelopes for mailing.

George came in, nodding once in my direction. His face was flushed, his eyes bright with anticipation. Daddy glanced up briefly at George, then turned back to his work without acknowledging him.

"L.J.," said George, "listen to this. I've—"

"Not now," Daddy interrupted. "I'm busy."

"I've been looking at boats," he continued. "I've found one that's beautiful. You've got to see it to believe it!"

"What do you need a boat for, George?"

"It's a great deal. I've got the figures right here with me."

"I'll tell you what, George. You say it's a great deal, you have the figures. Leave them here, and I'll go over them later." Daddy's voice was impatient.

"Look at them now," George pleaded. "I don't want to miss out on this deal. It won't last long."

"Oh, alright," said Daddy. He took the written estimate and looked it over. "It's good on paper, but you can't be too careful. Before I give you the money, I'll have to go down myself and check it out."

George grinned. I'd never seen him so excited and happy. "I knew you wouldn't let me down."

Daddy smiled at him. "There is one other thing I need before you leave, George."

"Anything you say."

"I want you to sign this. It's just some extra coverage I've added to your hospitalization policy."

"Sure thing," said George happily. Taking the pen from Daddy, he scribbled his name on the form. "Thanks, L.J. I'll never forget this."

When George left, Daddy looked at me. "Will Joanne ever learn?" he asked, taking me by surprise.

Pushing the swivel chair away from the desk, he got to his feet and began pacing restlessly back and forth across the room, ignoring me and the baby. Reaching over the collection of prescription bottles that had been steadily increasing since his heart attack, he removed several books from the section of bookshelves alongside the easy chair. Carefully he removed his forty-five-caliber service-issued automatic pistol from behind a row of books on the middle shelf. From the bottom drawer of his desk, he removed a soft cloth and began to run it smoothly over the dark blue surface of the barrel. He lovingly polished the handle, working the cloth between the lines and crevice of the grip. He pressed the gun to his cheek, lost in thought. I held my infant son closer, suddenly chilled. I didn't want to know what those thoughts might be.

One evening in early September 1969 I sat curled on the sofa in Joanne's apartment watching an old Abbott and Costello rerun while baby-sitting. The past seven months had been a dull routine. I worked at a health spa as an instructor during the day, came home at night to spend a few hours with my son until his bedtime, then whiled away the rest of the evening with a book or television. I loved my son, but he could not fill my emptiness. I felt as though I were living in suspended animation, my life put on hold. I was only nineteen, and my social life was nonexistent. Most of my friends were still single and dating. They often tried to drag me out to party, but I felt like a misfit, a fifth wheel. I missed having fun, I missed Bruce, and I was growing restless with boredom and inactivity. When Bruce called from Germany, I felt more and more distanced from him, and not only by miles.

I was startled out of my pity party by a loud rap on the door. I opened it to a tall, slim man whose arms were weighed down by several six-packs of beer. He had a wide grin on his face as he brazenly let himself in the door. He made his way to the kitchen, opened the refrigerator, and stuck the beer inside.

"Wait a minute—" I protested, following him. "Who are you, and what do you want?"

His eyes wandered appreciatively down the length of

my body. He turned. "I'm Mike Holland. Who are you?"

"I'm Carol, and I'm baby-sitting for my sister Joanne."

"Carol, huh? Well, you probably don't remember me, but I used to date Joanne, years ago. I remember you, though, and I have to say that you sure have grown up. You were just a scrawny little kid then. Look at you now." He flashed a grin at me.

I blushed with embarrassment and secret delight. It was nice to meet a man so sure of himself, and I couldn't help laughing at his charm.

"Do you know who you look like?" he continued, his blue eyes twinkling mischievously.

"Yes, Olivia Newton-John."

He laughed. "I know—everybody tells you that, right?"

"A lot of people have told me that, but I don't believe it. Actually," I said feigning an air of conceit, "I think I'm much better-looking."

Mike cracked up. I was intensely attracted to him, and a little warning bell went off in my head. I was a married woman. "Look, Mike, why don't you come back when Joanne and George are home?"

"Don't be mean," he coaxed. "Come on and have a drink with me."

I thought of how bored I'd been, how I had wished something interesting would happen in my life. "I guess so," I answered uncertainly.

He stayed for a couple of hours, and we chatted like long-lost friends. He told me that he was married and the father of one son, Jeffrey, then sixteen months old. "My wife's name is Anne," he explained. "We got married as soon as I was discharged from the navy. Things were good between us for a while, but now we seem to be going in opposite directions. Anne is so wrapped up in Jeffrey and me, so possessive of my every move, that I feel stifled. I'm a hell-raiser, always have been. She's the opposite. Her idea of a fun evening is playing cards with her parents. That's okay sometimes, but, Jesus, life has more to offer than that. Besides," he teased, "she has brown hair and brown eyes."

"What does that have to do with anything?" I asked.

Mike gazed intently into my eyes. "Everything. I've always been partial to blonds with big green eyes and sexy lips." He brushed his fingers lightly over my lips, and I felt a delicious shiver down my spine.

Flustered, I quickly changed the subject. "I have a ten-month-old son. His name is Bruce, just like his father's." I carefully enunciated the word *father's.*

"I noticed your wedding ring."

With that, I emptied my heart. I told him about my loneliness and frustration, about my strong belief that I should be by my husband's side. Mike was a good listener, sympathetic and caring. He was exactly what I needed, and I did not pretend to myself that he was otherwise.

He left that night with my phone number. The next day he called me at home. He began to call me a lot. And I began to look forward to his calls. I was playing with fire, and I knew it. I was so swept away by him that I ignored the fact that we were both married. I knew we had no future together, yet a bond formed between us, and it continued to grow stronger.

After two weeks of lengthy phone conversations, I agreed to meet him at Pat O'Brien's in the French Quarter of New Orleans. As we sipped hurricanes from tall glasses, I decided to throw caution to the wind and spend several hours with him at the Royal Orleans Hotel. We parted with mixed feelings. Daddy had finally relented and I would be leaving in three weeks to join Bruce in Germany. Mike would be going offshore the following day for a month as part of his job in the geological department of Shell Oil Company.

The next three weeks passed by in a rush of activity as I prepared for my trip to Germany. When the day arrived, the entire family went to the airport to see me off. We exchanged farewell kisses and hugs, thinking it would be two years before we would see each other again.

Daddy held little Bruce tightly. When the call to board my flight came, he escorted me onto the plane, his eyes shining with tears as he strapped the baby into the seat next to mine. I reached up to hug him one more time.

"I'm going to miss you, Daddy." He had directed my life for so long that I felt surprisingly panicked at the thought of being so far away from him.

"I know. Write often, and let me know if there's anything you need. I have to get off the plane now, or I'm going to wind up in Germany," he teased.

Eight days after my arrival in Germany I woke up feeling sick to my stomach. I barely had time to make it to the bathroom before I became violently ill. I crawled back into bed and threw the covers over my head, too miserable to move, knowing beyond any doubt that I was pregnant with Mike Holland's child. At first I toyed with the idea of telling Bruce the truth about the baby, but as time dragged on, telling him the truth became all the more difficult. Bruce was happy about the baby, and his love for me was so obvious that I couldn't bring myself to hurt him.

During my fifth month of pregnancy I received a letter from Mama asking me to come home and have the baby there. She didn't want the cesarean I would need to be performed on the army base. I discussed the situation with Bruce, and one week later I was headed back home.

What I found when I got there made me wonder if I could ever call it "home" again.

CHAPTER 4

SHIRLEY

A lawn mower roared to life. Its sound shattered the early morning stillness of our quiet residential community. The sun beat down upon my father's bare shoulders as he pushed the mower through the thick saint augustine grass, as meticulous as ever at the job. A stray piece of paper blew across the patio, and he bent to pick it up, glancing an accusation at me from the corner of his eye as he did so. I was his step-and-fetch-it girl, picking up small twigs and sticks from the ground that only Daddy would have noticed, and I'd missed something. He was a stickler for perfection. He inspected the property daily, always demanding that things be done according to his specifications. I'd tag along behind, following his orders. I had learned very early to do exactly what he told me, afraid of his anger toward me, aware that if I didn't perform perfectly, he would explode in a rage that left him seething with anger and me shaking and sobbing.

The baby of the family, I was the fourth daughter in a row. Since my father had been denied the pleasure of having a son, I think, he decided to mold me in the image of a perfect boy, complete with Levi's jeans and striped cotton shirts with plastic buttons. Cowboy boots would have completed the picture had my mother not interceded on my behalf, but her requests for more appropriate clothing, such as dresses and skirts, were always denied.

By the time I turned seven, I was the tomboy of the family, and my passion became horses. Sparky, a spirited brown gelding my father had purchased for Carol on her twelfth birthday, passed to me when Carol married and moved away. We also owned a chestnut mare, and my father and I spent hours in the stables grooming and caring for the animals. But what had started out as a hobby grew into a nightmare of never-ending chores, most of which required a great deal of physical strength. If I complained, Daddy pointed out the necessity of my developing a sense of responsibility and self-discipline, the qualities he admired most in others.

Soon he built an addition to the stables, with me as his helper. We sweated and toiled, hauled plywood and two-by-fours in the back of his blue Ford pickup truck. Perched on the top rung of the ladder, clutching the boards in a death grip above my head, I held my breath while he climbed onto the roof to make sure they were properly aligned before nailing them into place.

"Just one more," he'd tell me when I begged him to let me rest. Then another and another until my strength ran out, my arms became numb and lifeless, my legs blistered from the pressure of my shin against the ladder. He drove me relentlessly, and at night sometimes I couldn't sleep, I was so exhausted.

But there was a more tender side to his nature. His love of animals was evident in the gentle, careful way he handled them. It was oddly touching to see him crooning softly to the horses and calming them with a slight brush of his fingertips. It made him appear more human, more capable of caring, and it was what made me realize how much I loved him.

Memories are composed of many things—a word, an act, a certain gesture. But it is the act of remembering that brings these things to mind, the desire to store away experiences that have special meaning. Once, sitting on my father's knee at the age of five, I looked at him seriously and said, "Daddy, I don't want to grow up."

"One day you will," he promised. "But you'll always

be my little girl, because I'm the sun in your universe and everything you do revolves around me."

He could be the perfect father in my childish eyes. I was a happy child, too young to notice the underlying tension in our household. My world was filled with love, and I was safe and secure in the knowledge that I was cherished in a family whose members always expressed their feelings and truly cared for one another.

I was ten years old when the illusion died. Carol was pregnant with Bruce, Jr., that fall, so most of the attention in the house was paid to her. As I crossed the lot next door to our house on my way home from school, I noticed a tan Volkswagen parked in a small clearing in the woods. Curious, I stopped to investigate and caught my father making love to a young girl in the backseat. Hidden from view by the overgrown tangle of weeds and thick brush, I watched them lock in a passionate embrace, his hand on her naked breast.

Blinded by tears, I ran, scratching my ankles on thorns and brush in my desperate hurry to get away, to forget what I had just seen. Suddenly I felt a hand on my shoulder and struck out at it, landing a blow against a chest—*his* chest. Daddy turned me around to face him. He cupped my chin in his hands. "Shirley, what are you doing here?" he asked.

"I was on my way home from school when I saw you with her," I said, pushing him away.

His fingers closed fiercely on my arm. "Come with me," he said. "I want you to meet a friend of mine."

Inside the car sat a woman I had never seen before. Her skin was dark, her body boyishly thin. Now dressed in jeans and a red sweater, she gazed at me coolly, her left hand extended in a gesture of friendship.

"This is Marty," my father continued. "She'll be helping me work around the yard and in the stables. She loves horses as much as you do, so maybe the two of you can ride together sometime. What do you think?"

Unable to look either of them in the eye, I stared at the ground, my eyes fixed on the fallen leaves lying brown and wilted in the afternoon sunlight. Sensing my disapproval, Marty smiled in an attempt to put me at ease, but the smile seemed strange and cold, as though she were only faking it.

"Marty and I are just friends," he insisted. "But you mustn't tell your mother that you saw us together. Your mother gets a little jealous sometimes—you know what I mean—and I wouldn't want you to upset her. If you tell her about Marty, she will leave us, and it will be all your fault. Do you understand?"

A brief look of understanding passed between Marty and me. From that moment on, my dislike of her became an almost palpable thing, destined to draw a deadly line between us. "Yes, Daddy," I answered sullenly.

"Go on home now. But remember, Marty is our little secret." Giving me a slight nudge toward the house, he watched me slip through the hedges between the two properties.

It was difficult for me to keep Daddy's secret. I was not very good at deceiving Mama, who, noticing my expression of worry, often asked me what was wrong. The truth would cause her great pain, so I lied, and my guilt grew to enormous proportions as the weeks went by.

I couldn't sleep, constantly worried that my mother would find out about Marty and leave my father. I believed she would leave me, too, and that Marty would take her place. I became quiet and withdrawn, with the burden of my father's secret on my shoulders.

Marty and Daddy met often, staying for the most part in the stables and rear of our land. Marty had free run of the place and grew more daring as the months passed. She started parking her car behind the property every afternoon and sneaking along the path Daddy had cleared for her through the woods next to the stables. She lived only three streets over from our house, so I guess it was easy for her to slip over without being missed by her parents. Marty was an only child, her father a strict Baptist, her mother a soft-spoken, aloof woman. If I had not resented her so much, I might have pitied her.

Daddy began to give her things. He bought her clothes and jewelry, and gave her access to his credit cards. I often went shopping with Marty, who bought everything her heart desired. Daddy allowed her to swim in the pool and lounge about the patio when my mother and sisters weren't home. Floating in one of the white Styrofoam chairs, she would sip cola from a plastic cup and spread suntan oil liberally on her half-naked figure, clad only in a skimpy two-piece bathing suit. Whenever she had the chance, she would slip into the house and roam about as if she owned it, fingering Mama's personal items and touching other things, too.

Daddy hired several college boys from the neighborhood to work in the yard, something he had never done before. Like the ex–Marine drill sergeant he was, he followed them about, barked out orders, and supervised everything. Marty was soon flirting with the boys, wearing tight shorts and halter tops, secure in her position as Daddy's girlfriend.

Mama obviously smelled a rat, but Daddy stuck to the original story he'd given me. He told her that he'd hired Marty to work in the yard and in the stables. She was just a neighborhood girl who enjoyed riding the horses and swimming in the pool. Less than happy about the situation, my mother accepted his explanation, but as time went by and Marty became more blatant about their relationship, life at our house became a cold war. My parents began to have terrible fights.

Daddy still spent time in the stables, and I still had impossible tasks with impossible deadlines. He forced me to ride with Marty, who owned several horses herself, and occasionally we'd take the horses across Jefferson Highway to the levee on the bank of the Mississippi River. Inevitably when I returned home, I was forced to lie to my mother about my whereabouts. It was a never-ending cycle of lies and deceptions, and I was caught in the middle with no way out that I could see. And there was no way to ease the growing fear that began to take hold as I watched my father change from the loving man he'd once been to the cold stranger lurking just beneath the surface of his familiar facade.

My father's relationships with all of us became strained. He had little time for his family. Kelly and Lori, Joanne's children, had once been the highlight of his life, but he gave them little attention now when Joanne visited. He was rarely home to spend time with Nancy and me. He no longer seemed to take an interest in our welfare, at least not to the degree he always had before. His life had begun to revolve around Marty. She had a strange hold over him, something that seemed to me, even at eleven years old, to exceed the boundaries of love into something else completely.

Like Daddy, Marty tended to lose her temper easily, and her anger was always directed at my mother or my sisters. She was extremely jealous of them, constantly pointing out to him the lack of love he received, as though we had never shown him the least bit of affection. Her sarcastic comments never failed to bring out the worst in me, and when we argued over her words, Daddy always took her side.

Once, she pushed my temper too far, and I lost control. "I hate you!" I screamed. I didn't care that Daddy was there; with all my heart I wished that Marty would go away and leave us alone, leave us the way we were.

He was at her side in an instant to offer her sympathy and support. "Apologize," he demanded, pointing at me.

"No," I said stubbornly. It was the first time I'd ever refused to obey him.

"Apologize," he said again, "or you can forget you have a father."

Stunned, I looked at him, my heart breaking from the cruelty of his words. I was certain he meant it. "I'm sorry," I mumbled. To my humiliation, I began to cry.

Marty smiled in satisfaction as he placed his arm around her shoulder.

"Marty is my friend," he explained, his voice softening slightly. "You will treat her with respect and with the same decency you would your mother or me. Is that understood?"

I could only nod in reply, crushed by his lack of understanding. I began to wonder if he was still capable of loving and what I had done in particular to change his feelings. I tried harder than ever to please him, because I was afraid of losing him. It was the loneliest time of my life. Carol was in Germany with her husband, Bruce; Joanne had her own family; and Nancy, who was seven years older than me, was involved in high school and her friends. I spent more time than ever in the stables, in spite of Daddy's and Marty's presence. Miserable and desperate to please Daddy, I pretended to make peace with Marty and become her confidante. I would listen to her sarcastic verbal abuse of my family and feel like a traitor. Her greatest desire was to marry my father, and she made no secret about it. "One day I'll live in your house," she'd tell me. "And your mother and sisters will be out in the cold." It was only a matter of time before her feelings for Daddy made her interested in our lives to a much greater extent than ever before. She began to make judgments about my sisters and their husbands, children, and friends as though she had a right to an opinion. She was ruthless in her desire to bring them down in Daddy's eyes.

It was about this time that Daddy began having attacks of angina whenever my mother and Nancy left the house. I was always alone with him when the attacks occurred, and each time I had to administer the oxygen. I was terrified he would die in the process. It was a heavy burden for an eleven-year-old child, and often I'd stand vigil outside the library door so that if he needed me I would hear him cry out. Peeking through the louvered doors at the interior of the room, I would watch him read a book or magazine, his feet propped on the ottoman, a peaceful expression on his face. It seemed the moment I relaxed my guard he would call out for me, and when I raced to his side he would be slumped in the chair, his hands clutching his chest. I would remove his glasses and gently wipe away the tears that rolled down his cheeks. Heart thudding, I would pace nervously across the room, waiting for my mother to return home and praying his condition would remain stable until her arrival.

He always recovered as soon as she returned, and I began to realize that he was faking these attacks in order to manipulate her. Their relationship was on very rocky ground at this point, and I think he was trying to hold on to her, if only for a while. He did not really want to lose his family because of his relationship with Marty; she simply became an obsession he could not live without.

Carol returned home from Germany in the spring of 1970, which relieved the situation temporarily. Daddy was thrilled to have his favorite daughter back. He spent hours playing with little Bruce, and Joanne and George would stop by, often bringing Kelly and Lori with them. Marty seemed to come by the stables less often. Our house became a happy home again, filled with laughter and love.

Then the phone calls started. They came at all hours of the day and night. Sometimes the caller would hang up as soon as someone answered, but more often there would be only heavy breathing on the line, followed quickly by a dial tone. The calls were more annoying than they were frightening, but I came to dread them all the same. Whenever my mother received a call she became angry and upset. It seemed obvious to me that Daddy's girlfriend was doing her best to harass our household, but my family was at a loss as to how to deal with the situation.

Things rapidly became worse. Daddy began spending most of his time with Marty, only occasionally visiting his office in downtown New Orleans. His secretary would call to track him down. Clients were complaining; work was piling up on his desk. My mother went around the house thin-lipped and silent. Daddy didn't even seem to notice. His life became centered on Marty. I overheard him tell her that he would leave my mother; this deception set the wheels of violence in motion for the horror that would soon follow.

CHAPTER 5

CAROL

During my stay in Germany I received nothing but cheery letters from home, the only two exceptions being the news of Mama's having undergone unexpected surgery and of the death of Paw-Paw, my paternal grandfather. I was unprepared for the tension running through the house when I returned. It was a changed place. Everyone existed in an individual, private little world. Mama was tense and preoccupied. Shirley, now eleven, had always kept to herself a good deal, but now she seemed introverted and uncommunicative. Nancy, finishing her senior year of high school, was seldom at home. Even Ida Mae didn't seem her usual self, but appeared watchful as she silently observed the interactions between family members. Oddly enough, Daddy was more chipper than ever and peculiarly smug. Our home had become a house of shadows, electrically charged, much like the eye of a storm, deceiving in its calmness yet always followed by fury. The name of this particular storm, I quickly learned, was Marty.

She was on her knees pulling weeds beside Daddy in the rear of the property the first time I saw her, harmless enough at first appearance; but an unmistakable air of intimacy hung between them. I drew nearer to scrutinize Daddy's companion more closely. She seemed younger than I'd first thought. I judged her to be about my own age, twenty. From where I stood, I could see only her profile, and in the afternoon sunshine I was reminded of a thundercloud. She was dark-complected, almost Latin in appearance, with thick dark brows and the blackest eyes I'd ever seen. She was pencil thin, boyish really, with no visible feminine curves. I wondered where in the world she had come from. More to the point, I wondered why she and Daddy seemed so at ease, so cozy together.

I approached them tentatively. If I thought for one minute either of them might be embarrassed by my presence, I was sadly mistaken. Daddy jumped to his feet when he became aware of me. He was all smiles as he introduced us.

"This is Marty." He nodded in her direction. "And this," he said, putting his arm around my shoulders, "is my daughter Carol."

I stood beside him, feeling curiously awkward, as Marty stared defiantly at me. I felt a prickle of anger at her bold manner. At the same time, I sensed a wariness about her.

"I thought you two might become friends. That would be nice, since you're both the same age." Daddy was unmindful of the unexpressed yet obvious tension between Marty and me.

Not wishing to appear rude, I murmured, "It's nice to meet you."

"The pleasure is all mine," she answered. She unsettled me, though I couldn't have said why. I felt a pervading hostility about her that she made no attempt to conceal. I was a creature of instinct, and my every instinct warned me that Marty was trouble with a capital T. Daddy explained to me that she had attended Riverdale High School and that she lived only a few streets away. He went on to say with great pride that she was enrolled in Dominican College and was taking courses in elementary education. These odd bits of information did nothing to change my gut feeling.

Daddy made no effort that I knew of to keep Marty at bay. She roamed the grounds with great freedom, unconcerned that her presence might be wondered at by family members. Never once did Daddy admit to me that they were having an affair. As far as I was concerned, he didn't have to. Anyone with eyes would have noticed, and perception was one of my strong points. It was one of Mama's, too. That's why I felt certain she knew what was going on. At first I decided to stay out of it. I was hoping that it was an infatuation, that Daddy would soon get over it. But finally I realized that that was not likely to happen. Mama seemed so sad of late, but I knew that she would not seek me out to confide in. She would have felt that she was burdening me with things I was better off not knowing. She badly needed to talk things out.

We were alone in the house one afternoon in late April preparing dinner. We sat across from each other at the kitchen table, as I peeled shrimp and she chopped fresh vegetables. We worked in companiable silence for a time, while I tried desperately to think of a way to bring up the subject that had troubled me for weeks.

"Carol," she said suddenly. "Your Dad expects me to believe that Marty is employed by him to do the yard work. Have you ever heard a more ridiculous story in your life? Does he expect for one minute that I'm stupid enough to believe that?"

It was as if she had read my mind. Her eyes were questioning. She was waiting for my answer.

"I don't see how he can believe that you or any of us are that stupid, Mama."

"Yes, but then he seems to enjoy believing that we are that stupid." Her eyes had taken on a bitter cast.

"I don't know why he feels the need to flaunt this relationship with a girl young enough to be his daughter," I said. "I sometimes wonder if he's taken leave of his senses."

"That's because your father has always let his penis do his thinking for him."

My jaw dropped open.

"I'm sorry if I've shocked you, honey, but it's the

truth. He's been sleeping around for years. You'll never know how humiliated and degraded I've felt at times."

I was astonished. His faults were such obvious ones, I wondered how he could have managed to conceal this streak of infidelity from his kids all these years. "But I had no idea!"

"Well, of course not. It was the last thing in the world I would have wanted you girls to know. You all adored him so, and I'm sure you still do. But I know that you're not stupid, Carol. I know that you know what's going on. So what's the use of pretending anymore?" Her brow furrowed in anguish.

"But all these years! You can't feel the same about him!" I felt terrible for her. I couldn't believe my father would have treated Mama so badly. Would have wounded her over and over again in such a way.

"I've lost a lot of respect for him over the years. As well as a good measure of love. The other affairs were short-lived. I saw no reason to split my family apart because of my personal disappointments. But this time seems different somehow."

She gazed toward the sunroom, in the direction of the backyard. There was no sign of Marty.

"Different how?" I asked, worried.

"This is the first time he's ever planted one of his girlfriends on my doorstep."

Her words shook me. This time Daddy didn't care who knew about his affair. The implications disturbed me.

Despite Daddy's increasing preoccupation with Marty, he still found time to make my sister Joanne's life miserable. He harped on George's shortcomings, which led to more and more arguments between the two men. Strong-minded herself, Joanne defended her husband, but she was fighting a constant, wearying battle she couldn't hope to win. On more than one occasion she stormed out of the house vowing never to speak to

Daddy again. It was only a matter of time before she relented. Daddy's hold was too strong.

One Saturday afternoon several friends and family members were invited over for a combination swimming party and barbecue. Everyone sat outdoors enjoying the sunshine, chatting together. After a long day of sun and food, Joanne and George gathered their belongings and got the kids ready to go home. Daddy yelled across the patio to them, "Why don't you kids take some barbecue home with you?"

"No, thanks," Joanne yelled back. "The kids are tired, and we're all stuffed, anyway."

"Take the food," he insisted loudly. Then he jerked his thumb in George's direction. "With the jobless wonder here, who knows where your next meal will come from."

Joanne and George turned bright red—George from humiliation, Joanne from fury. It was simply not in George's nature to react adversely to Daddy's caustic comment. I could tell that Daddy's words had wounded him, but he only shrugged and continued to pack up their car. Joanne maintained her dignity in the face of this public humiliation, but I could see the tears in her eyes. I felt sorry for them both and had to blink back tears of my own.

Daddy's mean statement stayed in my craw for the rest of the day. That evening, after the last of the guests had left, I found myself alone with him on the patio. The anger simmering inside me suddenly came boiling over.

"How could you be so cruel?"

His eyebrows lifted in genuine puzzlement. "What the hell are you talking about?"

"Your comment today, about Joanne not knowing where her next meal is coming from. It was a cruel and pointless thing to say, and it really hurt her. She was about to cry."

"Well, there's going to be a lot more tears in her eyes as long as she's married to that little shit."

"But *you're* the one who hurt her!" Why wouldn't he see that?

"I gave her the best of everything. She married a loser. That's all there is to it. She deserves better than that."

I didn't bother to answer him, but I thought that he probably meant someone like himself. That was the crux of the problem—George was not of the same mold as Daddy. He was not an achiever, nor was he ruthless enough to spark the slightest bit of admiration from my father. George was a product of the turbulent sixties generation—unmotivated, with no real direction in life at age twenty-four. I felt certain that given time, George would find his niche in life. I could not have known that fate would intervene and forever rob him of the chance.

May 15, 1970, was a lovely spring day—much too pretty for any of us to be indoors. I was sitting on the step of the pool, watching little Bruce splash in the water. Daddy had crossed the patio a few minutes before with a large cardboard box under his arm, then disappeared toward the stables. A little while later Mama and George walked out onto the patio. Daddy came strolling across the wide expanse of lawn toward the three of us. He stopped a short distance from the patio and yelled impatiently to George to get a move on, he'd been waiting for him, and he was in a hurry.

"Where are you off to, Len?" asked Mama.

"I'm trying to make it to an early matinee, and I'm running late," Daddy replied. "Come on, George. I'll show you where to put these floodlights.

George said, "I guess I'd better get going. See you later, Tubby," he teased. I was far along by now with my second child. He ran his fingers through my hair on the way by.

Mama was telling me that she was going to have her hair done and then make a quick stop at the grocery when Daddy came running from the back. He waved as he hurried past us to his car.

"He sure is in a rush," I commented.

"I guess he doesn't want to keep his girlfriend waiting."

A half-hour or so later I went into the house to put Bruce down for his nap. I decided to lie down awhile myself. In my seventh month of pregnancy, I tired easily.

The ringing telephone woke me. I snatched up the receiver, groggy. It was exactly two P.M. by the digital clock on the bedstand.

"Hey, it's me—Joanne. Did I wake you up? Sorry. I wanted to talk to George for a minute. Would you get him for me?"

"Sure, hold on. I'm going to have to round him up. Be right back."

I set the receiver on the bedstand and went downstairs. I looked first to see if George was in the house, but little Bruce and I were the only ones home. I went out the back door and called for George. No answer. I headed out toward the stables and called his name again several times, but there was still no George. I returned to the house.

"I didn't see him anywhere," I told Joanne, "but I know he was here earlier."

"Yeah, he said he'd be there most of the afternoon installing the floodlights. When you see him, would you tell him to give me a call? I need him to pick up a few things at the store on his way home."

Shirley arrived home at about three-fifteen, and twenty minutes later Joanne called again. Shirley ran out back and checked for George. He had to be around the house, because his red Caprice was still parked in the front driveway. When she returned without him, I told Joanne that he didn't seem to be around. Something was strange here. Mama returned at five o'clock, and as she was setting a bag of groceries on the counter, Joanne phoned again. She mentioned to Mama that she had tried us several times and nobody could find George. Mama said his car was out front. Maybe some of his friends had come by and he had taken off with them. It seemed a likely explanation. Mama promised to have him call as soon as he showed up, then added that she would send Shirley out to look for him once more. Mama placed the receiver back into the cradle, and the phone immediately rang again. It was Daddy this time, and I heard her tell him no, it wouldn't be necessary to bring sandwiches home. Mama had a puzzled look. Why would Daddy, never one to be considerate these days, call with such a question? Her expression deepened as she asked him exactly where George was installing the lights out back. Joanne had called several times, she told him, and we hadn't been able to find him. When she hung up, her expression was of pure fear.

"Shirley," Mama said, "Daddy wants you to go out back and look for George again on . . ." Shirley slipped out the patio door before Mama could even finish the sentence.

"Look for George on what?" I asked, confused.

"Daddy said to look on the Hassells' side of the stables," she replied. The Hassells' property bordered ours.

I have never believed in telepathy, but at that moment, as I looked into my mother's eyes, I knew we shared the same horrible thought.

Mama whirled and headed out the patio doors in the direction of Shirley, whose slim form was halfway across the wide lawn. I tagged behind Mama, slowed by my pregnancy but mentally willing Shirley to stop, to turn around, to do anything but head for the rear of the stables. Mama closed the distance between them, but Shirley was fast, and she turned onto the fenced walkway that ran beside the corral to the rear of the stables. Within seconds I rounded the bend of the corral and came face-to-face with the horror that nightmares are made of. George lay on his stomach, his head turned to one side, the top of it almost touching the wall of the stable. His hands were folded neatly under his cheek, and his blue eyes were open. A thin line of congealed blood ran from his nose to his mouth. His body was so white and still, it might have been carved from wax. I felt the hysteria bubble up in me as I noticed his wallet lying to his right, opened flat to photographs of Kelly and Lori. Some distance to the right of his head sat a cement block with a small stain of blood on its surface. A length of heavily insulated wiring lay across his back haphazardly. Dappled shadows from the tree overhead danced on his back. My stomach lurched. Through a red haze I saw Mama sink to her knees in the grass, as though struck down by some giant, unseen hand. The colors of our garden spun around me—red, pink, white, yellow. The heady, cloying smell of flowers in bloom rushed into my nostrils. Shirley's eyes were a vivid blue contrast to the white of her face and the sprinkle of freckles across her nose. It is a tableau forever etched in my memory.

We stood rooted to the spot, frozen. Mama broke the yawning silence. "Police. We have to call the police."

Her words brought me back to reality. I held on to Shirley's hand, and together we followed Mama back to the house. Shirley was sobbing, and I did my best to comfort her along the way. Once inside, Mama called the Jefferson Parish sheriff's office. She then insisted that I stay indoors with Shirley and little Bruce to wait for the police. She would return to George. I watched through the glass walls of the sunroom as she made her way across the lawn to the back of the stables. I understood why she felt the need to go back to that terrible place. She did not want to leave George alone.

I heard the ambulance long before it pulled into the driveway. Two Jefferson Parish police cars sped behind and into the front drive, red lights flashing. I met the officers in the side driveway and instructed them to follow the drive all the way around to where it dead-ended at the stables.

I returned to the sunroom, where Shirley stood, small

and desolate, with Bruce on her hip. We stared out the windows, but unable and unwilling to see what was happening. Mama finally emerged from the stable area, flanked by two police officers, one of whom had his arm around her to support her. I offered a silent prayer to God to please let George be alive, but I knew in my heart that God would not be able to answer it.

The police officers came inside and bustled about, their conferences hushed and in corners. Mama called George Whitlow, a dear friend of the family and a neighbor of Joanne and George's, who offered to drive Joanne over. He suggested it would be best to tell Joanne simply that there had been an accident at home and not mention any of the details. Mama agreed. She then called Nancy at a girlfriend's house and asked that she come home. Nancy got back quickly and burst into tears when Mama broke the news to her.

It was useless to try to contact Daddy. We had no idea where to find him. We knew only that he had gone to a matinee, and there was no way to track him down.

The police officers questioned us as we sat in the living room in a daze. One of the officers, a tall, dark man, not much older than me, asked us when we had last seen George alive. I said that I had seen him around noon that day and that he'd been on his way to the stables. Mama filled the officer in on the reason George had been working in the back. The questioning continued, and Mama explained how the three of us had found his body after repeatedly trying to find him for several hours. The officer paused and spoke briefly into his walkie-talkie with another officer, one apparently still back at the stables. I heard him mention the coroner's wagon and George's estimated time of death. I bit down hard on my bottom lip to keep from sobbing.

He told us they had found a ladder lying on the rooftop of the stables and glass from a shattered floodlight, along with ragged strips of bark torn from the tree. It would appear that George had fallen from a tree to the rooftop before falling another eight feet to the ground.

The officer's words brought a fresh round of sobbing from my younger sisters, who sat huddled together on the sofa.

As George Whitlow's white station wagon pulled into the front driveway, Mama got to her feet. In a panicky voice, she said, "Oh, God. How am I going to tell Joanne this?"

"Try to calm down, Mrs. Fagot," said the officer. "The other officers and myself are here to help in any way we can. If you're not up to it, I'll handle it."

Joanne rushed through the front door. She wore a pair of blue shorts, a plaid shirt, and sandals. She stopped short at the sight of the two police officers. "What is it?" she asked. "Is it Daddy? There's an ambulance in the driveway—I saw it . . ." Her voice trailed off as she became aware of the awful silence in the room. We looked at her helplessly, unable to say the words.

"Mrs. Westerfield?" asked the officer. Joanne nodded. She was starting to understand. "I'm sorry to have to tell you this, but your husband is dead. There was an accident." The officer's face was truly compassionate. "I'm sorry."

Joanne began to shake. "Is he at the hospital? I want to see him now—I have to see him."

"Joanne, you don't understand." Mama moved forward. She tried to put her arms around her, but Joanne slapped her hands away impatiently. She turned and began fumbling for her purse and her car keys. "I know George will want to see me. He needs me." Her eyes were wild and unfocused. Her small shoulders were slumped, arms folded across her chest as if protecting her from the terrible reality of Mama's words.

Mama grabbed Joanne from behind by both arms and spun her around to face her. "Joanne, honey, please listen to me. George is dead. You can't help him now."

Joanne collapsed then, as if all the life had gone out of her. "No, it's not true. He can't be dead." Her voice rose hysterically as her breath began coming in tight little gasps.

"Get her on the sofa—she's hyperventilating," said one officer. "Somebody get a paper bag!"

Somebody grabbed a lunch bag out of the kitchen. The officer placed it over Joanne's nose and mouth and told her to breathe slowly. After a few minutes she began breathing normally, but she still trembled violently. Another young officer came in the back door and sat beside her. He handed her George's wallet and wedding band. She held them in her hands, and after a moment she started to weep softly. I began to cry again.

Daddy came rushing through the front door, his face a mask of concern. "My God, what's happening?" he demanded. He spoke directly to the two policemen, since we were obviously too distraught to answer.

"This is my husband, Leonard Fagot," Mama said.

The shorter of the two officers nodded in Daddy's direction. "Mr. Fagot, there's been an accident. Your son-in-law George was killed in a fall on your property today. Your wife and daughters discovered his body. We understand he was installing some lights for you; is that correct?"

Daddy stared at him. "Yes, that's correct," he replied, rubbing his left arm and leaning on the stairwell.

"When did you last see him, Mr. Fagot?" The officer jotted down Daddy's words in a notebook he held.

There was hesitation in Daddy's reply. "Earlier today. I left to go to the movies and then my office. I'm an attorney."

"Yes. Well, the coroner has arrived. He's of the opinion your son-in-law broke his neck when he fell. Of course, we'll have to wait until the autopsy report is completed to make certain, but as of now there is nothing to indicate that this was anything more than a tragic accident."

Suddenly Daddy sagged to the floor. He clutched at his pockets, searching for his nitroglycerin pills. He found them in a top pocket, opened the bottle, and shook one of the small white pills into his hand. He placed the pill under his tongue, then fell heavily over on his side. Even now, I can still hear the little white pills in the bottle scatter over the floor. For the second time that day an ambulance pulled into the driveway of 279 Citrus Road. Daddy was released within a couple of hours after admission to the emergency room at Touro Infirmary.

The next morning an article appeared in the New Orleans *Times-Picayune.* "A twenty-four-year-old Jefferson Parish man, George Safely Westerfield, Jr., fell to his death yesterday while doing some electrical work at the home of his father-in-law, noted Jefferson Parish attorney, Leonard Fagot. Family members confirmed that Westerfield was last seen alive at approximately noon on Friday. The Coroner's Office has ruled the death as accidental. Westerfield is survived by his wife, Joanne, and his two daughters, Kelly Lynn, aged two and a half, and Lori Ann, aged one year."

I called Bruce in Germany and passed along the sad news. He was shocked, but he tried his best to comfort me long-distance.

Since Daddy was unwell, George Whitlow stepped in and took control of the situation. He brought Joanne and Mama to select a casket and make all the necessary arrangements at the Leitz Eagan Funeral Home. It was not an easy job for him. For one, Joanne didn't want George buried in his parents' family plot because she felt he should be in a place where she might one day join him. Mr. Whitlow had to explain gently that she was only twenty-two years old and would in all probability marry again some day. George would always be his parents' son, though, and he belonged with them. We are eternally grateful to Mr. Whitlow for his kindness and caring in seeing us through this troubled time.

Word of George's death traveled quickly. Mama's phone rang nonstop as friends, relatives, and neighbors called to offer their condolences. Even Mike called from offshore. His wife, Anne, had told him the sad news. Since he was in Anchorage, Alaska, he wouldn't be able to attend George's funeral, no matter how much he wanted to. Shell Oil Company needed him too much to let him make the trip. I was sorry I wouldn't see him.

My maternal grandmother, Mom-Mom, a sixty-year-old widow, arrived by plane from her home in Baltimore to attend the funeral. Ida Mae gave up her weekend off to stay at the house and do whatever she could. She bustled about, fixed meals, and badgered me to rest. I had a baby on the way to think about, and taking care of little Bruce was a job itself. Joanne's children, Kelly and Lori, were too young to understand what was going on, so for the time being explanations were one less thing to worry about.

Joanne was inconsolable. The funeral services were scheduled to be held on Monday, so she stayed at Mama's house over the weekend. She insisted that following the funeral she would return to the small house she and George had been renting. Ida Mae agreed to stay and watch all three children until the funeral was over.

On Sunday evening, as we were preparing to leave for the wake, Daddy painfully dragged himself out of bed, insistent on going with us. He'd been knocked out on tranquilizers since his return from the hospital, so I wondered why he felt such urgency to attend George's wake. It was sure to be an emotionally draining experience. By the time we arrived at the funeral home, friends and loved ones had already turned out in large numbers to mourn the death of the quiet young man they had cared for.

The older adults comforted each other, incapable of accepting the death of one so young. The younger adults, many of them facing for the first time the reality of the death of a peer, were shaken by the knowledge that such tragedy could happen suddenly and swiftly to one of them.

The Westerfields were sitting beside their son's casket, and although clearly stricken with grief, they maintained a calm dignity.

The top half of the casket was left open for viewing. I'd never seen anyone dead before. I approached the casket in morbid fascination. George was dressed in a dark suit and tie with a white shirt. Beside me, I heard a woman I didn't know say, "Doesn't he look good." I turned to stare at her. What was she saying? I gazed down at George. By no stretch of the imagination did he look good. There were no disfiguring marks on him, granted, and maybe if I tried real hard I could convince myself that he appeared to be only sleeping. But, look good? Never. He looked lifeless—small and shriveled, somehow. I shuddered, wondering what perversity in man compels him to display his dead loved ones in such a horrible way. It was too obscene, too cruel—like stripping away one's last vestige of human dignity. Surely there was a purpose to it, this paying of last respects, but I couldn't find it. I would pay my last respects to George by keeping him alive in my memory, not by standing there gawking at his dead body.

At Daddy's urging, Joanne knelt beside the casket. She shivered slightly. I felt sick with compassion for her. Daddy's secretary, Ann, draped a red jacket around her shoulders.

My eyes were on Daddy as he made his way through the throng of mourners. He shook hands and agreed whenever someone said it was a terrible tragedy. After making the rounds he joined us once again beside the casket. He stared in consternation at Joanne, then leaned toward us.

"Why is she wearing that red jacket?" he asked, exasperated. "Widows wear *black.*"

"She's wearing it because she's shivering," answered Mama. She couldn't hide her disgust for him.

Daddy's lips thinned. "I don't care whether or not she's shivering. She can just pull herself together until this is over."

"Come on, honey," Mama said to Joanne. She ignored Daddy as she helped Joanne to her feet. "Come with me."

Daddy blocked their way. "She isn't going anywhere," he said through clenched teeth. "Her place is here, where she can speak with people. It's proper protocol at a wake, and I won't have my family behaving improperly in front of everyone."

"She's on the verge of collapse," hissed Mama. "The stress is unbearable for her. You're a cruel human being. You're worried more about what strangers might think than you are about the welfare of your own daughter."

"She can have a break for a few minutes, but I'm warning you, she will take her proper place without the red jacket."

I could have cried with shame at Daddy's cold manner. From the disbelieving expressions on Mama's, Nancy's, and Shirley's faces, I knew we all felt the same way.

Pausing beside the coffin, Daddy gazed down at George. He kneeled, then folded his hands in an attitude of prayer. I felt my grandmother stiffen beside me as Daddy leaned over and kissed George on the lips in a final farewell.

George was buried the next day in the Westerfield family plot. As we were getting into the limousine for the ride to the cemetery, Daddy clutched at his chest and again collapsed. All was in turmoil once more, with Shirley running to retrieve the oxygen tank from his car and the frantic efforts to revive him, but he recovered in a short time. We left him in the capable hands of a good friend of his.

The burial service was brief and simple. Joanne watched in silence. As the American flag was folded and presented to the young widow, Daddy's car pulled up beside the crowd of mourners. Daddy's friend emerged from the front and proceeded to open the back door of the car. Daddy stumbled from the backseat of the vehicle. In the process of getting out, he slammed the front seat forward, where it came to rest on the horn. A loud blare shattered the stillness of the cemetery.

All eyes were on him as he slowly made his way to Joanne's side. His hand came to rest on her shoulder in a gesture of comfort. Joanne looked up at him with sorrowful eyes. Her arms slowly came up from her sides, and she clung to Daddy as if he were a lifeline.

"I told you I would always take care of you," I heard him say. His voice was somber above the hush of the gathered mourners. "You'll never have to worry about anything again."

CHAPTER 6

CAROL

I have always been at odds with the night. Especially deep night. Those vast and silent hours between midnight and dawn, when darkness seems to swallow the world whole and I'm left alone with my thoughts. Maybe I would sleep better at night, as most people do, if it weren't for my compulsion to analyze everything. I've never been content to accept anything at face value. I have to dissect things, break them down, study their nature and their relationships. By doing so I display the individual parts and pieces of any particular problem for scrutiny and discover the true nature of the problem. And then my rational thinking goes beyond, to disarming, frightening thoughts that strip away the protective, sensible layer of mind. My innermost fears, those easily buried by daylight, are laid bare.

Night after night, then, I thought about the nature of George's death. He died alone a hundred yards from where I lay napping. I should have known somehow. I wondered how long he might have lived. I lay in bed for hours every night replaying the events surrounding his death over and over again in my mind. Nagging little memories kept surfacing—Daddy's mad dash from the stables and the fact that no one ever saw George alive after that; Daddy's words to Mama over the phone to look for him "on the Hassells' side of the stables"; and, the darkest thought of all, Daddy leaning over to kiss his dead son-in-law, a son-in-law for whom I knew he had nothing but disdain. Even the words he spoke to Joanne at the funeral, his assurance that he would always take care of her and the children and that she'd "never have to worry about anything again"—words meant to reassure and comfort—took on a sinister air. The more rational part of me argued that I had to be out of my mind to even consider the possibility of Daddy's involvement in George's death. You're just upset, I told myself, these are just the paranoid notions of a pregnant woman. I tried to tuck the thoughts away, afraid to examine them more closely.

On the Friday following the funeral I was rushed to the hospital in premature labor. My physician, Dr. Samuels, said it was due to stress and shock. Fortunately, he was able to arrest the labor. I was scheduled for cesarean section surgery on June 12, and hoped I could hold on until then.

My grandmother postponed her return trip to Baltimore for another week. On the day she left, she hugged each of us tightly, her eyes wet with tears. "I hate to leave you all," she said. "There are so many things I worry about." I thought of her reaction to Daddy's odd behavior at the wake.

My daughter, Kimberly, was born on June 12, 1970. She was not a strikingly beautiful baby, as Bruce had been. She was adorable in a rakish, urchin-like way, with a headful of red-gold hair that stood up in wisps and blue eyes so round, they seemed to swallow her tiny face. The first time the nurse on duty brought her to me to bottle-feed, I carefully counted her miniature toes and fingers. As I was wrapping the baby back in her pink blanket, she smiled a great big lopsided grin and instantly stole my heart.

Bruce had managed to swing a few days leave from his duties in Germany, and one day, moments after he had left at the end of visiting hours, a nurse burst into my room. She cheerfully announced that my husband was here to see me and that even though visiting hours were over, she was going to bend the rules this once. Mike Holland was right behind her with a large bouquet of red roses and a grin on his face. I couldn't help laughing at the absurdity of the situation.

"How am I going to explain these?" I said.

"Just tell the truth," he replied, his face suddenly gone serious.

"You know there's no way I can do that."

"There's always a way," he answered simply. "I love you. Right or wrong, that's the way it is."

He'd brought joy into my life, had made me feel alive. I couldn't bear to see him so distressed.

"I've been to see my daughter. Now that I've seen her, I can't bear the thought of living without her. She's part of me. Part of us. I love you, Carol."

After he'd gone the tears came. I loved Mike. But Bruce was my husband, and I loved him, too. I'd woven myself a tangled web. Mike was married, with a son of his own. His family no doubt loved and needed him every bit as much as Bruce loved and needed his. I think I grew up a little bit that day in the hospital, because while the thought of losing Mike brought a pain so fierce to my heart I thought I might die, I was able to recognize the pain that our love would cause others. We had no right to happiness that came from another's sorrow. I made up my mind then and there to end it.

A week after Kimberly was born, Bruce left to go back to Germany, and the baby and I returned home to Citrus Road.

At the time of George's death, he and Joanne had been renting a house in Westgate, a small subdivision located in Metairie, next door to Daddy and Mama's former home. The house was owned by Bill and Jan Wilson. Joanne insisted on returning to her house the night of the funeral. She felt she had to face the loss and get on with her life for the sake of her children. I thought her terribly brave to face things head-on, but I wasn't fooled for one minute by her stoic demeanor. There was a perpetual shadow of sadness about her. We grew very close in those troubled days. While I understood that I couldn't possibly conceive of the pain her loss had brought, I had a very deep understanding of her loneliness. I visited her often, and we spent long afternoons together. We talked about everything under the sun—everything except George. At the mention of George's name her eyes would cloud over, as if she'd pulled a window shade down over them to keep me from prying into her soul. George was a taboo subject, an invisible barrier between us that she would not allow me to breach.

Six weeks after Kimberly's birth, near the end of July, I worked alongside Daddy in the library, helping him to arrange the hundreds of books that lined the shelves. Right in the middle of the project, he took a break and called Joanne to ask her to come over to the house. Joanne arrived a half-hour later. Daddy handed her a check as soon as she walked into the library.

"This is for twenty thousand dollars," he told her. "I had George purchase a life insurance policy to protect you. He may not have mentioned it. The check is payment in full; it includes the ten-thousand-dollar face value and an additional ten-thousand-dollar double indemnity for accidental death. It's not a fortune, but if you handle it the right way, it'll get you by until you're back on your feet."

"I had no idea George had gotten insurance coverage," Joanne said. She gazed at the check in her hand, stunned.

"Well, he wouldn't have, except that I made the premium payments. By the way, Carol," he said, turning to me. "I think it would be wise of you to suggest that Bruce do the same thing. I think we all know now that death can strike right out of the blue. Now, Joanne, Bill and Jan Wilson want to sell the house you're living in, and they're only asking for six thousand dollars down. I strongly suggest you take advantage of this opportunity to buy the house: You now have the means to do so, and the monthly payments will run you no more than rent. It will offer security for you and the children, and that

would make me happy. If you agree, I'll have the necessary papers drawn up, and the house will be yours, in
your name."

"I don't know how to thank you," said Joanne, her
eyes filling with tears.

"There's no need to thank me, baby. I know how hard
all of this has been for you, and I want you to know that
I'm always here if you need me."

In early August Daddy surprised Mama and me by
offering to treat us to an all-expenses-paid month-long
trip to Europe.

"I think it will do you good to get away for a while,"
he explained. "I haven't mentioned this to Nancy yet,
but she's welcome to join you. Shirley will have to stay
here, of course, since she can't possibly miss that much
school. Since Bruce is being discharged soon, this seems
like the perfect time to see as much of Europe as possible. Who knows—you may never have the opportunity
again."

Mama's eyes were dancing with excitement. "I think
it's a wonderful idea. But won't it be terribly expensive,
Len?"

"You let me worry about that. You can use the credit
cards for car rentals and lodging. Pick up some trav-
eler's checks, and I'll make arrangements with the airline."

Nancy, who had recently gone to work at a local
department store in the junior petite department,
asked for a leave of absence. Joanne offered to care for
Kim and Bruce for me. We departed September 8, and
Bruce met us at the Frankfurt airport. Happily, Bruce
managed to obtain a thirty-day leave, so he accompanied us on our tour of all the great sights of Europe.

It was a terrific experience that left me with memories I will always cherish. But as wonderful as our jour-
ney was, we became weary and were eager to return
home by the fourth week.

We returned from Europe by way of Belgium, viewing the quaint windmills that dotted the countryside.

We spent the night in Brussels and arrived in New York on a 747.

After a few days back home, I noticed that Shirley was spending more time than ever in the stables. If I tried to strike up a conversation with her, she seemed ill at ease and preoccupied. If she wasn't in the stables, she was alone in her bedroom. I became worried about my little sister. I knew George's death had been a traumatic experience for her, especially since she had discovered his body. I wondered if it were possible that she was suffering more than any of us realized, and watching her thin, weary face, I determined to get to the bottom of the situation.

One afternoon, after dumping her schoolbooks in a heap on the sofa and changing her clothes, she headed immediately for the stables. I gave her a few minutes alone before trailing her. I paused at the corral fence and silently observed her. She was briskly grooming one of the horses, a pretty little brown mare named Cinnamon. Her face had a grim expression, and there was an air of despondency about her, as if she carried the weight of the world on her frail shoulders. My heart went out to her as she suddenly hugged the horse's neck, burying her face in its tangled mane. I called her name, and she jumped, startled.

"I didn't mean to scare you," I said.

"I thought you were someone else," she said, relief washing over her face.

"Who?" I asked curiously.

She ignored me and turned away, her attention once again on the horse.

"Shirley, I know something's bothering you," I persisted. "Do you want to talk about it?"

"It's not something I can talk about. Daddy wouldn't like it."

"So, it concerns Daddy," I said thoughtfully. Taking a guess, I asked, "Does it concern Marty, too?"

She looked at me, pure panic on her face. I pulled her close to me, upset by her reaction to Marty's name.

Tears began to roll down her cheeks, and she spoke in a faltering voice. "When Marty first started coming around here, Daddy said Mama would leave us if she ever found out about her. He said it was our little secret. I tried to keep his secret, I really tried. He thinks I'm the one who told Mama about her. It's all my fault."

It hit me then that the poor kid had been carrying this burden, trying to protect Daddy. I hated the thought that she had felt responsible for Daddy's actions. I knew my father could be self-centered, but I could not believe he would have been so cruel. "Shirley, in the first place, this is Daddy's fault, not yours. And Mama would never leave you or abandon us for any reason. Never. When did Daddy tell you this?"

Her face reddened, and she looked down at her feet. "I saw them in the woods back there, months ago. They were kissing and hugging and doing other things," she stammered. "Daddy saw me and said that she was just a friend. Marty is always sneaking around here. That's why I was afraid you were her."

"Are you afraid of her?"

"I hate her! And I hate telling lies to Mama, but Daddy makes me. After Mama found out about Marty and they had all those fights, Daddy promised Mama she'd never come over here again, and Mama believed him, so I couldn't tell her the truth. The whole time you and Mama were gone, Marty was here and acting like she owned the place. She bossed me around like she was my mother. She even slept in Mama's bed!" she said, clearly horrified at the thought.

I hugged her close and reassured her that everything was going to be alright. But as I held her, I knew that nothing was ever going to be right again.

In the next few weeks, the situation disintegrated. Marty became more blatant than ever. Any secrecy Daddy intended to keep up was blown away by her sheer determination to make certain we all knew exactly where she stood in the scheme of our lives. Gone was the tan Volkswagen, replaced by a brand new shiny blue Corvette, and to me it didn't take an Einstein to figure out where that had come from. Marty began following the family around town in her new car. She would tail Mama and her friend Joy Whitlow to the drugstore, the cleaner's, and the bank. All one had to do was glance in the rearview mirror, and there she was. On one occasion she went so far as to follow Nancy to work. Nancy had pulled over to park her gray Camaro, a graduation present from Daddy, and Marty slammed the Corvette in reverse. She traveled backward like a shot, nearly hitting a coworker of Nancy's who had just turned the corner in her haste to get away.

She passed our house regularly, like a city bus on schedule, seemingly fascinated by our daily lives. Several times I came across her pulled over and parked on a neighboring street, just sitting. Whenever one of us complained to Daddy about her ridiculously childish behavior, he simply laughed as if it were all very funny. He appeared to get a kick out of all the contention going on around him, delighted by the thought of our vying for his attention. The fact that Marty was creating chaos in our lives was irrelevant to him.

We had long been receiving phone calls in which the caller just breathed heavily and hung up. Now when the telephone rang at odd hours, a female voice would utter, "Bitch!" before hanging up. I had no doubt as to the identity of the caller, especially after Mama answered the phone one Sunday afternoon and was shocked to hear the same female voice whispering eerily, "Why, oh why, did I have to get *her?*"

I was feeding the baby at the dining room table, and I winced as Mama slammed the receiver on the kitchen counter. Grabbing her car keys, she headed for the library. I heard her voice ring loud and clear. "Your girlfriend belongs in a loony bin." She marched from the room, her mouth set in a white line of fury. Daddy was right on her heels.

"Just hold on a minute, Shirley," he said in a placating voice.

Mama ignored him as she slammed the front door in his face. He turned to me with an aggrieved look on his face. "What in the world was that all about?"

"I think Goofy just made one of her calls to Mama again," I answered.

He looked puzzled. "Goofy?"

"Marty, Daddy. I think that girl has a screw loose. You know—the lights are on, but no one's home?" I said.

He laughed. I ignored him and went back to feeding the baby. How could he condone such outrageous behavior from Marty, and why did he actually seem to revel in being a party to it? To him the situation may have seemed humorous, but to me it was menacing, as if the two were involved in some sadistic game for which they made all the rules.

By now the situation was taking its toll on Mama. Although she tried her best to hide it, her pain and humiliation were plain to see. I'd chosen to conceal from her everything that Shirley had told me. There was no need to compound Mama's misery by telling her that Marty had been staying at the house during our European trip. Mama was so opposite Daddy in nature that I'd often wondered what strange force had conspired to draw them together. She was as temperate as he was extreme, and though she was more than his intellectual equal, she lacked the ruthlessness that served him so well. I knew her feminine pride would eventually prod her into a confrontation with Daddy. And I knew with equal certainty that she would not walk away the winner.

One night in early December 1970 the sound of crying woke me. My daughter, then six months old, was teething and had been restless throughout the night. I scooped her up from her crib and rocked her until she fell into a deep sleep. I placed her back in the crib, tucked a blanket around her, then went downstairs to make a cup of hot tea. The house was silent and dark as I descended the stairway. On my way to the kitchen I noticed a light in the sunroom. Who would be up at such a late hour? I eased open the sliding glass patio door. Mama, in her robe, sat on one of the rattan sofas, her back to me. A nearby lamp cast reddish shadows on her dark hair as she gazed through the parted curtains at the cold, somber night. The Christmas tree lights reflected off the glass panes like miniature stars trapped in the frosted panes.

I sat down beside her on the sofa. Several minutes went by with neither of us speaking. Mama just stared out at the night. When she finally spoke, her words stunned me.

"Have you ever wondered about George's death?"

She turned to look at me then, and her eyes were filled with despair. I wanted to run from those eyes. To stay would mean voicing the impossible. My glance strayed to the cold, impenetrable walls of the windows and to the shadows that lay outside, searching for an answer. "Yes, I have wondered."

Mama nodded. "Did you ever think that perhaps George's death wasn't accidental?"

I knew the question was coming, but I was still unprepared to answer. Mama watched me intently. I knew the time had come for truthful answers, no matter how insane they may sound. "I'm not sure I believe his death was an accident, but I'm afraid of what that might mean."

There was a dead silence as tears rolled down her cheeks. "I believed it was an accident," she said so softly that I had to lean forward to hear her. "A needless, tragic accident. It never occurred to me until today that it could be anything else."

An icy stab of fear sliced through me. I waited for her to go on.

"Several days ago I made up my mind to find proof that your father bought the Corvette for Marty. I knew he keeps his bank statements and canceled checks in the library, so I began searching there for evidence of the purchase. He's always hidden things he doesn't want me to know about behind the books on the shelves. I began to pull books out . . . Carol, it was like opening Pandora's box."

She paused to light a cigarette. Her fingers trembled. Taking a deep breath, she continued, "I came across an autopsy report on George. It totally unnerved me. I know that, being a lawyer, he may have had a very logical reason for requesting it, but in my heart I don't believe that."

Surely, I wondered desperately, it was only Daddy's passion for order that made him ask for a copy of George's autopsy report. Maybe it had to do with settling some legal matters. Maybe the authorities routinely give the autopsy report to the dead man's family. Maybe he just wants to spare Joanne the pain of seeing it . . .

But Mama went on, "I found several insurance policies covering the lives of every member of this family. He is the beneficiary of every one. They're substantial policies, all carrying double-indemnity coverage."

The words struck a chord of fear inside me. What was she leading up to?

Her quiet voice was relentless, unnervingly dispassionate. "I found no proof that he had purchased Marty's car, but I did find on the July bank statement a deposit in the amount of one hundred sixty-eight thousand dollars."

"Well, where did that come from?" I was confused.

"At the time I couldn't figure that out myself. Since his heart attack, he hasn't handled many cases—certainly none of that magnitude," she said, her face deathly pale. We both knew that he had once received substantial fees. But those days had been over for years. "A phone call from the friend who handles the majority of your father's insurance gave me the answer. He said that he had something he wanted to discuss with me, something that he had promised your father he wouldn't mention unless Daddy in some way hurt our family. With that, something clicked in my mind. I asked him if what he was going to tell me had anything to do with one hundred sixty-eight thousand dollars. He was amazed at my question and wanted to know how I knew about the money, so I told him about finding the bank statement with the deposit in that amount. He quickly said that the money came from no illegal source. He said his company had written a double-indemnity life insurance policy on George for one hundred thousand dollars, with Daddy as the beneficiary, and 'lo and behold, the boy died eight or nine months later!' Then he added, 'Hell, Shirley, how could I know that he would die just a few months later?' I can't tell you how sick I felt when I hung up the phone." Her words were stiff and formal, as if she were talking about a stranger.

"Two hundred thousand dollars?" It was impossible that Daddy had collected such a vast amount of money from George's death and mentioned it to no one, especially not Joanne. "My God, are you telling me you think he killed him?"

Mama leaned back and closed her eyes. The lamplight gleamed on her dark hair, her drawn face. "I asked your father that. I told him I knew about the money, and his only answer was that it was because of this kind of thinking on my part that we could no longer live together."

"But he didn't deny it?" I said, incredulous.

"No, he didn't deny it. He only laughed and asked me, 'How do you think I paid for your trip to Europe?' "

I felt as though I'd been kicked in the stomach. What I thought had been a kind and generous gesture on my father's part had instead been a trip paid for with blood money.

"He didn't even care about Joanne, or Kelly and Lori," she continued. "I asked him, " 'How can you just wipe out a young boy's life and leave your own grandchildren fatherless? How can you rob your daughter of the man she loved, as though you were God?' He said, 'When are you going to grow up, Shirley? Don't you know there's a price for everything?' "

That was how I learned that the price of George's life was two hundred thousand dollars.

CHAPTER 7

CAROL

In early January 1971 Daddy purchased the Hassell house, next door at 275 Citrus Road. During the next several weeks he renovated the older home. I assumed he was planning to either sell the house for a profit or possibly rent it for additional income, so I was surprised when he took me aside and explained that he'd purchased it for Bruce and me. At first, despite my suspicions about him, I was touched by his thoughtfulness. Surely that was proof that Mama was wrong about his involvement in George's death. And besides, just because he had an insurance policy on George's life that he had told no one about didn't mean he was a murderer. But the more I thought about it, the more leery I became of living so close to Daddy. Not only was I disturbed by all that I knew, but I remembered very well Daddy's interference in Joanne's marriage. Living in such close proximity to him could not possibly enhance my already tenuous marriage. In light of my past relationship with Mike Holland, I felt that I owed both Bruce and myself the chance to make the best of our marriage. For the time being, I decided, I would put the decision to move next door on hold.

Bruce was discharged from the army in early February, and the children and I were at the airport to greet him when he arrived home. When we got to the house, Daddy met us at the door and shook Bruce's hand heartily.

"Welcome home, son," he said, steering us toward the library.

"It's good to be home, Mr. Fagot," answered Bruce with a wide grin. It was obvious to see that Bruce was thrilled to be home again.

"No need to be formal, Bruce. Just call me L.J. All the kids do. Here, have a seat on the sofa. So, now you're an army man, huh?" said Daddy, as he settled into his leather recliner.

"Was an army man," corrected Bruce. "I understand you were a marine."

Daddy nodded. "That's right, the only way to go. Seven years' active duty, thirteen years' reserve."

Bruce nodded respectfully. "You must have been a damned good one," he said with admiration. He eyed the display of medals on the wall. "The Silver and Bronze stars."

I had been nervously anticipating this reunion to see if Bruce and Daddy would still have the same rapport they had displayed in the early months of my marriage. I relaxed as they talked easily together.

"I earned those in the Pacific," said Daddy, beaming. "The service isn't like it used to be, though. But, then, serving time in a war is a lot different from peacetime military service on base somewhere."

"Maybe so, but I was just as happy not to go to Vietnam."

Daddy shrugged. "Well, people are different. I would rather be in the thick of things. I hated to see the war end. I was called back to active duty for the Korean War, but as luck would have it, I didn't make it past California. Seems like somebody thought I'd make a good instructor." He chuckled. "What are your plans now, Bruce?"

"College, I guess. Since Uncle Sam's paying for it, I might as well give it a try."

"Good decision, son. I did the same thing myself. It was tough going, but it was worth it. If you set some high goals for yourself, you'll go far in this world. Believe me, there's no satisfaction like achievement and nothing worse than working at some penny-ante job all your life." He paused a moment, then looked my way. "Carol, have you mentioned anything to Bruce about my surprise?"

"No. I haven't had the chance to discuss it yet," I said casually.

"What's there to discuss?" asked Daddy in a puzzled tone. "I've purchased the house next door for you two to live in. I'm not going to charge rent. I'll pay your utility bills, and that will be that much less you'll have to worry about."

"I don't know what to say or how to thank you," said Bruce, taken aback by such a generous offer.

"Actually, you'll be doing me a favor. You can help me keep up the place, and I'll have my grandkids right next door."

"What do you think, Carol? It sounds sensible to me," said Bruce.

"It looks to me like you two have pretty much made up your minds, so I guess that's it." My sarcasm fell on deaf ears.

We made the move the following weekend. Bruce promptly enrolled as a full-time student at the University of New Orleans on the Lakefront. Daddy offered him part-time work doing odd jobs around the two properties to help us out financially, and I took on a full-time job at Blue Cross Insurance in the claims processing department. Joanne volunteered to baby-sit for little Bruce and Kim during the day, which eased my apprehension about leaving them with strangers at such a tender age.

Bruce, at twenty-two years old, was a dreamer by nature, with his head in the clouds and his feet less than firmly planted on the ground. He dabbled in art and spoke openly of the day when he would set sail around the world in his own sailboat. He was convinced that one day he would write the great American novel and jet off into the sunset piloting his own plane. He was a handsome blond with twinkling blue eyes and even features. His face was impossibly revealing, his every feeling stamped on it clearly. Before long he and Daddy were fast friends, and it was easy to see why. Bruce held the deepest respect and admiration for Daddy. It was understandable that Daddy would offer his hand in friendship to this bright young man who obviously thought the world of him.

So deep did Bruce's loyalty to my father go that at times it completely overrode his common sense. It seemed to me that he felt whatever Daddy did was fine, no matter who got hurt in the process. He found Daddy and Marty's antics every bit as funny as Daddy thought they were, and it hurt me to think that Bruce could be amused by a situation that was painful to me and to everyone else involved.

He soon dropped out of college and devoted all of his time to helping Daddy in the yard and tinkering in the garage with his 1956 Jaguar, a car in a constant state of repair. I felt keenly that he was not living up to his potential and that Daddy was partially responsible. It was ironic that Daddy was cultivating in Bruce the very qualities he professed to dislike in George.

In Bruce I saw my own weaknesses. His interactions with Daddy so closely mirrored my own that I felt oddly threatened. It was very disconcerting to watch my husband fall victim to my father's strange and powerful charm. It was as if Daddy now had double the power over me.

In the hope of making some sense of my marital situation, I finally made up my mind to bring my feelings out in the open. One day in early spring of 1971, when Bruce lay roughhousing on the living room floor with little Bruce, I confronted him.

"Bruce, I want to talk to you," I said.

"What's up?" he asked teasingly. He tried to pull me down on the rug beside him.

"Come on. I'm serious," I warned, and stepped away from him. "I want to know if you're going back to college and if not, what your plans are for the future."

He looked away from me, spread his arms out on the

floor, and stared at the ceiling. "I don't know. There's plenty of time to think about the future. What's the rush?"

"Do you plan to live next door to Daddy forever?"

He stared at me, amazed. My anger surprised him. "What kind of a thing is that to say? Your father has been very generous to us, Carol. The least you could do is be appreciative."

"I do appreciate the things he's done for us, but I'm worried about the things he's taken away from us. You've given up everything you ever hoped for to help Daddy." Tears of anger and frustration began to well in my eyes.

"Carol, you're not being fair. Your father needs me."

It was my turn to stare in disbelief. "What about what *I* need? Does that matter to you?"

"Certainly it matters to me, but I think you're being unreasonable, honey. Don't you love your father?"

"Of course I love him. I'm just tired of living under his thumb, and I think the way he's treated Mama is unforgivable."

"He can't help it if he's fallen in love with another woman. It happens all the time." He refused to look at me. His answer was weak, and he knew it.

"He could at least have been discreet, and you know it, Bruce. He has to have it all, no matter who he hurts in the bargain."

"I still say you're not being fair. We owe him something," he said stubbornly.

"Okay. Have it your way. Only I hope I'm not around the day he demands a payback!" I stormed from the room before Bruce could say anything else.

The saddest thing I have ever witnessed was the deterioration of my parents' marriage. I've often heard divorce is harder on a young child than a grown one, but I'm not sure I believe that. I think it's much easier to lose something we've known only briefly than it is to lose a thing we have shared and built on from the cradle to adulthood. It is especially hard for a grown daughter to witness the pain and disillusionment of her mother in the face of impending divorce. A line is crossed, and suddenly you are no longer just mother and daughter, but two women sharing one heartache.

I was not really surprised when Mama first mentioned divorce to me. She had walked over for a visit, and we were in the kitchen sipping a cup of tea. She looked tired.

"I've asked your father for a divorce." She spoke softly, her voice barely more than a whisper. I reached across the table and patted her hand. I felt as though a knife had sliced into my heart. "He refused to even consider it," she continued. "He became very upset. He warned me how unpleasant he could make things if I insisted on pursuing this."

How could he say that? "Why should he care if you divorce him? Does he really think you're going to live with him while he keeps running around with Marty?"

"It isn't Marty at this point. I don't even care about her anymore. I might even have been able to live with him despite her, but I can't live with him now or ever again because of what I know about George." Her face seemed pale, almost translucent in the late afternoon sunlight that filtered through the window shade above the kitchen sink.

"Will you file for divorce, anyway?"

She ran her hands wearily through her hair. "I don't know. The only thing I do know is that I won't live with him any longer. I've lived with him for twenty-five years of marriage, and now I don't think I ever knew him at all."

It was a sad commentary for twenty-five years of marriage, but I understood what she meant. I had been his daughter for twenty-one years, and I didn't know him, either.

Daddy was in the habit of popping up on my doorstep several times a week. He would play a few hands of

cards with Bruce and me or visit with the kids, sometimes staying to tuck them into bed after reading them
a bedtime story. Several days after Mama had told me
that Daddy had refused to give her a divorce, he
showed up unannounced at my back door. I offered to
make him a cup of tea, and he seemed pleased at my
suggestion. Bruce was visiting his parents, who lived
only a few miles away in Metairie, and the kids were in
bed, so we chatted for a while. He was in an unusually
relaxed mood, and I dared to bring up the subject of
Mama's request for a divorce.

"Daddy," I said as tactfully as possible, "you know
that I love you and Mama very much and I wish that
things were different, but I don't believe they ever will
be." I waited for his response.

His face took on a pained expression. "You'll never
know how much your mother hurt me when she asked
for a divorce. All I have done for her, and to think she'd
consider walking out on me, a sick man! I'll never understand women. What can she possibly want from
me?"

I thought about that one for a moment before answering. "Why don't we stop kidding each other,
Daddy? She wants a divorce just as any woman in her
right mind would if her husband were seeing another
woman."

He chuckled. "I know your mother better than that,
and believe me, the last thing she wants is a divorce.
She has everything she can possibly need. There's no
reason on earth why we can't continue to live together
the way we always have," he said.

"I think you're looking at this a little one-sidedly,
don't you? Are you trying to tell me you honestly expect
that Mama will adjust to this and everything will just
smooth itself out in time?" He couldn't possibly believe
that. Could he?

"Why not?" he asked. "We've always worked out our
differences in the past."

"Because I think this time is different." I was getting

tired of parrying with him and decided to get right to the point. "I'm sorry if what I say hurts you, but I think you have embarrassed and humiliated not only Mama but every other member of this family, as well."

He stiffened at my words. "And I think I'm surrounded by a bunch of jealous, selfish females who are goddamned determined to make my life miserable."

I felt a white, hot anger flare in me. "Selfish? You're the selfish one! You don't care about anything but yourself. If I were Mama, I'd go out the first thing tomorrow and hire the best damned lawyer around. And I'd make damned certain I got half of everything you own!"

There was dead silence. I was so angry, I was trembling. Then he smiled at me, a tight, cold smile that never reached his eyes. "If you think for one minute that I would allow some snoopy lawyer to dig into my personal affairs, think again." There was menace in his eyes as he leaned across the table, only inches from my face. "If your mother makes the mistake of hiring a lawyer, I'll bury her six feet under so fast, she won't know what hit her."

I could only gape at him as an icy chill raced down my spine. I was still trying to absorb his shocking words when he rose to his feet and threw a parting shot in my direction. "Tell your mother for me that we can separate, I'll even buy her another house to live in, but there won't be a divorce. She can take it or leave it. The choice is up to her."

Long after he'd gone I lay awake in the darkest hours of the night, praying he was bluffing and knowing in my heart that he was not.

Several weeks later Daddy bought a three-bedroom split-level home built of wood and old brick for Mama at 10112 St. Paul Avenue. It was in an area on the outskirts of River Ridge known as Paradise Manor. Sparing no expense, he had the interior completely remodeled to suit Mama's taste. He ordered new carpets, draperies, appliances, and anything else necessary for her comfort and convenience. Beamed cathedral ceilings on the ground floor gave the house an airy spaciousness that matched its cheery, modern decor. Large glass windows overlooked the front and rear of the property, which was enclosed by a high wooden fence. Polished hardwood floors gleamed in the living room and dining area, both decorated in muted shades of peach, brown, and ivory, for a warm, comfortable look.

Mama, Nancy, and Shirley moved into the house on St. Paul Avenue in the summer of 1971. Within days Marty moved in with Daddy, next door to Bruce and me. I saw her often, as she worked in the yard, swam in the pool, or lounged about the patio in bright bikinis. We spoke very little, and neither of us made an effort, since my animosity toward Marty was obvious. Every time I caught a glimpse of her, I felt heartsick. She had taken my mother's rightful place—a girl young enough to be my sister, someone who had never sacrificed or struggled for the things that Mama had and who, I felt, was not entitled to them. Shirley often visited me, since it was still her job to care for the horses. Each afternoon she pedaled the two miles from Mama's house to mine and did her best to avoid Daddy and Marty.

Nancy was dating a young man by the name of Gary Gonzales, whom she had met when he installed new kitchen cabinets at Mama's house. A lean, good-looking guy, he dressed the way most young people did in the early seventies. Gary wasn't a hippie, but his hair was shoulder length and curly, and he wore tie-dyed cotton shirts and faded blue jeans. Nancy, at nineteen was completely smitten with his good looks and charm. Mama accepted the situation and allowed Nancy to see Gary whenever she wanted to. After all, Nancy was no longer a child, and Gary seemed nice enough. Daddy, caught up completely in his affair with Marty, was too preoccupied to care what any of us did. He never even commented on the new romance.

Then Nancy announced that she was moving into

Gary's apartment in uptown New Orleans. I was at Mama's house when she broke the news.

Mama walked across the bedroom and sat beside Nancy, who was perched on the edge of the bed, her face set.

"Why?" Mama asked simply.

"Because I love him," Nancy answered. Looking Mama right in the eye, she continued, "Right or wrong, that's the way it is."

I was struck by the memory of Mike Holland's words to me when he had visited me in the hospital following Kimberly's birth. I felt a sense of loss, and I reminded myself that I had put him out of my life forever.

CHAPTER 8

CAROL

My mother's leaving was a turning point in my life. When she left, she took the heart and soul of the house on Citrus Road with her, along with a decade of memories.

I stood on the back porch of my home and gazed across at the silhouette of the house next door. I had lived there for ten years. I knew every inch of that place, and now I shuddered at how suddenly cold and gloomy it seemed, how bleached of warmth and life. My thoughts strayed to the image of my father rattling around in that huge mausoleum of a house with only Marty for company, and I wondered if he lay in bed at night grieving, as I did, for the loss of family unity over the last year and a half.

Why had this man, whose love I'd cherished, allowed things to come to this? He'd crossed over some barrier, broken ties with loved ones that could never be mended. He'd become brooding and more callous than ever. I'd thought that love would help him, but I was wrong. I didn't know him anymore, if in fact I ever did.

Two weeks later, in early August, Daddy purchased two professionally trained beagles and a Winchester twelve-gauge shotgun. He said he was taking up rabbit hunting as a hobby. For days he and Bruce busied themselves building the beagles' kennel.

The Friday after Daddy bought the two dogs and the shotgun I overheard Bruce and him discussing the idea of trying the dogs out the following morning.

It sounded like fun to me, and I called out, "Can I come?"

"I don't see why not," answered Bruce. He glanced at Daddy for an okay.

Daddy's answer was to the point. "No."

Bruce shrugged his shoulders and refused to meet my eyes. Their attitudes made me angry, so I decided to push. "Why not?"

"You'd only be in the way," said Daddy firmly. The conversation was over.

The alarm went off at five-thirty the next morning. I jumped up in bed and jabbed viciously at the alarm button to shut it off. Beside me, Bruce lay snoring, and I thought briefly of not waking him, to get even. But I knew that wouldn't cut it with Daddy. I'd never hear the end of it if Bruce were late, and no doubt they'd both blame me.

Once I woke him, Bruce dressed quickly and grabbed his rifle from the hall closet. The headlights of Daddy's truck shone in our driveway, and on Bruce's way out the door I grudgingly gave him a thermos of coffee. From the open doorway I watched him toss his rifle into the back of the pickup. He then hopped into the cab of the truck beside Marty, who was wedged against Daddy as if permanently affixed by glue.

I slammed the back door and prayed for rain.

Shortly before eleven o'clock that morning Bruce telephoned. He spoke rapidly, his words tumbling over each other in his hurry to get them out.

"L.J.'s been shot! My God, I thought he was going to die. Jesus! I don't know how I managed to get him to the hospital. We're at Oschsner Hospital, and I think you'd better get over here. The doctors are talking about removing his hand." On that note he hung up the phone. I was speechless.

I put in a call to my in-laws, the Applegarths, who offered to keep Kim and Bruce. Then I telephoned Mama to ask her to call my sisters to let them know what had happened. I drove my children to the Apple-garths', and from there went on to Oschsner Hospital, on Jefferson Highway in Metairie. A feeling of pure panic bloomed in me at the thought of Daddy's dying before I could get there. I made every kind of bargain with God, if only He would spare my father's life.

When I entered the emergency room, the nurse on duty told me that Daddy was being prepped for surgery. She reassured me that family members would be allowed to see him briefly before the operation.

Mama arrived, along with Joanne, Nancy, and Shirley. As soon as they spotted me, they rushed in my direction and began tossing questions at me.

"Wait, slow down," I said. "I don't know anything at this point other than that he is being prepared for surgery and that we'll be able to see him for a minute before they move him to the operating room."

Just then Bruce rounded a bend in the corridor, headed in our direction. The front of his shirt and jeans were caked with blood, and his face was pinched and pale. As he ran his hands through his hair, it stood up in spikes around his forehead.

"What a nightmare!" He shook his head and rubbed his fingers over his eyes. "I've never seen so much blood. It was everywhere."

"How did it happen?" I asked.

"I wish I knew. He was ahead of me, and I heard a shotgun go off. By the time I got to him, he was on his knees, trying to tie a strip of leather around his upper forearm. There was blood everywhere. At first I was so shocked, I didn't know what was happening. Then I saw his hand."

He paused, his face blanched. "It was his left hand, and it was dangling from his wrist, barely attached. I saw a small stick on the ground and grabbed it with the piece of leather and made a tourniquet." He stopped again to catch his breath. "I knew I had to get him to a hospital, so I hauled him to his feet, and Marty helped me sling him over my shoulders. My God, he weighed a ton. I don't know how many times I fell down with him on the way to the truck. But I broke just about every traffic law in the book trying to get him here before he bled to death." Bruce sat down heavily into a chair. Carrying Daddy, who outweighed Bruce by an easy twenty-five pounds, must have been an ordeal.

A nurse entered the waiting room and informed us that we would now be able to spend a few minutes with Daddy before surgery. Only two visitors at a time would be allowed in the preop room.

Mama and I went into the room. We were nervous about what we would find, but Daddy looked surprisingly well, considering. He lay in the crisp white hospital bed, his damaged arm covered by a blanket and his good arm resting atop the coverlet. Two plastic tubes beside the bed fed medication into his veins.

He was conscious and appeared to be clear-minded as he acknowledged us. He looked so vulnerable. I leaned over and kissed him on the cheek. We'd been very wrong about him, I thought. He couldn't be capable of what Mama and I suspected.

"I guess your old man isn't as good with a weapon as he used to be." His words were light, but there was a catch in his voice.

I managed to reply, despite the lump in my throat. "Even the pros screw up sometimes."

He nodded, and took on a bewildered expression. "I don't know how it happened. I seem to remember slipping on a bottle of some kind." He shook his head, as if trying to clear his thoughts. "It all seems so vague. The dogs, I remember they were tangled around my legs. I heard a shot, and at first I didn't realize it had been my own gun going off. Then my hand felt like it was on fire. After that, everything is a blur. I can vaguely recall Bruce carrying me to the truck, but I don't see how he could have possibly done that on his own."

"That's just what he did," said Mama. "And then he

drove you here to the hospital. You were very lucky he was there, Len."

"You're right. I could never have made it on my own. I guess I owe him my life. Where is he? I'd like to thank him."

"He was here a few minutes ago," I replied, "but he may have gone home to change his clothes. He was a mess."

Daddy struggled to raise himself off the pillow. "Don't tell me he's not here!" There was an odd note of panic in his voice.

I tried to reassure him. "Calm down. I'll find him for you."

"Do it now. I have to speak with him immediately. The hospital will report this shooting to the police; it's standard procedure, and they'll want to question Bruce. You go find him for me now," he demanded.

"What's the rush, Daddy? You can talk after surgery. You're getting upset over nothing."

"I can't wait that long," he thundered. "I have a lot at stake here, including a substantial amount of insurance that I can't afford to lose. FIND HIM NOW!"

There was no pacifying him, so I went searching for Bruce. I found him still slouched in the same chair I'd left him in only moments earlier and passed on Daddy's message. He went straight into Daddy's room. Mama came out and joined me in the hallway, and ten minutes later Bruce emerged, a grim expression on his face. He didn't volunteer any specifics of his little meeting with Daddy, and I didn't ask.

An hour into the surgery a nurse came to the waiting room and informed us that they would have to amputate Daddy's hand. The accident had all but severed it from the wrist. He was holding up well otherwise, though, and his heart condition had not added any complications to the surgery. Daddy's loss saddened me, but I was grateful that he would survive. I kept picturing the tattoo that had been on his left arm:

PEARL HARBOR DEC. 7, 1941

If he survived Pearl Harbor, he could make it through this.

"Hand me my pain pills, Carol."

"You just took one a half-hour ago, Daddy."

"I know what I took. Now, just hand me the pills."

I snatched the bottle of codeine and read from the label. "Take one every four hours as needed for pain. It's right here on the label," I said. His stubbornness was driving me crazy.

"I know what's on the label, and I'm telling you for the last time to hand me the goddamned pills!"

"Give them to him," said Bruce.

"You give them to him," I said angrily. I threw the bottle at Bruce and caught him right in the chest with it.

Bruce ignored me and instead turned to Daddy. "Are you having a lot of pain?"

"Hell, yes. It gets worse all the time. I have to double the dose just to take the edge off."

Another of Daddy's attempts to make me feel guilty. I'd had stitches in my hand once, and I'd cried like a baby, so I could well imagine the pain he must be feeling after losing his hand. I was more concerned for his long-term welfare. Someone had to be sure that he didn't take too many painkillers.

"You only have a couple of these left," commented Bruce. He shook the bottle for emphasis.

"Damn." Daddy sighed. "Tell me what's left in the other bottles."

Bruce pulled the curtains aside and began inspecting the contents of several bottles lined up on the window ledge.

"You have two Darvons left," he reported, "and a couple of Seconals. All the other bottles are empty."

"Great," said Daddy with sarcasm. "That ought to get me through the night."

"Why don't you ask for some refills?"

"Forget it. I can't get any of them refilled for another two weeks. Believe me, it took every bit of persuasion I had to get my damned doctor to give me all that he did. Then I had to call my cardiologist to get the rest. Doctors are such tight asses, if any of them came close to suffering the kind of pain I'm having, you can bet they'd keep their own asses doped up."

"I wish there was something I could do."

It took only a few seconds for Daddy to come up with that something. "Maybe there is. You must know someone who can find pills out there."

Bruce looked confused. "I don't follow you."

"Street drugs, Bruce. Pills, weed, cocaine. The kind of stuff you kids eat like candy nowadays."

He looked from Bruce to me expectantly. "Don't tell me neither of you know where to find that stuff!"

Daddy was actually suggesting that Bruce and I solicit drugs for him. I couldn't believe it. Bruce, on the spot, just shrugged. "I don't fool with that stuff, L.J."

"But you probably know someone who does, right?" Daddy wouldn't let up.

"I guess I could call around and check."

Bruce and his lame answer to Daddy disgusted me. I had to stop this. "Bruce and I don't take drugs, Daddy. Not only is it illegal, but the pushers would rip you off. They'll charge you an arm and a leg."

"You can't put a price tag on this kind of pain," he shot back at me.

"I know you're in a lot of pain, Daddy. But your doctor knows what he's doing. I think if you would just take the medication according to directions—"

"Who the fuck asked you to think, anyway?" he exploded.

Infuriated, I turned to leave the room. If I stayed, I knew, I would say something I'd regret.

Daddy was up and out of his chair immediately. "You're not going anywhere yet. There's something I've been meaning to discuss with you."

He crossed the room to his desk and began furiously punching the keys on the calculator. "House notes, electric bills, insurance, credit card receipts! Christ, the list goes on and on, and you pay no attention to it! You've never had to! Do you have the faintest idea what all this costs? I'm surrounded by women who are trying to drive me to the poorhouse." He whirled around and pointed the bandaged stub of his arm only inches from my face. "Have any one of you bothered to notice that I have no source of income other than my investment company? Have you noticed that I've quit practicing law? Or do you think that money grows on fucking trees?"

Out of habit I backed away from him. But I was incensed that he had the audacity to blame his money problems on us—and, in particular, on me. I pushed myself forward again. "Daddy, it was your decision to pay the note on the house for Bruce and me, and you're the one who offered to pay the electric bills. You're the one who gave me credit cards to charge the things I needed, and never once have you told me that you resented doing any of it," I said bitterly.

"Well, I certainly never expected my children to take advantage of me the way they have." He took on an injured expression, but for once I wasn't going to be buffaloed by his theatrics.

"If anyone is taking advantage of you, it's your girlfriend. Marty's the one riding around in a new Corvette, not me. Maybe if you didn't blow every dime you had on her, you wouldn't be so broke."

He looked at me as if I'd lost my mind. "Do you really think I'd be able to keep her if I didn't occasionally treat her to something nice?"

"Knowing her, I doubt it." I'd gone too far, and I knew it.

"I'll spend my money any fucking way I please, and neither you nor anyone else is going to tell me otherwise."

The doctor had asked that we keep him calm, so I let

up. "Why don't you start taking on some new cases? I can't remember the last time you've been to work."

"You know damned well I've referred ninety percent of my caseload to associates. I am a sick man, dammit. I could fall over dead from a heart attack just like that!" He snapped his fingers with a flourish.

Sure, I thought. Work is going to kill you when you've survived jumping in the sack with a girl twenty-seven years younger than you.

He took off in a new direction. "I wouldn't be in this position now if that stupid fucking insurance company would pay for the loss of my hand. Those sons of bitches! I pay more money per year on insurance premiums than most people earn per year. Well, I'm not going to sit around and wait for some pansy ass to decide to pay me. Let them learn the hard way that they're jacking around the wrong man. I'll sue those assholes for triple what they owe me if I don't get what's due me. Christ, the way they're acting, you'd think I'd shot my own hand off!"

CHAPTER 9

CAROL

In mid-September of 1971 Joanne surprised us all by remarrying. Her new husband was James Joseph Tracy; everyone who knew him called him Joe. I had met Joe on several occasions at Joanne's house, but I never dreamed their relationship had become so serious.

Joe had grown up in the neighboring area of Metairie and knew some of the same people Joanne did. He was a dark-haired, blue-eyed, twenty-four-year-old former navy man, strong and assertive. Divorced, with a three-year-old daughter of his own, he seemed very attached to Kelly and Lori. He and Joanne had a lot in common, so I thought they were a good match. More than anything, I was glad to see her happy again.

Daddy and Joe got along fabulously. Both were direct and outspoken, and they had the same ribald sense of humor. Joe owned a Labrador retriever he had spent a great deal of time and patience training. Duck hunting was his passion, and he spent weekends in a pirogue in the marshes, dog at his side. Daddy liked that.

One evening in late November while I was visiting Joanne, Joe mentioned that he was going to run by Daddy's house and borrow a shotgun to take on a hunting trip. He'd agreed to lend his own gun to a friend, and Daddy had offered Joe use of his. It didn't occur to me then that the borrowed shotgun was the same one involved in Daddy's accident.

It had been three months since the accident, and I was acutely aware that the insurance company handling the claim for the loss of his hand had steadfastly refused to pay. According to Daddy, they were incompetent assholes who would live to rue the day they ever gave Leonard J. Fagot the runaround. I was still unsure about why they were holding out, but I was sure there was more to their reasoning than Daddy was willing to admit. According to Bruce, the shooting had happened just the way Daddy had said. He'd slipped on a soft-drink bottle, and the gun had gun off. If that was the case, why wouldn't the company pay the claim? It made no sense to me that they would not settle a claim that seemed so cut and dried, or that they wouldn't have exercised good sense and dealt squarely with Daddy, an attorney who had firmly stated his intention to file suit for compensation. There were just too many vagaries involved to figure it all out.

One week after Joe returned from his hunting expedition a very elated Daddy stopped by my house. He was beaming as he came into the kitchen.

"I can finally force those idiots to pay!"

Bruce looked up from his dinner plate. "You mean the insurance people?"

Daddy nodded.

"How?" I asked.

He slid a chair out from under the table and plopped down. A smug smile spread across his face. "Can you believe the damned gun has a faulty trigger?"

"No shit!" Bruce slammed his fist on the table.

"No shit. Joe took that gun duck hunting, and the son of a bitch kept jamming on him. He didn't shoot any ducks, but he sure made my day!"

He laughed, and Bruce joined in. I watched them both in silence, intrigued by this latest tidbit of information.

"This is the best part," Daddy crowed. "Joe gets back home and takes the gun to a guy he knows, an expert. The guy checks the gun out and finds metal filings in the trigger mechanism."

"What does that mean?" I asked.

Daddy turned to me. "Those filings came from the

trigger mechanism. Apparently there was some sort of friction in the components. But the kicker is, when this guy slammed the stock of the gun on the ground, it discharged with the safety on." He looked for all the world as if he expected us to applaud.

"So the gun is defective, right?" asked Bruce. "I mean, hell, it's a brand-new gun."

"Damned straight it's defective. This guy is going to sign a statement to that effect."

"What happens now?" I asked.

"Now I send that baby to White Laboratories. It's the same lab that did the ballistics on the rifle used in JFK's assassination. I'll get them to examine mine and then sign a statement about their findings. There's no chance that the insurance company won't pay."

True to his word, Daddy shipped the Winchester twelve-gauge shotgun to White Laboratories, buoyed with confidence.

In the days that followed, he spent his time deriding the insurance company and trying to convince anyone who had the patience to listen that the lab's findings would grant him the leverage he needed to claim the two hundred thousand dollars worth of insurance due him.

He tried too hard. The more he talked, the more convinced I became that there was a reason for his dramatic overkill.

Although Marty lived with Daddy, she usually parked her car around the corner or in the woods, no doubt for her parents' sake. It was sad and ludicrous for me to see her, an awkward, thin young woman, sitting in Mama's favorite chair. She seemed to be in awe of Daddy's house and its plush surroundings, and her dark eyes would roam over the contents of the rooms, lovingly, possessively. I spoke only the barest of pleasantries to her. I was well aware that if I cared to have any relationship with Daddy, I would have to tolerate her presence.

I saw only two aspects to her personality: Either she

giggled and chattered, all full of nervous energy, or she pouted and acted sullen. She seemed peculiar to me at times. When Daddy and I would talk, she would mutter under her breath. Her words were too soft to be heard, and I often wondered if she was even aware that she was speaking, though it did occur to me that she might simply be doing it to annoy me. If the latter was the case, then she succeeded. She also had the strange habit of making faces behind my back. On more than one occasion, sensing that she was doing this, I spun around quickly and caught her sticking her tongue out at me.

Despite her imperious attitude and the pleasure I sensed she got in playing mistress of the manor, she always seemed jealous of Daddy's girls, and particularly of my mother. Whenever she was with my sisters or me her face would turn to a bright red and her eyes would darken.

Of course, I could understand her position. It couldn't have been easy for her to fill the shoes of my graceful, charming mother, who'd shared Daddy's life for twenty-five years. Nor could it have been easy to replace his four children. I did not hate her in those days. I only hated the role she played in separating the people I loved and the perverse pleasure she seemed to derive in doing so. I saw her as an interloper, who had first invaded, then taken over, my familiar world.

On Thanksgiving Day 1971 we sisters all gathered with our loved ones at Mama's house for dinner. It was the first time that Daddy wasn't there to share this special day. The table was splendidly set, and the air was rich with good food, but there was a pall. Even the little ones seemed aware of the empty chair at the head of the table that neither Joe, Bruce, nor Gary Gonzales was willing to occupy.

"That's Paw-Paw's chair," piped Kelly. Her light brown hair, streaked with gold, curled in ringlets around her heart-shaped face, and her blue eyes were questioning. "Why isn't he here, Nana?"

Mama smiled at her. Nana was the name she had chosen to be called by her grandchildren. "Paw-Paw's not here because he's eating dinner at his own house."

"I bet he comes to see us later."

My throat caught at her innocent conviction. At four, there was no way she could possibly understand that her Paw-Paw would not be showing up for Thanksgiving.

Kelly hopped into the empty chair at the head of the table, arms folded across her small chest. "I'll save this chair for him, in case he does come," she said. My heart went out to her, this tiny sentinel waiting for the unlikely to happen.

The weeks passed, and Christmas arrived. While helping Bruce and the kids decorate the tree, I thought about Christmases gone by. Trimming the tree had been an almost sacred ritual in my parents' home. Our tree always stood two stories high, and as we girls would decorate the lower half, Daddy would do the top from his perch on a ladder. We'd stand on tiptoe to pass the ornaments up to him. With Christmas carols playing in the background and a fire blazing in the hearth, we'd drink mugs of warm, spicy eggnog that Mama would prepare. It was a special time of year, filled with a special warmth.

Kim's voice pulled me back to the present. I felt ashamed. I should have been making every attempt to create special holidays for my family, and instead I was daydreaming about the past. Would I ever grow up and let go of the past? Would I ever accept the simple truth that all things change with time, including our family?

Daddy was as generous with his grandchildren as he'd been with us. For Christmas he gave an expensive swing set, complete with ladders and slide, to Bruce and Kim, and one just like it to Kelly and Lori. To my surprise, he gave Nancy, Shirley, Joanne, and me each one thousand dollars in cash. I knew that he was strapped for money, and I felt that the lavish gifts were his way of making amends.

As New Year's Eve approached, Bruce and I decided to throw a party. Actually, it was an impromptu decision on my part, an attempt to cheer myself up and lessen the painful awareness that I would never again be attending one of my parents' famous New Year's Eve parties. We invited a crowd over, including Nancy, Gary, Joanne, and Joe. Mama had plans of her own, and Shirley was spending the night with friends. Still, I was happy that at least part of my family would be by my side to ring in the new year.

By the time midnight drew near, the party was in full swing. As the disc jockey on the radio announced the approach of midnight, the laughing, drunk crowd inside my home surged through the front door to light fireworks. It was a bitterly cold night. I hugged my jacket to my shoulders and laughed at the antics of the men in the group as they lined up Roman candles, determined to blast each one into the sky precisely at the stroke of midnight. From the open doorway I could hear the first strains of "Auld Lang Syne" coming from the stereo speakers. As if on cue, the men lit the rows of fireworks, and we welcomed 1972 with a fantastic display.

Amid the noise and laughter I found myself gazing at the house next door. I saw the sleek outline of Marty's Corvette in the driveway and felt a tightness behind my eyelids. I felt a hand on my arm and turned to look at Nancy. She looked in the direction of Daddy's house with longing in her eyes, and I knew that she felt as sad as I did.

It was after two A.M. when the last of the partyers left and I escorted my very drunk husband to bed. I made a halfhearted attempt to pick up the mess everyone had left, but I quit before too long. Tired, and a little tipsy myself, I went to bed.

I had just fallen into a light sleep when the pressure of a hand upon my shoulder woke me.

Startled, I opened my bleary eyes to find Daddy

standing over my bed. In the dim light he appeared wraithlike in his white pajamas.

"Daddy, you scared me half to death," I whispered.

He stared at me, his face a pale blue in the moonlight shining through the sheer curtains. "I never meant to scare you." He spoke haltingly, his words slurred. His body swayed suddenly, as if off balance, and I made a quick grab for him. He clung to my arm for support.

I snatched my robe from the foot of the bed and stood beside him, still half supporting his weight. I led him down the hallway and into the spare bedroom toward the bed. I switched on the bedside lamp and noticed in its muted glow that his pupils were wide and dilated, his eyelids heavy. There was no mistaking that he was drugged.

"Daddy, why don't you lie down and get some sleep," I suggested. I patted the bed and prayed he would listen to me.

He chuckled then, a raw sound without humor. "I can't sleep. No sleep for me."

He rubbed his injured arm, but it was an absent-minded stroking.

"Is it your arm? Does the pain keep you awake?"

He stared at the wall as if he hadn't heard my question. When he finally spoke, his voice was flat. "Pain is all in the mind. I've seen men injured on the battlefield die, when there was no need for them to die. They just gave in to the pain, let it take control. Pain causes fear, and that fear spreads just like a cancer eating away at your sanity. Sometimes it's easier for a man to die than it is for him to suffer."

I was fascinated by his words and the hypnotic cadence in which he delivered them.

"Take this arm, for instance," he continued. "Some people might not have survived this." He held out his injured arm, which was covered by a white sock. There was a strange light in his eyes, and the conversation was beginning to make me feel more uneasy than fascinated.

Without warning he whisked the sock from the stump of his arm and held the arm up to the lamp. It was the first time I'd seen his injury laid bare. I gasped. The hand, along with a quarter of his forearm, had been removed, and at the end of the forearm, flaps of skin had been surgically folded inward, barely covering the remaining bone. The skin surrounding the injury was the shiny pink of scars that have only lately begun to heal, and crisscross patterns where stitches had been removed flared an angry red. Part of his tattoo—the date, *Dec. 7, 1941*— remained, the lettering now puckered and shriveled. I closed my eyes.

"Open your eyes and take a good look, Carol. It's an ugly sight, but I want you to remember it so you will always know how I've suffered for you and for all of my family."

I suddenly felt bone weary. All the stress and anxiety of the last year sank onto my mind. "Daddy, please lie back and get some rest now."

He nodded, and swung his legs onto the bed. I helped him crawl between the covers, then sat beside him, stroking his hand. In a short while his body began to twitch as his muscles relaxed. Once I thought he was asleep, I switched off the bedside lamp and got up to leave the darkened room.

As I turned, I felt a hand clutch the back of my robe. "I've dug myself a hole I can't get out of."

His words hung in the darkness, cloaking me in a suffocating, irrational dread. I couldn't stay in that dark room one second longer, so I kept walking, and shut the door behind myself.

In the early light of dawn I arose to check on him, but the bedroom was empty, the bedcovers neatly folded. It was as if he'd never been there.

CHAPTER 10

CAROL

One evening in late January there was an insistent rapping on my front door. I was in the middle of bathing Kimberly, so I scooped her out of the tub, wrapped her in a warm towel, then ran to answer the door.

As soon as I unlatched the lock, the doorknob twisted and Joanne burst in.

"Do you know what he's done?" she screamed in a shrill voice.

"Who?"

"Daddy. I can't believe my own father would do this to me!" She slammed her purse down hard enough on the kitchen table to make her car keys fall out and skitter across the glass top.

"Here," I said. "Sit down and tell me what this is all about." Kimberly came into the room, pajamas in hand, so I seated myself across the table from Joanne and began to dress my daughter as Joanne dug around inside her purse and took out a pack of Winstons.

I watched her light the cigarette. She took a deep drag to calm herself, then exhaled a thin stream of smoke that curled lazily around her head. "He sold my house right out from under me. Can you believe it? Because I can't!"

"You can't be serious! How could he do that? The house is in your name, isn't it?"

"He said it was," she replied. She stabbed her cigarette out in the ashtray. "You were sitting right there when he said it."

"I certainly was. Do you mean to say that it was never put in your name?"

"Obviously not. At the time of the act of sale he handed me a paper and said, 'Here. Sign this Joanne, and the house will be in your name.' So like an ass, I signed the damned paper. I took him at his word, and he lied to me." She lit up another Winston and had a few short puffs.

"I still don't understand," I said. "What was it you signed then?"

"I signed power of attorney over to him, which gave him the right to sell the damned house."

"He told you this?"

"Yes. He looked me right in the eye and said, 'Now, honey, how could you have possibly thought the house was in your name? You have no collateral and no established credit. I thought I made that very clear at the time I bought the house.' He tricked me. And stupid, stupid me—I fell for it." She slumped forward and buried her head in her hands.

"God knows Daddy has done his share of rotten things," I said, "but I can't believe that even he could stoop this low."

"I'll tell you how low he's stooped," she said through the cloud of smoke around us. "I have thirty days to vacate my house! Thirty days to pack up everything I own and get the hell out! And you don't think for one minute that I'll ever see a penny of the six thousand dollars I put up for the down payment, do you?"

I shrugged my shoulders. She was probably right.

"I asked him point blank for my six thousand dollars, and do you know what he said?" Her eyebrows arched.

"No."

"He said that I would be forfeiting that money in lieu of the house notes he's been paying for me all along. That's the name of the game with Daddy. He offers to do something nice for you, and you agree because you believe that's what he wants to do. Then one day, out of the total blue, you find out that what he did had nothing to do with generosity." There was fury in her words, but she couldn't hide the hurt in her eyes.

"I don't know what to say," I said.

She ground out the cigarette slowly, resigned to it all. "What is there to say, really? I've lost the house. But I'm going to tell you something, Carol. There's something wrong inside of Daddy. Something's changed; he's not the same person. It's just like that movie we saw when we were kids, *Invasion of the Body Snatchers*—you remember that, don't you?"

I had to laugh. "It scared the hell out of me."

"Well, that's what he reminds me of. He's the same on the outside, but different on the inside. I don't trust him any more than I'd trust a rattlesnake. I told him that as far as I'm concerned, he can sell the damned house, do whatever he wants, as long as he stays the hell out of my life." She started sobbing. I could only thank God that she didn't know about the two hundred thousand dollars Daddy had collected for George's death. That would have been just too much for her to bear.

After she'd gone, I thought about all she'd said. My father's selling Joanne's house was despicable and cruel. Knowing him, he could have done this for only one reason. He needed money. That could mean just one thing—he still hadn't received the money from the insurance company for the loss of his hand. I wondered if he'd received any word from White Laboratories.

I wasn't about to risk stirring up a hornet's nest by asking Daddy directly, so I decided to hit on the next best source of information.

I cornered Bruce in our garage, where he was, as usual, tinkering with his Jaguar. He was half-buried under the hood of the car, apparently fiddling with the engine. When he saw me, he pulled out from under the hood and began wiping his hands on a clean rag.

I got straight to the point. "Bruce, has Daddy heard anything from White Laboratories?"

As I waited for his reply, he continued to wipe his hands as if he were totally engrossed in it.

"Well?" No weaseling out this time.

"Yeah. Yeah, he got the report back," he said as though it were no big deal.

Getting a straight answer out of him would be like pulling teeth. I pushed on. "What did the report say?"

"Nothing much, really. It just stated their findings on the gun." He inched away from me and slid toward his workbench.

I dogged his footsteps. "What did they find?"

"Oh, you know." He waved his hand vaguely. "They found the same metal shavings in the trigger mechanism as Joe's friend did."

He made himself busy arranging tools, his back to me.

"About these metal shavings," I said. "How did they get there?"

He studied his feet as if there were something terribly interesting about his blue-and-white sneakers. "Well, they probably came from some kind of friction, sort of a grinding effect, like maybe one of the components in the trigger mechanism grinding against another."

"You mean like metal grinding against metal and producing metal shavings?"

"Something like that." He began briskly rubbing a clean cloth over the surface of the Jaguar.

I felt like a prosecutor grilling a witness. "Would this type of friction cause the components to wear down, making the gun fire defectively?"

He chewed on that for a second. "Yes, I suppose so. But then, I'm not a gun expert."

"Could the gun have been deliberately tampered with?" I hadn't planned to ask him that; it just popped out.

He seemed startled. The question had caught him off guard. "What an imagination." He attempted a laugh, but it came out more a nervous giggle. "Now, who on earth would deliberately sabotage your father's gun?"

"No one I can think of," I said slowly. "It just seems odd to me that a new gun that had hardly been used would have worn-down components. And why hasn't the insurance company paid the claim yet? I'm wondering if there might have been some problem with the gun. Just tell me this: Could there be some way, hypothetically speaking, of tampering with a shotgun that would wear down the components and cause metal shavings to be present in the trigger mechanism?"

"Hypothetically speaking, all you would have to do would be to file the components down. That would produce the wear-and-tear effect and account for the metal shavings. By the way, the insurance people have already paid your Dad."

Well, that blew my theory that Daddy had sold Joanne's house because he needed money. "I didn't know that. Did he get what he was hoping for?"

"He settled out of court for only a quarter of the face value."

"But why? He had two statements given by experts, and you as an eyewitness. Why wouldn't he be entitled to the whole sum?"

I watched, mesmerized, as Bruce's jaw grew slack and his face paled. "Now, wait a minute," he said. "I never said I was an eyewitness. No way could I have witnessed anything. I was deep in the woods by the time it happened."

"But I thought you said in the hospital that you were behind him. You didn't say anything about being off in the woods."

"You misunderstood me. The way it happened was, when I got out of the truck your Dad told me to go one way, into the woods, and he told Marty to go the opposite way. He was still at the truck fooling with the dogs when Marty and I took off. I heard the gun go off once, then twice more; that's the distress signal hunters use. I ran toward the sound of the shots, and there he was, on his knees, tying a piece of leather around his arm." Bruce's eyes were deadly serious.

I knew I couldn't pump anything further out of

Bruce, so I left him to his tinkering and returned to the house.

Inside, I tried to unravel the bits of information I'd gleaned from Bruce. I couldn't shake the feeling that he was hiding something. But for whom? Only one person I could think of, and that was Daddy.

As I replayed the day in August Daddy shot his hand, I remembered how adamant he'd been about my not joining them. But he'd brought Marty. Why hadn't he wanted me there? My memory flashed back to the hospital when the most urgent thing on Daddy's mind was that I find Bruce. Had Daddy been worried about the possibility of losing his hand? Hell, no. He'd been worried about insurance money, and finding Bruce, and making statements to the police. I did not like where my thoughts were leading me. A persistent little voice in my mind whispered, Why was he worried about insurance money? Doesn't that seem odd? Damned right it seemed odd. Very odd. But not as odd as finding metal shavings in a brand-new shotgun.

"Alright," I said aloud. "What is it you don't like about these metal shavings?

The fact that they existed.

And the insurance company wouldn't pay. Even with two statements given by experts, it still wouldn't pay. Why in God's name not?

My mind was whirling now. I remembered Bruce's words: "Hypothetically speaking, all you would have to do would be to file the components down."

And I remembered Daddy's, on New Year's Eve: "Take a good look, Carol . . . so you will always know how I've suffered for you and for all of my family."

Not for me, Daddy. Please don't say you did that for me.

Did what?

My fevered brain demanded an answer. Did what?

Shot off your own hand. The thought was like a scream ricocheting off the walls of my mind. You didn't want me to go that day, did you, Daddy? Because you knew ahead of time what would happen. Because you planned it, and only God knows how long you planned it. That's why you bought the dogs and, of course, the shotgun, the Winchester twelve-gauge shotgun with the metal filings in it. Because, hypothetically speaking, all you had to do was to file down the components, and while White Laboratories did find the filings, they couldn't say for certain where they had come from. That's why you told Bruce to go one way and Marty another. That's why you were already tying a piece of leather around your arm when Bruce reached your side. You even tried to tell me, in your own way, didn't you? Hell, you almost spelled it out, only I didn't catch it. Well, I've caught it now, Daddy. And how the hell am I supposed to live with it?

CHAPTER 11

CAROL

The road to my adulthood had been paved with traditional values. Truth and integrity were the moral bread and butter of my upbringing, fed me by my father, the one person I most believed in. With the absolute faith that only a child can possess, I believed heart and soul in the righteousness of the law, fought for and defended by my dad, a powerful and noble advocate.

Now, at age twenty-two, I had learned that truth is sometimes impossible to find, and integrity easily sold for the right price.

I believed my father had committed atrocities that dulled the senses. Accepting this belief seemed the road to madness; denial, the road to self-deceit. If I could have reached these conclusions through reason alone, I might have been able to fall back on that legal loophole called reasonable doubt and judge him not guilty. As it was, my ability to analyze the situation rationally, combined with a long knowledge of him as a unique and often irrational person, left me without recourse.

There was nothing in this world that could ease the pain of that knowledge, no miracle potion, no magic cure. I was shattered and, worse, unable to turn to my husband for comfort. Bruce was far too caught up in Daddy's powerful charisma to be objective. How could I blame him? In that respect we were completely alike. I had spent a lifetime caught in that same spider's web of blind devotion. I could no more abandon this man who had given me life than I could have abandoned my own children for being something less than what they should have been.

It was time to take stock of my life. Save for my children, I was lonelier than I had ever been. I loved my husband dearly as a person, but not nearly enough as a man. It was no more his fault than it was mine, just a fact that I could no longer ignore. My world was falling apart around me, and I sent up a little prayer that happiness might come my way. Someone must have been listening, because Mike Holland called me not long after. Two years earlier I'd made the decision to put him out of my life, but I hadn't learned how to put him out of my heart.

I agreed to meet with him the following day in Audubon Park, part of the beautiful garden district of Old New Orleans. He was sitting on a park bench when I arrived. He smiled up at me, eyes crinkling, and there was no apology in their blue depths, only love. I wondered then how I could have ever blinded myself to how very much I loved him.

We talked for hours. He told me he had recently left his wife, Anne, who had begun to stifle him, as if she "breathed every bit of air in the room," in his words. Unable to make her understand, and unwilling to mold himself to her expectations, he'd finally left her and the son he loved dearly.

I could understand his situation. It was not so different from my own. I knew what it felt like to be trapped in a marriage that was no longer fulfilling. Though I could not have known him as well as Anne did, having spent years with him, I knew him well enough to understand that there was a freedom of spirit within his soul that would not be possessed by any woman. It was that quality that had drawn me to him from the very start. There was a strength of character in Mike Holland that I admired much as I'd admired the strong side of Daddy. At that point in my life I felt so depleted of emotional strength that I desperately needed someone to lean on. It was the sweetest feeling in the world to admit that I loved this tall, rangy man who had the courage to be himself. This sweetness was surpassed only by my instinct that he would move heaven and earth to have me by his side, the place I now knew I most wanted to be.

Now I had to tell Bruce. It would have been so much easier to tell him that I wanted a separation, some time to myself, than to tell him that I loved another man. But then I remembered all the opportunities I'd let pass when I'd tried to tell him the truth about my daughter's conception. I knew that I would only inflict more misery on both of us if I put it off.

He was in the den, tending to his aquarium, one of his favorite hobbies, when I finally summoned up the courage. I struggled to make the words come out right. "Bruce, there's something I have to say. Please believe me when I tell you that I never meant to hurt you."

His eyes met mine, and I knew that I had to speak then or I never would. "I want a divorce."

He exhaled as if the wind had been knocked out of him. "You don't mean that." His voice was shaky, low in timbre.

"Yes, I do. I don't love you the way you deserve to be loved. But it's not only that—there's someone else in my life."

His eyes grew dark and solemn. "I don't care what you've done, or who you've done it with."

I felt helpless. If only he would yell or scream, anything but stare at me with that hurt look in his eyes.

"It's more than an affair." My voice was pleading, its sound begging him to understand if the words were too hard for him to hear. "I'm in love with him."

Without warning he punched the paneled wall. I winced. "I don't want to hear this," he said slowly. "Go to him, tell him that it's over. Tell him fucking anything."

"I won't do that," I said. "You and I have a marriage in name only, Bruce. I know you won't be able to settle for that. No one could."

"I'll settle for whatever I have to!" He slammed his fist into the wall again.

He was making it too hard, and God knows it was hard enough. "I don't think I'm getting through to you," I said, firmly but gently. "I don't plan to spend my life with you. It isn't fair to either one of us. You can't possibly want to hang on to someone who doesn't love you."

He sank into a chair and buried his head in his hands. Sadness welled up in me, and I had to fight back the tears. "I don't know what to say; you're my life, Carol."

"I don't want to be your life, Bruce. I want you to have a life of your own, a full, happy one."

He nodded in a slow, dejected way.

"There's something else I need to say. Something I should have said a long time ago, only I didn't have the guts."

As I spoke he just sat there, motionless, head between his hands. I was grateful that he wasn't looking at me, and I wished for all the world that I did not have to say these words to him. "I became involved with Mike while you were in Germany, before I ever joined you there. By the time I got to Germany I was pregnant, although I didn't know it until a week later."

He sat up in the chair, and his head snapped straight. "Are you trying to say that Kimberly is not my daughter?"

"Yes," I said. "God, there were so many times I wanted to tell you, but I couldn't do it, couldn't stand the thought of telling you. So I've kept it to myself all this time, and now I'm so damned tired of lies." I couldn't stop the tears then.

"You can't know it for sure." His eyes begged me to agree, to allow him that one fragile hope, but I remained silent.

The next few days were very exhausting ones for me. With an ache in my heart I watched Bruce pack his belongings. I had truly cared for him, and if he was heartbroken, then he was no more so than I.

Daddy was shocked to hear of the breakup of my marriage. He accepted with resignation my decision to leave Bruce and asked me to stay on at the house. I gratefully accepted, since I had nowhere else to go, and my job would never support me and two children. I felt guilty, ashamed, and oddly lonely without Bruce in the days after his departure. I'd cleared the path that led to Mike Holland's side, but I hadn't been prepared for the brambles that tore at my heart along the way.

On July 20, 1972, Joanne gave birth to a third daughter. The baby was born seven weeks prematurely, a tiny, three-pound eight-ounce, precious scrap of humanity named Jamie Lee Tracy. Looking through the glass walls of her incubator, at her small form attached to wires and feeding tubes, I could only feel that if there truly were a God in heaven, then He would spare this infant's life. Surely he owed Joanne that much, two years after her first husband's death.

In the weeks to follow, whether through divine intervention or Jamie Lee Tracy's sheer determination to live, the baby began to improve, even gaining a few much-needed ounces. One day, through the nursery window, I watched Joanne tenderly stroke the baby's tiny hand, and I felt a great well of joy and happiness surge through me as the delicate pink fingers curled around Joanne's. I knew then that Jamie would make it, and I prayed with all my heart that her life would be a happy one, free of the violence and deceit wrenching ours.

In late November Gary Gonzales, Nancy's live-in love, was busted for possession and intent to distribute marijuana. According to Nancy's account, the police kicked in the front door of the apartment they shared and dragged Gary handcuffed from the premises. Beside herself, she'd called Daddy at two A.M. to tell him what happened and begged him to come down to the Jefferson Parish central lockup to bail Gary out.

Daddy did better than that. He made a phone call to a judge, a close personal friend of his, and as Gary had never been arrested before, he was released on his own recognizance that night. Gary never did go to trial for the arrest. Daddy handled the whole affair, and by the time all the legal red tape had been cut through, the charges were reduced to simple possession since it was a first offense. Gary pleaded guilty and got off with only a slap on the wrist.

While he may have been lucky in that respect, Gary did not fare so well in other areas. He had thus far managed very well to keep a low profile in regard to Daddy. This was no doubt a result of Nancy's carefully thought-out plan to keep it that way. She was no fool. She was certainly aware that the old adage "Out of sight, out of mind" held a lot of water. Prior to Gary's arrest he'd been nothing more to Daddy than a kid who shared Nancy's living space. But Gary Gonzales became a household word afterward. Daddy, who had never been shy of cuss words, became a veritable fountain of foul language. He spewed forth expletives at a dizzying speed, all aimed at Gary.

The foul language was bad, but it did little damage other than to assault my senses and set my ears to burning. Daddy's threats were what bothered me. "I'll bury that motherfucker six feet under" was the one that got to me the most. It was the same one he'd used to discourage Mama from filing for divorce. The deadly, sinister tone in which he said the words alarmed me. My every instinct warned me to pay heed, and I knew well enough from experience that a threat from Daddy almost always led to action.

I told Nancy about Daddy's outbursts and threats. My only thought was to warn her and, if possible, ward off a chance encounter between the two men. Unfortunately, my plan backfired because Nancy did the last thing in the world I expected her to do. She decided to confront the issue head-on.

It was a Friday night, and I was at Daddy's, along with

Joe and Joanne. Joanne and I were in the dining room chatting over a cup of coffee, and Daddy and Joe were in the library watching a basketball game on television. They had bet each other on the outcome of the game, and every so often one of them would let out a loud whoop.

By an act of God, none of the kids were there to witness what happened next.

Nancy and Gary walked in the front door without even knocking. Nancy's face was set in serious lines, and she appeared ready to do battle. Gary seemed a bit nervous, but not unduly so. Why should he have been—he'd never been exposed to Daddy's terrible temper. But I was sure that he was about to be.

Nancy glanced in my direction, her blue eyes solemn. "Where's Daddy?"

Another loud whoop came from the library. Grabbing Gary by the arm, she steered him toward the hallway leading to the library. After they disappeared from sight, I held my breath and waited for Daddy's explosion. Nothing. The house was ominously quiet, and I strained my ears for any sounds from the library. Then I heard a series of loud thumping sounds, followed by a piercing shriek from Nancy.

I was up and out of my chair in a heartbeat. Halfway down the hallway I collided with Nancy, who was ashen-faced and wild-eyed. "He's going to kill Gary," she shrieked. "Stop him! Somebody stop him!"

I could hear Joe screaming, "L.J., calm down! Come on, man, back off!" I suddenly felt bloodless, as if my bones were made of jelly. I could feel Joanne's breath on the back of my neck, and when I turned to look at her, her eyes were as big as saucers.

Joe's voice came down the hall again, high-pitched, pleading. "Come on, man, you don't want to do this. Give me the gun, man."

I wasted no more time. As I yanked open the louvered doors, I felt the hair on my neck stand on end at the sight before me. Gary was seated in Daddy's easy chair. Daddy towered over him, his forty-five pistol only inches from Gary's face. The barrel of the gun shone wickedly in the lamplight, which seemed to surround Gary in a halo. The sight of the gun was terrifying, but it was nothing compared with the look on Daddy's face. His features were distorted, twisted into an ugly snarl of rage, his eyes slit and dark with menace, his lips compressed in a tight line of fury.

Joe shook his head and waved a silent warning for us to leave the room. The fear in his eyes only deepened my own fear and rooted me to the spot.

Daddy was oblivious to our presence. Suddenly he placed the barrel of the gun to Gary's mouth.

"Open your mouth, you son of a bitch!" he demanded.

Gary began to cry. "Please, Mr. Fagot—"

Daddy leaned forward with his stump of an arm and mashed Gary's head into the back of the chair. With his other hand he shoved the barrel of the gun against Gary's closed lips. "Open your mouth, you bastard, or I'll blow you the fuck away, right now."

Gary parted his lips to let the barrel in. His body heaved violently as the barrel entered. Saliva drooled in thick strands from his lips. Daddy forced the gun down his throat.

Joe stepped forward and grabbed Daddy by the shoulders. "L.J., that's enough! Come on, give it up before you do something you'll regret!"

Daddy didn't even bother to look in Joe's direction. "Get the fuck away from me or you'll be next, I fucking promise you that."

Joe backed away. Joanne and I stood paralyzed with fear, transfixed by the sickening display before us.

"Get up," Daddy ordered Gary. "On your fucking knees."

Gary rose from the chair, his hands gripping the arms on either side so tightly I could see his knuckles whiten from the effort. My mind raced frantically as I tried to come up with some plan of action. There was no doubt in my mind that Daddy was completely out of control. The slightest movement might set him off.

Gary sank to the floor on his knees, sweat staining his shirt as he twitched and jerked.

"Nobody puts one of my daughters in a situation like you did," said Daddy. "Now, I'm going to pull this trigger and blow your brains all over the place, and you can think about what you've done on your way to hell."

Nancy, who had been hovering in the open doorway, whimpered. Time came to an abrupt standstill as I watched Daddy's thumb flip back the hammer on the forty-five before curling around the trigger.

"No, Daddy!" Nancy yelled as she flung herself at him.

Daddy pulled the trigger. There was only a loud click as the empty chamber fired. Gary fell, as if in slow motion, onto his side. I closed my eyes. From across the room I heard Daddy chuckle.

"This time was only a warning," he said.

CHAPTER 12

CAROL

It was no surprise to me that Daddy was once again plagued by financial difficulties. How could he expect not to be, since he continued to enjoy the same lavish life-style he'd led while he was working. It made no sense to me that he had given up a successful, lucrative practice at the pinnacle of his career. His excuse for quitting—ill health—just didn't ring true with me. I did not believe him to be too ill to work after his heart attack, especially since the doctor had advised all of us to avoid treating him as though he were an invalid and to urge him to resume a normal life. It seemed obvious to me that Daddy had simply grown lazy and accustomed to answering to no one. Too many times I had answered the phone at his house to find a client on the other end in need of legal assistance, only to hear Daddy say, "Tell him I'm not here."

The money problems came to my attention through Mama. She told me that Daddy hadn't paid the mortgage notes for the past three months on her new home on St. Paul Avenue and that she'd recently received a letter from the homestead threatening default of the loan if the notes were not paid in short order. She asked if I would speak with Daddy about it, but I firmly declined. There was nothing in the world I wanted less than to get involved in a free-for-all with my father on the subject of money.

Without my support, Mama was forced to take matters into her own hands. I was surprised as hell when she reported to me the gist of that conversation: Daddy had actually offered to give up his residence, the pride and joy of his life, and move into the smaller house next door, where I was living. He would have Mama move back to 279 Citrus Road, and he'd rent out the house on St. Paul Avenue. That way, he'd explained, he would have one less note to pay.

I wasn't the slightest bit concerned about giving up my residence, but I was most worried about the inane idea of Mama's and Daddy's living next door to each other. With Marty's presence rounding out the cozy picture, the setup was as ludicrous and as potentially dangerous as giving a child a book of matches and a case of dynamite to play with.

On top of it all, Mama was badgering me to move into the house with her. Though she said that there was no point in letting all that room go to waste, I could see right through her. She wanted me there as a buffer and as an intermediary between her and Daddy. I couldn't blame her, and I wouldn't abandon her, so I packed my belongings and began hauling them next door in preparation for the move. Likewise, Daddy began to cart his more prized possessions over to my house. It all seemed funny, like a game of musical houses. To make the game all the more interesting, Joanne and Joe decided to rent the house on St. Paul Avenue.

This all was in November of 1972. Around the same time, Bruce Applegarth fell madly in love. The lady of his affection was not of the flesh and blood variety, but she definitely had all the right curves. She was a forty-foot racing sloop with clean lines and graceful symmetry, aptly named *Stiletto*. I went with Bruce and Daddy to the New Orleans Lakefront Marina to get my first eyeful of the lady who'd captured Bruce's heart.

The vessel had seen better days, and her owner's neglect was obvious. The solid teakwood cabin and deck had faded to a lackluster finish, the paint on her wooden hull cracked and blistered with age. Still, it was easy to see how graceful and majestic she must have once been. The job of restoring her would not be an easy one, but it would be well worth the effort.

"You're really sold on the idea of this boat?" Daddy stood beside me on the pier, his left arm encased in a sling he'd taken to wearing lately.

Bruce's eyes sparkled. "I'm in love with this boat. You know, she sailed all the way here from Denmark over thirty years ago. She's solid as a rock. With the right amount of work, she could be worth an easy forty grand, not that I'd ever dream of selling her."

"If I do buy the boat, I want you to understand that it will be put in Shirley's name for tax purposes. It will belong to her on paper, but of course you'll have complete control over it. Do we have a deal?"

"You bet we have a deal!" said Bruce, pumping Daddy's hand.

The price was agreed upon, the papers signed, and on the day Mama made the move back to Citrus Road, Daddy proudly presented her with the title to the *Stiletto.* Mama and I were in the kitchen unpacking boxes of dishes when he breezed through the back doorway.

I felt Mama tense beside me at his casual entry into what was now supposed to be her home. "Don't you know how to knock?" she asked as she continued to unpack the silverware.

He answered with a wide grin. "I don't know why you have to be this way. Here I go and do something nice for you, and you have to be sarcastic. The simple truth is, I know you got a little shortchanged in the separation, and now I'd like to make amends."

"Oh, good," she replied snidely. "Then you've come to give me a divorce, right?"

He laughed. "What a sense of humor you have, Shirley. Actually, I've brought you something that I'm sure will please you very much."

"What might that be?" she asked, her face deadpan.

"Your own sailboat. Or, I should say, yours and Bruce's. You'll own even shares in the boat. He'll make the necessary repairs and keep the boat in running condition, and you'll be able to use it at your discretion."

"Somehow I can't see you being so generous, Len. What's the catch? What do you have up your sleeve?" She looked in my direction, as if I were in on some conspiracy. I shrugged my shoulders and began stacking dishes in the cabinet.

"No catch," he said, smiling. "I happen to still care for you. Why look a gift horse in the mouth?"

"Spare me, Len. Give it to Marty—she'll appreciate it more."

"Don't be ridiculous," he replied. "I want you to have it. Think of it as my gift to you."

Relaxing beside the pool in lounge chairs, my sister Shirley and I gazed across the hedges dividing the two properties. Today was moving day. Marty teetered unsteadily on high heels as she struggled to balance a heavy box in her arms. Pausing a moment to catch her breath on her way up the steps, she leaned against the wrought-iron railing of the porch.

"Check out the outfit she's wearing!" Shirley joked. "Hot pants and high heels!"

I couldn't stop myself. "Look! She's stamping her feet at us!"

A few minutes later Marty entered the house. Shirley's face was resentful as she turned to me. "I don't know why she has to live right next door to us."

"Well, she does," I said gently, "so you might as well get used to the idea."

She crossed her arms. "I don't want to visit Daddy if she's always going to be there."

"Don't be like that. You have the right to see Daddy any time you want to, and if Marty's around, just try to ignore her."

Shirley's sun-bleached hair fell across her cheekbones. She pushed it away impatiently. "I guess you're right."

"Why don't you go over there now? I'm sure Daddy would like to see you."

I thought a visit would make her feel a little better. I watched her hop from one stepping-stone to the next along the path Daddy had made between the two houses. In a bound she was up the brick steps and tapping lightly on the glass panes of the back door.

Ten minutes later she was back. Her face was streaked with tears, and she held her chin up defiantly. "I went to see Daddy, but I had to push my way inside because Marty wouldn't let me in the door. I sat in a chair in the kitchen, waiting for him." Her eyes were hard, a frightening thing to see in one so young. Her voice was filled with sarcasm as she continued. "When he came in, he sat down across from me, and Marty plopped down on his lap, just staring at me. She twirled the hairs on his chest with her fingers and smiled. Then she mouthed, 'Get out,' moving her lips like this." Shirley did her imitation. "I told Daddy to make her stop, but he just looked surprised and asked me what I was talking about! I told him what she did, and he called me a liar. He said that if I couldn't be any nicer to Marty, I could leave. So I did."

"That bitch!" I said. "I'm going over there!"

"What are you going to do?" she asked.

"I'll be back in a little while."

I crossed the yard and knocked on Daddy's back door. When Marty opened it, we carefully sized each other up.

"What do you want?" she demanded.

I exploded. "Now, you listen to me! Just because you have my father wrapped around your little finger, you think you can do whatever you want to!"

Suddenly Daddy appeared in the open doorway leading from the hallway to the kitchen. "What's going on here?"

"Marty had no right to treat Shirley that way! The kid was in tears. Don't you even care about her?"

"Of course I care about her," he answered smoothly, "but I won't have her starting trouble over Marty."

"You've never stopped to think about what effect your relationship with Marty might have on the poor kid, have you? Getting your own way is the only thing that matters to you!" I could have slapped him for his selfishness.

Daddy glared at me. A tiny vein in the corner of his temple began to throb as he fought to control himself. "I will not have you girls punishing Marty on your mother's behalf. Now, get this straight once and for all: If you can't get along with Marty, plan on staying away."

"Fine," I said, looking at Marty. "You can have the little slut. I'm leaving."

For several weeks I avoided Daddy and spent most of my time with my two children and with Mama and Shirley. I saw Bruce's truck parked in Daddy's driveway a lot. I knew he was making arrangements to have the *Stiletto* delivered and set up on an acre of land adjacent to the big house.

When the *Stiletto* did arrive, she was an awesome sight. Having seen her only at the boat slip, I was unprepared for the actual size of the vessel. She towered over everything on the property. Bruce went to work on her right away. He would put in hours sanding the hull and restoring the wood to its original luster before tossing in the towel at the end of the day and returning to his apartment uptown. Occasionally I watched him work from a distance, certain that he was unaware of my scrutiny and somewhat surprised by his obvious zeal to get a job done for once.

One night in May 1973 I stared at the moonlight filtering through the narrow skylights, unable to fall asleep. Shirley was stretched out comfortably in the twin bed beside me, the outline of her body illuminated by the faint glow of light.

Suddenly I heard a sound, a rhythmic creaking, coming through the open window. Sitting up, I parted the curtains and peered into the darkness. Moisture ran in tiny rivulets down the aluminum roof of the sunroom, located directly below. Beyond it lay the patio, all but hidden in the darkness. A shadow passed by the pool, then quickly disappeared as clouds passed over the moon and obscured what little light it had to offer.

The sound continued, a steady creaking that set my nerves on edge. I realized it was coming from beyond the patio and immediately thought of the swing Daddy had set up in the yard for the kids. I thought someone was out there, patiently swinging, waiting for God knew what.

"Shirley, wake up," I said nervously. The house was silent, foreboding somehow in the darkness. I nudged her side and made her get up.

"What is it?" she mumbled, annoyed. She turned onto her side.

"I heard something outside. I think someone's out there."

"Go to sleep," she replied. Her head was now under the covers.

"Listen. I'm telling you someone's out there."

More than half asleep, she sat up and leaned toward the window. "It's the swing," she said, her blue eyes wide with fear. "Who would be out there at this time of night?"

"Did we lock the doors?" I asked. I was scared.

Shirley looked at me, her face serious. She was wide awake now. "I don't know."

"We've got to check them." I drummed up my courage and entered the hallway. I had always hated being alone in the house at night, it was so large and rambling, filled with shadows. Mama had gone out to dinner with friends, and I found myself hoping that she would soon return. I thought of calling Daddy, then remembered that he was in the hospital overnight following surgery on his arm. Feeling like a child facing the bogeyman, I went downstairs, with Shirley staying close to my side.

The dining room seemed exposed, surrounded as it was by glass. I had the unshakable sensation that someone was peering in at us. The grandfather clock near the foyer struck twelve o'clock, a deep baritone that broke the stillness of the room.

I checked the front door, then headed for the sunroom. The patio beyond the glass doors was dark. I reached out my hand and locked the back door, afraid that whoever had been out there had entered the house.

"Let's go upstairs," I suggested, "and wait for Mama to get home." I had a horrible feeling of impending disaster, a premonition of something bad yet to happen. We passed through the dining room and went back upstairs. I locked the bedroom door behind us. Maybe our imaginations were working overtime—I hoped they were—but something felt very wrong in the house.

We waited for Mama to return. Shirley sat beside me, tense and uneasy. About an hour later I heard a sound in front of the house and assumed that it was Mama pulling into the drive. After ten minutes, when she had not entered the house, I got nervous and decided to go downstairs to see if Mama had driven up. Once again Shirley and I crept down the hallway to the top of the stairs, then paused on the landing.

There was a sound like that of a puppy scratching at the front door. I was stuck, petrified. Shirley, braver than I, moved to the bottom of the stairs, and I followed.

"Help me . . ." The sound was pitiful. "Please . . ."

With shaking fingers, and filled with dread at the thought of what might be outside, I fumbled with the dead bolt. Shirley flipped on the outside floodlights. The door opened, and there were Mama and Marty, silhouetted in the sudden glare. Mama was crawling up the brick steps, her face and hair matted with blood. Marty towered over her, a large rock in her hand.

Marty dropped the rock and scrambled away as I rushed to Mama's side. Not far away, Marty suddenly sat down, hugging her arms across her chest and pulling her knees together. Slowly she began to rock back and forth. "I'm so sorry," she said, "so sorry. I don't know what came over me." My first instinct was to strangle Marty with my bare hands, to throw her to the ground and stomp her senseless, but before I could react, she fled around the side of the house and disappeared into the bushes. On the ground beside me Mama moaned. Shirley helped me lift her into a sitting position, and between us we managed to get her into the house by half dragging her and half supporting her with our arms.

By the living room light I was able to better assess her injuries, the blood ran freely down her face from a wound in the center of her forehead. Her pale, blue-green eyes were hysterical with pain and fear.

"She came out of the darkness and hit me twice, then tried to strangle me! She said she wanted to talk. I thought your father might have taken ill. I turned to open the door, and . . ." She collapsed in a fit of tears, unable to go on.

"Shirley, stay with Mama," I said. "I'm going next door."

"No!" shrieked Mama. "She'll kill you!"

"Not if I kill her first."

"Please," she begged, "don't go over there. She's crazy, out of control. She blames me for not giving your father a divorce."

"Is that what she said?" I was incredulous. "Is that the kind of crap he's been feeding her? Goddamn him! I'm calling the police; let them handle her. She belongs in a mental institution, but prison will suit me just fine."

I stormed to the phone and called the police. While waiting for them to arrive, I bathed Mama's face in warm water. The cut on her forehead had stopped bleeding and did not appear to be too deep, but I had no way of knowing about any other injury, as Mama said she had been hit twice in the head. Her chestnut hair was slick with blood, so it was impossible for me to locate another wound. I knew that she should go to the hospital, be checked for concussion, and have the wounds properly cleaned as soon as we had talked to the police.

Twenty minutes after I'd placed the call to the police station, two Jefferson Parish officers arrived. We briefed them on what had happened, and they proceeded to search for Marty, beginning at the house next door. Shirley and I stood on the back patio as the two officers made their way to the back door. They knocked loudly, but apparently received no reply.

"This is your last chance to open the door!" We heard one of the officers yell. There was a long silence, followed by a loud splintering of glass and wood as the younger of the two policemen kicked in the door. From the open doorway came the sounds of scuffling and cursing, then the sight of both officers leading Marty, handcuffed and flailing, from the house. Although flanked by the officers, Marty lunged forward and cursed viciously. "Motherfuckers!" she screamed. A struggle broke out, and she was subdued by the officers, who took hold of her by both arms and led her to the waiting police car.

The younger officer appeared at our front door several minutes later to advise us that Marty was being taken to the East Jefferson central lockup, where she would be booked for aggravated battery and resisting arrest. He needed a statement from us as to what had occurred.

After listening to our story, he nodded in sympathy. He'd just had his own run-in with Marty. "You're very lucky, Mrs. Fagot. She could have killed you. Off the record, I think she's a very seriously disturbed young woman. She failed to respond to our request that she open the door, and we had to break it down to get in. We found her sitting in a corner of the kitchen and staring like she was in some kind of trance. There was a loaded forty-five on the table next to her. I suggest you go to an emergency room and have that forehead checked out. A head injury is nothing to fool around with. I can give you a ride to the hospital if you like."

Mama smiled her thanks as she held a towel to her injured head. Her hair was disheveled and bloodied, as was the front of her shirt, but she remained gracious. "No. I can manage, thank you, anyway."

An hour later I drove Mama to the hospital, where she was examined. Luckily, the cut on her forehead did not require stitches, though it had bled freely in the way head wounds often do. By the time I got her home, she was ready to drop from nervous exhaustion. Shirley and I tucked her into bed, then went downstairs.

Dawn was just beginning to streak the sky as Shirley and I went outside to look around at the site where Marty had attacked Mama. It wasn't long before we found a large aquarium rock that still bore traces of blood. I recognized the rock immediately. It came from Bruce's aquarium, which was now disassembled and stored in the garage next door. The rock proved one thing to me. Marty had come over to our house in possession of a weapon. She had lied when she said she hadn't meant to harm Mama.

Deciding to play amateur detective, Shirley and I let ourselves into the empty house next door. The police had set the back door on its hinges, but it was no longer attached to the frame, so we had no difficulty getting in. Once inside, we found a pair of Levi's, a dark windbreaker, and a pair of navy blue tennis shoes—all ladies' clothing with bloodstains on them. I was shocked. Marty apparently had intended to blend with the shadows in order not to be seen. I imagined her patiently waiting in the backyard for Mama to come home, swinging back and forth until she heard the sound of her car in the driveway. I could see her, moving with deadly purpose through the shadows to the front of the house, the rock clutched in her hands.

Daddy was released from the hospital the following day. When he got home, he made a beeline for Mama's. He came in through the sunroom door, then stopped short at the sight of Mama and me as we sat on the rattan sofa.

"Would anyone care to tell me what's going on around here?" He looked from Mama to me, his hazel eyes taking in the bandage on Mama's forehead before quickly turning away.

"Nothing much, except that your girlfriend tried to kill my mother." I almost hated him for the pain he had brought us. The feelings of sympathy and concern I'd felt for so long were gone.

"Let's not get carried away. I've talked to Marty, and she's explained to me that your mother took the first swing, and that she hit back at you, Shirley, only in self-defense."

Mama laughed curtly. "And you believe her, right?"

"It was obviously nothing more than a cat fight between two jealous women."

I refused to hold my tongue any longer. "Knock it off, Daddy. Your girlfriend tried to kill her. I know it, and the police know it. She's been arrested for battery and resisting arrest, and I hope they send her ass right down the river."

He whirled on me. "Cut the dramatics, Carol. Your mother is perfectly fine. I've bailed Marty out of jail, and those charges aren't worth the paper they're written on."

"What you mean is that you've personally had them taken care of, right?" I threw back at him.

"What if I have? This is none of your business, anyway, young lady, so just butt out."

"You have no right to speak to her that way." Mama's eyes were blazing. "Your girlfriend is dangerous, Len, and I wouldn't put anything past either one of you."

He sensed her fury and composed himself. "She's immature and hotheaded, I'll grant you that, but she most certainly is not dangerous."

Mama rose to her feet, a five-foot-two storm of indignation. "How dare you come over here and defend that crazy bitch to me! You have no control over her. Now, something set her off, and if you know what's driven her over the edge, then maybe you'd care to enlighten me."

He pursed his lips in thought. "She came to visit me last night in the hospital, and I said that I wouldn't marry her."

"Then why didn't she hit *you* in the head with a goddamned rock?" I yelled.

He laughed then, as if it were all very funny. "Alright," he said. "Let's all just calm down. I agree with you that she needs some counseling, and I promise she'll get it."

"Do what you will, but I've had enough of living around that loony tune. My mind is made up. I want out of here. I'll move to Covington or somewhere else in the country. You'll buy me another house or I'll have her locked up, I swear it. It's a fair trade, Len—this monument you've built to yourself," she said sarcastically, with a sweeping gesture about the room, "in exchange for my peace of mind."

She'd backed him into a corner, and he knew it. The last thing in the world he needed was to have charges pressed against Marty. "Okay. You've got a deal. I'll give you the property on St. Paul, as well as the house next door, and I'll buy you a house in Covington. But there won't be any charges pressed, understand me?" His voice was tempered with warning.

"I read you loud and clear," she replied evenly.

"Then you're certain you want to go through with this?"

"Dead certain."

In early June Nancy announced her plans to wed Gary. Daddy conceded. During the last three painful years in our family, he had, no doubt, given up all of the grand plans he'd once had for his children's future.

The wedding was set for August 1, Nancy's birthday. Mama, who was still house hunting in the country, agreed to stick it out on Citrus Road until after the wedding.

Over a hundred guests attended the evening ceremony, held outdoors amid stands of beautiful flowers and dozens of tiki torches. The young couple was striking. The groom was tall and lanky in white tails, his dark hair curling around his collar. His six-foot-four frame dwarfed his petite bride as he slipped the wedding band on her finger. Her blue eyes reflected all the happiness in the world, and she was lovely in her charming, old-fashioned wedding gown interlaced with yellow satin ribbons along the hemline and the cuffs of the puffed sleeves.

At the reception Daddy, never one to drink before, downed a couple of bourbons and water. The liquor put him in a sentimental, almost maudlin mood, and he stayed close on Mama's heels all night. It was a beautiful, sultry evening, the sky filled with stars—an evening made for romance. I'd invited Mike Holland to the wedding, and I escorted him over to where my parents sat in order to introduce him. As I drew nearer to them I overheard Daddy saying to Mama, "You know, I've always loved you, Shirley. Maybe we could live together." Mama rolled her eyes in exasperation and smiled tolerantly. It was Nancy's evening, and she wasn't going to say a thing that might set Daddy off and spoil it. I made introductions all around and strolled off with Mama. Mike and Daddy became engaged in animated conversation.

The newlyweds took off in a shower of rice, headed for Florida for a week. It was not until Nancy's return that she mentioned to me that Daddy had presented her with a gift of two thousand dollars and a forty-thousand-dollar life insurance policy covering Gary's life. I congratulated her. Nancy didn't need to know about George.

In the weeks following the wedding, after looking at dozens of properties, Mama decided to buy a home in Covington, located on Old Military Road in the heart of horse country. The property was owned by Buck and

Bonnie Taylor. Buck was a thin man of few words, and Bonnie a displaced Iowan, a sweet and charming lady who constantly talked about returning to her midwestern birthplace.

Bonnie finally did return to Iowa, but, sadly enough, in a casket. A week before the act of sale she locked herself in her young daughter's bedroom. She then sat down in a rocking chair, placed a thirty-eight automatic to her heart, and pulled the trigger. Her husband did not find her body for several hours, nor did he feel the need to tell Mama. She didn't find out until the closing, whereupon he politely informed her of what had happened. He reassured her that the bedroom carpet had been thoroughly cleaned, and remarked at how lucky he was not to have had to replace it.

Mama was totally flabbergasted at Buck's news, but she signed the papers for the house on Old Military Road. No doubt she felt that there were worse things in life to contend with than the possibility of Bonnie Taylor's ghost appearing on her doorstep some dark, wintry night.

CHAPTER 13

CAROL

The house in Covington was situated on thirteen beautiful acres of wooded land complete with a barn and a stream that ran from one end of the property to the other. The town of Covington, fifty miles north of New Orleans, is inhabited for the most part by simple, down-to-earth country people. At the time, it hadn't been invaded yet by get-rich-quick developers building waterfront condominiums, so it offered Mama the peace of mind for which I knew she had been searching. Meanwhile, Mike and I had decided to live together. Mama expressed nothing in the way of criticism of our decision, but instead offered us a portion of her land on which to set up a mobile home. She seemed quite pleased to have our company and no doubt was relieved when Mike volunteered to take care of the grounds.

Several weeks after we all had settled in, Mama and I stood on the carport gazing across the rolling pastureland. Shirley cantered by on one of the horses, her copper hair streaming behind her, before she disappeared into the barn.

Mama waved to Shirley a few minutes later, when she reappeared on the path leading to the house. "Did you have a nice ride?" she called out.

Shirley ignored her and walked across the carport to the side entrance. Mama approached her, obviously worried about Shirley's unhappiness. "Why don't you put the past behind you now?" she asked. "You're starting a new school, you'll make new friends."

Shirley walked away without a word. Mama's eyes misted.

I was worried about Shirley, too, but much to my later regret I was too caught up in my newfound happiness to pay her much attention. Mike worked two weeks each month offshore for Shell Oil Company and spent the following two weeks at home. During those days off we spent our time combing every inch of the surrounding countryside with Kim and Bruce, often packing a picnic lunch. We rode on horseback, and there is nothing in the world that spells freedom so clearly as cantering across an open meadow with the sun warm on your face and the wind blowing through your hair. It was the next best thing to heaven. I discovered a whole new world, different from any I had ever known before. My senses awoke again, and I felt as if I'd been sleeping for years. I became finely attuned to the sights and sounds around me.

I woke in the morning to bird songs, and went to bed at night lulled by chirping crickets and cicadas, and the occasional hoot of an owl. At times we entered the bayou by pirogue. Deep in the bowels of Black Bayou there lay a quietude like none other. Being there was like entering some exotic jungle. Giant oaks bent down majestic limbs so thick with hanging moss, they formed a narrow tunnel impossible to pass through at some points. Only the cry of a bird and the gentle rhythm of lapping water against the pirogue would break the silence. Turtles sunned themselves on fallen logs. When I first entered the bayou, I was horrified by the sight of thick snakes swimming through water or sunning on overhanging branches of trees, but I soon learned to tell the dangerous ones from the harmless, and that there's no need to fear either as long as you don't invade their space.

Under Mike's patient guidance, I learned how to cast a fly rod in Black Bayou, and after hours of practice, I reeled in a large-mouth bass. Mike was a wonderful teacher, and I was a most willing pupil. I'd never handled a gun before, but I soon learned how to shoot a rifle, if not expertly, then well enough. Raised on steak and baked potatoes, I never could develop a taste for wild meat, but I did learn how to cook rabbit, squirrel, and robin breast in a savory brown gravy for Mike. We also planted a garden, and it was with great pride and accomplishment that I served my first harvest of home-grown tomatoes. They weren't perfect hothouse ones, but I had grown them. It was a good feeling to know that I was able to finally fend for myself, physically and emotionally.

I owed much of that to Mike. More important than anything else I learned in the country, I came to know that I was capable of a true and lasting ability to love. As surely as I thrived on the country air, I thrived on my love for Mike. There was a strength and caring in him that brought out the best in me, a kindness in his soul that was evident in small things that he did. No matter how small and insignificant my problems were, he made them his own and helped me to see my way through them.

And for the first time in their young lives, my son and daughter learned to amuse themselves without expensive toys. At five and four years of age, they had sturdy bodies that turned honey brown in the summer sunshine, and dark blond hair that streaked with new gold. They built a tree house with Mike, and played inside it for hours. They'd come down occasionally to forage for small treasures, like abandoned bird nests and cocoons, wild berries, and small pebbles. When the summer heat forced the two down from their perch, they splashed in the creek, built dams, sailed toy boats, or poked sticks in the crawfish holes along the banks of the creek. The children tagged along behind Mike, like baby chicks after a hen. They learned how to feed and care for their growing menagerie. All told, we had seven dogs, two rabbits, three horses, a piglet, a half-grown calf, and a calico cat named Scrounger, so called because she lived on whatever small, hapless creature she came across.

As is the way with most people, there was another, private side to Mike Holland, a side that was as remote and exclusive as an island. Though he possessed all the spit and polish of a city boy on the surface, his heart belonged to wide, open spaces. He would disappear for hours into the woods, as comfortable in its depths as the creatures that made their home there. He hunted rabbit, squirrel, and quail, and unlike some hunters, he ate what he caught, sometimes roasting his catch over a small fire. That was a habit I could not begin to fathom. But, then, I only embraced nature—for Mike it was a need as vital as breathing.

It was natural that we should wed. When our divorces became final at the end of the summer, Mike proposed to me, and I accepted. We were married in late November 1973, in a small, quaint chapel in downtown Covington. The church was alight with candles, and tall stands of autumn flowers decked the altar. I wore a long ivory dress made of soft cashmere with tiny pearl buttons from the waist to throat, and a spray of baby's breath in my long blond hair. My bouquet was made of pink and white sweetheart roses, offset by sprigs of baby's breath. Mike wore a camel-colored suit, beautifully tailored, that complimented his dark blond hair and lean frame.

I had chosen my best friend, Gari Pence, to be my maid of honor. A petite brunet with deep blue eyes, Gari looked wonderful in her rose-colored gown with bellied sleeves and a long sash that tied in the back. Larry Achord, Mike's dear, lifelong friend, stood as best man, and since Gari and Larry were in love, there was a doubly romantic overtone in the air that evening.

Shirley had offered to play the church organ, and she gave a splendid rendition of the "Wedding March" as Daddy walked me down the aisle and presented me to my husband-to-be. He kissed me on the cheek, then shook hands with Mike before taking his seat in the front pew.

By candlelight Mike and I repeated our vows to love, honor, and cherish each other till death did us part. We sealed them with a kiss, and as I gazed into my husband's eyes, I was filled with wonder that such happiness should have come my way after so much pain.

We left the church in a flurry of rice. Since we had invited only family and close friends to share in our special moment, we'd accepted Mama's offer to have the reception at her house.

In the middle of the party I spotted Daddy leaning against the fireplace in the den. He looked out of place, unsure of this new ground that belonged to Mama. I'd invited him to the wedding because he hadn't been there to give me away when I'd married Bruce. It seemed unnecessarily cruel and almost disrespectful to exclude him from this happy day. He was beautifully dressed, elegant as ever. Nostalgia tugged at my heart. I left Mike's side and went over to him.

"I love you, Daddy. I'm glad you came." I encircled his waist with my arms and laid my head upon his chest.

He patted my back and hugged me close. "I was afraid my presence would upset you with the way things are between your mother and me." His expression seemed thoughtful, almost sad. "I want you to know, sweetheart, that I wish you only the best."

I felt a strange sadness at his words. "I know you do, Daddy."

His eyes suddenly brightened, and he cupped my chin in his hand, tilting it upward to gaze directly into my eyes. "I have a wedding present for you."

"What is it?"

His answer was like a cold dash of water in my face. "I've purchased a life insurance policy."

"A life insurance policy? What for? I don't plan to die, not anytime soon." My voice was light, but my heart felt heavy.

"The policy doesn't cover your life, baby. It covers

Mike's. Life insurance is something you kids don't give much thought to." He smiled encouragingly.

"Well, it's not something I care to think about on my wedding day. Most people view marriage as a beginning, but somehow I get the feeling you don't see it that way."

"Beginnings are nice, honey, but I'm a realist. And believe me, there's nothing more final than death. I'll keep the policy and make the payments on it."

He winked at me. "By the way, have I told you that you make a beautiful bride?"

CHAPTER 14

SHIRLEY

The serenity of the country brought out a feeling of contentment in me that I had not felt for years. Tense and anxious by nature, I started to relax, happy to roam freely about our property on the horses or to lie peacefully in the upper pasture gazing at the clouds and daydreaming. Wildlife was abundant in the area, and often I would see rabbits, squirrels, raccoons, and other animals that stopped to drink from the creek bordering the woods.

Since we had thirteen acres and a four-stall barn on the property, Daddy had allowed me to take the horses with me when we moved. He also had given me a small red Honda motorcycle to ride. Our house was located thirteen miles from Covington's city limits, and because at fourteen I was too young to drive a car, the bike came in handy when I wanted to visit my friends, most of whom lived in town.

The summer passed quickly. Carol and Mike settled down and seemed happy to be together. Mama was more relaxed and happier than I could ever remember. I saw little of Daddy. It was a relief not to be caught in the middle of his manipulative games, and I found myself hoping that without Marty around to stir things up, Mama would find some measure of peace, as well. Life took on a quiet, dreamlike quality that was really only the calm before the storm.

I attended tenth grade in the fall at Covington High School, a typical country school surrounded by oak trees and weeping willows nestled in the heart of town. I made new friends and tackled my schoolwork. On my fifteenth birthday Mama threw a wonderful party, complete with cake, ice cream, and decorations. Carol, Mike, Kim, and little Bruce attended. Daddy's present was a Wurlitzer organ, something I'd wanted for a long time. He also sent me flowers, with a short note attached that read, "All my love, Daddy."

Later that evening I called him to thank him for my gift. He sounded impatient and annoyed when he answered. "What do you want?"

Offended, I answered with hesitation. "I wanted to thank you for the organ, Daddy. It's beautiful."

"I'm glad you like it," he said coldly.

There was an awkward silence following his words. I was trying to think of something to say that would ease the situation, but he hung up. I listened to the silence on the other end of the line for a moment, unable to believe what he had just done. I wanted to cry, or shout, do anything to express the awful feeling of not being wanted.

Something changed inside of me after that. I became sullen and resentful in the way of many teenage girls. I challenged Mama's authority at every opportunity. She was patient at first. She'd already raised three teenage daughters and knew these adolescent phases, but my stubbornness surpassed even her good temper. We had terrible arguments that usually ended in tears of frustration on her part. No matter how hard she tried, I refused to listen to her advice. A part of me blamed her for Daddy's relationship with Marty—unfairly, I knew. Nonetheless, it made it even more difficult for me to reach out to her. She was at a loss as to how to deal with me, and as time went by the situation grew worse, until there was little communication between us.

In November, a week or two after Carol's wedding, I met Ray Tresch, an eighteen-year-old senior attending Covington High. He was a slim, dark-haired boy with big blue eyes and a gentleness that attracted me from the very start. We began meeting between classes and at lunch to talk about our problems. Both of us were in need of a good friend. I finally had someone objective I could talk to. I explained to him my relationship with my mother and how difficult it was for us to get along. I admitted that I loved her very much but simply couldn't understand her at times.

Mama completely disapproved of Ray when I introduced them. She felt that I was far too young to carry on with a boy old enough to be in college. Determined to have my own way, I continued to see Ray, despite her objections. I wanted to prove to myself that real love did exist, even if I had rarely seen it displayed by my parents. I envied my sisters their early memories of the loving years my parents had spent together, free from the constant whirlwind of hate and jealousy that had become the center of all our lives.

Things came to a head when the school principal contacted Mama and informed her that I had been skipping classes. When I got home, she confronted me in the den, determined, I think, to keep the situation in hand as best she could.

She began with an accusation. "You're still seeing Ray, aren't you?"

"What difference does it make?" I answered. I tried to push my way past her, but she stood her ground, barring me from the hallway leading to the bedroom.

"You're going to flunk out of school," she said, almost in tears. "Don't you realize you've got your future to think about?"

"I can handle it," I said stubbornly, my jaw set.

She must have sensed a seriousness in my voice, because she became wary. Or maybe she didn't recognize me as the same daughter she once had. "You don't know what you're talking about, Shirley. You're only fifteen years old—you're still a child. Think about what you're doing."

"It's my life, don't forget."

"Yes, and you're throwing it all away. Don't you realize that?"

All I realized then was how angry I was and how sorry I felt for myself. "Leave me alone! You don't have any idea what I think or how I feel."

"Why don't you tell me?" She was sincere, but still I held back.

"Forget it," I said. "It doesn't matter."

"I give up!" She threw up her hands. "I'm calling your father. Maybe he can get through to you."

I walked away and into my bedroom. The only sound I made was the slam of the door. I glanced around, small and alone, at my room. Books and papers were scattered on the white dresser and matching hutch; a sweater was carelessly thrown across the back of the chair. There were no pictures of the family displayed and no posters of rock and roll stars pinned to the walls. There was no expression of personal taste anywhere in the room, and I preferred it that way. To me, those things made no difference. Life was too serious for those kinds of things.

I flopped down on the bed, eyes on the door. It was the first time I'd ever given my parents any real trouble, and I wasn't sure how Daddy would react to Mama's news. He didn't know about my relationship with Ray, and he also had no inkling of the trouble between Mama and me. There was no way of knowing how much she would tell him, given the circumstances, so I tried to compose myself, desperately wanting to appear calm and in control when Mama called me to the telephone.

When fifteen minutes had passed and she hadn't returned, my patience ran out. I went down the hallway and stopped before her bedroom door. I eased it open, went into the room, and stood at the foot of the bed.

"Shirley's having problems," she said into the phone, her back to me. "I need your help, Len."

I felt sorry for her. It must have been hard for her to swallow her pride and call Daddy. I knew she had done it only out of concern for me. Suddenly, for the first time in a long time, I felt ashamed of my actions and guilty because of the pain I'd caused her. I may not have liked everything she did, but she was trying.

"She's been skipping classes! Talk to her!" Mama said angrily. I approached the bed and stood before her, my hand outstretched for the telephone. I thought that if I could only talk to Daddy, I could smooth things over.

Mama ignored me. Two bright spots of color appeared in her cheeks. "She's also your daughter, Len, in case you've forgotten!"

"Let me talk to Daddy," I begged. The depth of anger on her face alarmed me.

She passed the phone to me and left the room. Taking a deep breath, I said, "Hello, Daddy. It's Shirley."

"What's going on?" he asked in a put-out tone.

"I need to talk to you," I explained. "I want to come stay with you for a while." I was hoping that if I put some distance between Mama and myself, things would get better. I felt a desperate need to belong somewhere, and the house on Citrus Road had always been home to me. Most of all, I wanted Daddy's sympathy and concern.

"I'd like to see you, but right now I just don't have the time. Maybe next week I can give you an appointment. How about Friday at three P.M. ?"

I hung up the telephone. I realized at that moment that I could never count on him to be there for me when I needed him. He no longer loved me. That was a reality I forced myself to accept, and in doing so I lost the childish innocence that had sustained me for fifteen years.

The following morning I packed a few belongings in a duffel bag and tossed it through my bedroom window. It landed in a heap behind some azaleas. Picking up my books, I sneaked down the hallway to the kitchen, and almost jumped to the ceiling when Mama appeared in the doorway, a cup of tea in her hand.

I had been hoping to avoid her, but I was glad to see her before I left. The sight of her face almost made me change my mind and stay. I thought of all the times she had been there for me to lean on, the times when I was sick or unhappy and she had cared for me. I thought of Carol and Mike, and wished I had the chance to say good-bye to them. But I was afraid to let anyone know what I was doing. Frightened, and very much confused, I was unable to ask for help, even from those I loved and who I knew loved me.

Halfway out the door I turned to Mama. "I love you," I said. "I just wanted you to know."

She smiled, somewhat surprised by my sudden words. "I love you, too."

I felt like a heel. I fetched the duffel bag from the side of the house and slung it over my shoulder. I walked quietly along the gravel driveway to the bus stop, over the cattle guards set in the ground along the way.

I was still considering my decision to leave when I got to school. I stuffed the bag inside my locker and checked into homeroom class. Daddy's words to me kept coming to mind, along with the memory of all his previous lies and deceptions. Everyone, it seemed, was getting on with life—Mama was free, and Carol had Mike. Joanne and Joe were happy. Where did I fit into it all? What part of their lives could I share?

I made up my mind. I was definitely going. When I explained my plan to Ray, he immediately decided to go with me, so we left his yellow Mazda in the school parking lot, pooled our money—a total of sixty-eight dollars—and walked to the bus stop in the center of town. We bribed an old man in the street into buying tickets for us and boarded a bus leaving for New Orleans.

In New Orleans we switched to another bus heading for Houma, a small town like Covington eighty miles from New Orleans. Friends of Ray's we had called met us when we arrived, tired, anxious, and hungry from the long trip.

CHAPTER 15

CAROL

A man I'll call John Smith was a clever fellow in his early thirties who probably could have gone far in life had he not been cursed with both an incurable lazy streak and wealthy parents. He was a friend of Mike's and spent many days visiting us in Covington. Like Mike, John was prone to restlessness and convinced that the world had so much more to offer than a mundane life of working nine to five. He had a keen wit and a sense of adventure, living his life with as few encumbrances as possible. He accepted the breakup of his marriage with the same easy aplomb with which he accepted most things life tossed his way.

One Saturday John showed up at my front door high on the idea of making fantastic bucks. His plan involved buying marijuana in Mexico and smuggling it back into the United States. The idea was not as shocking then to Mike and me as it would be now. We were in our twenties, and both of us spent a fair amount of time getting high, just as most of our friends did.

John had done his homework well. He presented a complete aerial map of the interior of Mexico and of the Rio Grande along the U.S.-Mexico border. According to the plan, two guys would purchase the pot in Guadalajara, then drive it through Mexico via the back roads, to the border town of Beauquias, a hodgepodge of tiny adobe shacks squatting desolately in the hot desert sun. From Beauquias it was about a two-mile hike through the desert to the Rio Grande. Under cover of darkness, they would carry the marijuana in backpacks across the

Rio Grande and into the wilderness of Big Bend National Park, near Marathon, Texas. A third party would be waiting there with a camper truck. They would transfer the marijuana to the camper, then make their way back across the river to Beauquias. After picking up their own truck, the two would reenter the United States at the official border station in Laredo, Texas. The third party would drive leisurely out of the park with the marijuana cleverly hidden in the back of the camper.

It was an intriguing plan. The idea looked thrilling and extremely profitable. It was easy for us to convince ourselves that we would be dealing in a basically harmless commodity. After all, everyone smoked pot in those days. With all the abandon of youth we gave ourselves over to the scheme, unaware of the fatal results smuggling drugs would eventually bring.

The first trip to Mexico was to be strictly a dry run, a one-shot effort to test the plan before actually purchasing any weed. Mark Wright, a close personal friend of both John's and Mike's, was chosen as a third partner. A black-eyed hell-raiser with a heart of gold, Mark was ready to do anything to make enough money to keep his ex-wife happy so she'd let him see his two children. The threesome set a departure date, and one week later I saw them off in a flurry of good-bye kisses.

During Mike's ten-day absence from home I searched for Shirley, who had disappeared two weeks before. I contacted every person that came to mind who might have any idea of her whereabouts. Either her friends were truly unaware of what had become of her, or they were damned good liars. Mama was beside herself with worry and guilt. She felt that with all the upheaval in her young daughter's life, Shirley had run off to ease the confusion and pain she couldn't cope with. Although we had no leads, the one thing we were certain of was that Shirley was with Ray Tresch, who had disappeared on the same day. The police were contacted, but there was little they could do, and we were forced to deal with the situation on our own.

Finally, in desperation, Mama decided to tell Daddy about Shirley's disappearance. Up until that point she'd not wanted to tell him that his daughter of fifteen had flown the nest with a nineteen-year-old man we knew virtually nothing about.

I agreed to accompany her to Daddy's to break the news. I thought Mama would need my support. And I was right. Daddy reacted just the way I had anticipated he would.

"I should have known you couldn't handle her," he accused Mama. "This is all your fault."

Mama looked as if she'd been slapped. "How dare you say that to me when you were the one who refused to even see her when she needed you. It's no wonder she felt unwanted." Her voice quavered, and I knew she was on the verge of tears.

Sensing her mood, Daddy backed off. When he spoke next, his voice was calmer. "Have you contacted her friends?"

"I've talked to everyone I could possibly think of, but no one has seen or heard from her," I said. "We do know that she's with her boyfriend."

"But what if she's not?" said Mama. "What if she's been abducted?"

"Use your head, Shirley, and try to calm down. Any fool can see that she's with the boy. What's his name, anyway?" Daddy's lips compressed into a thin line.

"Ray Tresch," answered Mama. "His parents live right outside of Covington. I've already spoken with them, and they know no more than I do, other than that their son has disappeared."

"When I get my hands on that punk, he'll disappear alright. Permanently," said Daddy. His voice made me remember his horrible threats against Gary, threats that came too close to coming true.

"Don't even say things like that, Len."

"Why not? I can easily have him taken care of, if you like."

Despite the chilling statement he had just made, Daddy's tone was as casual as if he were discussing the weather. Mama and I exchanged glances.

Finally she spoke up. "Hire a private detective to find them."

Daddy shrugged. "No problem. I'll keep you abreast of the situation."

As the days flew by, Mama worried more and more. I'm certain she wondered if she would ever see Shirley again. I know I did, and the thought almost killed me. When the private eye Daddy hired failed to come up with any information about Shirley, Mama caved in from the sheer weight of her sorrow. In despair, she moved out of the house in Covington to a small apartment in New Orleans, where memories of her lost daughter would not intrude so often.

Mike, John, and Mark returned from their trip to Mexico full of good cheer. While drinking tequila and cold beer in a cantina in the center of Guadalajara, they'd met a smartly dressed, smooth-talking young man by the name of Rueben. When John had casually asked the Mexican if he might know where they could score some weed, Rueben had looked him dead in the eye and replied, "How many kilos do you need?"

They assured me that they had the route down pat and the perfect contact. Now they were ready for the real thing. All three quit their jobs and put together the money they needed to finance the trip, and John borrowed a camper. The truck was the perfect vehicle, since it had enough space to hold not only the marijuana but the backpacks, spare gasoline cans, rope, canteens, binoculars, and other paraphernalia, too. They left after only a few days, confident and happy. My job was to hold down the fort and stay near the phone in case of emergency.

* * *

By now Nancy had moved into the house next door to Daddy. It was a move that would very soon destroy her marriage. I could see it coming when she came to Covington for a visit one day during Mike's absence. She was very concerned about Daddy's increasingly bizarre behavior.

"He's taking too many pills, and he's very moody," she said. "One day he's kind and loving, on top of the world. The next he's morose and totally silent. On his worst days he goes on about how all of us are using him for his money."

"Where is he getting his drugs?" I asked.

"I can't be sure, but I know it's illegal. He has bottles of Empirin with codeine, and there must be three hundred pills in each one. And he's taking Valium; I've seen little bags of them lying around the house."

"You'd think that if Marty cared so much for him, she'd be trying to discourage all this pill popping."

"I don't think she cares for him at all. I think she's the one who keeps filling his head with all this nonsense about nobody caring for him but her. She's apparently trying her best to convince him that none of us love him anymore."

Nancy twirled a long blond strand of hair as she spoke. "I'm worried that he'll really begin to believe her, especially with all these drugs." She tucked the lock of hair behind her ear.

"You're probably right. I know how Daddy is when he gets on one of his self-pity jags, and if he's loaded on drugs, he's going to be twice as vulnerable to any suggestions she makes. The problem is, what can we do about it? You know how tough Daddy is. He isn't going to appreciate either one of us sticking our noses into his and Marty's business."

"Don't I know it." Nancy sighed. "I don't understand him at all. He defends her, and then he turns right around and calls me in the middle of the night to moon about losing Mama. Of course, it might just be the drugs talking, but he even said that he regretted his relationship with Marty, but that she knew too much to just let her walk away. I tried to get to the bottom of what he was saying, but it was useless. When he gets like that, he talks in circles. He's getting worse all the time, Carol. You just don't know what I've been going through being right next door to him. Twice he's called me late at night, and I've been right in the middle of talking to him and realized that he wasn't on the phone anymore. I called his name into the receiver over and over again, and got no response from him. Scared me shitless. Both times I ran next door, and there he was, passed out in the chair, with a bottle of pills nearby, and Marty was just sitting on the sofa as if nothing were wrong."

"Is she stupid or something?" Maybe she truly just wasn't that smart.

"I don't buy that she's stupid," she retorted. "Just unconcerned. Both times I actually had to ask her to help me get him to bed. There's something wrong going on over there, and I suspect that she wants him drugged out of his mind. Otherwise she'd hide the damned pills or throw them away. I'd do it myself if I could get in there without her following me around from room to room."

"I'll tell you what I think, Nancy. I think she's determined to have what she wants. I can't say for certain what that might be, but I'll give you an educated guess. I think she wants everything we have. I mean, she's done everything in her power to break our family apart. She was probably delighted when she finally ran Mama off. Then Mama moved back into the house. It must have driven Marty up the wall."

"So, you think that's why she attacked Mama that night?"

"Maybe, but I don't think that's all there was to it. Marty went to see Daddy that night in the hospital. I know, because Daddy told me and Mama. He said he'd broken the news to Marty that he wouldn't marry her. Of course, knowing Daddy, he probably twisted the facts. He probably really told Marty that Mama wouldn't give him a divorce, and that's why she snapped. Maybe she sees Mama as being in the way of her getting what she wants. And you can believe one thing—people like Marty don't stop until they get what they want."

"I guess you're right," Nancy said. "I only wish I had thought more about moving next door to them. I thought he was being kind, you know, trying to apologize for the way he's treated Gary. But now I'm not so sure."

"How are they getting along? I'm surprised that after all that bullshit with the gun Gary wants to be anywhere near Daddy."

"They get along pretty well for the most part. Gary does some work around the yard in his spare time, but they really don't have a whole lot of contact with each other. The only time things got rough was when Gary bought his dogs."

"I didn't know Gary had any dogs."

Nancy laughed. "Yeah. He had four beagles and was thinking about a side business, raising them and training them to hunt."

"He *had* four beagles? I take it he doesn't have them anymore?"

"No. He got rid of them. Daddy complained that their barking kept him up at night. When I told Gary he should give them away instead of causing trouble, he accused me of siding with Daddy. You know how it is when you've got your dad on one side and your husband on the other. You can't win, any way you slice it."

When Nancy left she seemed a bit more lighthearted than she had been when she'd arrived, and I hoped she wouldn't let her problems with Daddy and Gary get her down. I was glad that I was not in her shoes. It was selfish of me, but the house on Citrus Road and its two occupants was the last thing I cared to dwell on. I decided that I'd left all that craziness behind me, totally unaware that before too long the menace that dwelled there would reach out across the miles to destroy all that I held dear.

Ten days after their departure Mike, John, and Mark made their way back home. They arrived at three-thirty in the morning, exhausted and euphoric, with a camperful of pot.

The pot was disposed of in two days' time, leaving each of them some ten thousand dollars richer. They immediately began to plan their next trip, and it was obvious from the look of pleasure on Mike's face that for us, smuggling marijuana was now a way of life.

CHAPTER 16

SHIRLEY

For three months Ray and I survived on our own. We rented a small room in an old building in the center of Houma. Our landlady, a dark-haired, heavy woman in her early thirties, asked few questions of her "newly-wed" tenants, making it that much easier for us to lie low.

I thought of my family often and missed them very much. But I tried to put these feelings from my mind. I was unwilling to return to the situation I felt I had escaped from. I also knew that if my father found us, he would have Ray thrown in jail and prosecuted for statutory rape.

Ray and I were in a drugstore shopping one day when I noticed a man dressed in a light tweed suit watching us. I caught his eye and figured he'd stop, but he continued to check us out. I started to feel nervous. We made our purchases and left the shop. A minute later the man followed. I ducked into a nearby doorway, and Ray, who was walking a few paces ahead of me, stopped and turned around.

"What's wrong?" he asked, puzzled by my strange behavior.

"There was a man in the store. I think he's following us. Daddy must have hired him."

Ray just brushed my suspicion aside. "Come on. Don't act so paranoid."

"He was following us, I know he was. I think we should go back."

"What are you talking about?"

I couldn't shake a feeling of uneasiness. "I want to go home. Let's leave everything behind. We don't have to go back to the apartment."

"Are you out of your mind?" He stared at me. "How are we going to get to New Orleans? We don't have the money for a bus ticket."

I kept at it. "We'll hitchhike. Someone will stop and give us a ride."

"What about your father?" Ray's face was sad, as though he couldn't believe what I was saying. "What about me?"

I looked at him and put up a facade of courage that I really didn't feel. "I can handle Daddy."

The stubborn set to my face made him realize that arguing with me would be pointless. When I stood near the road and held out my thumb, he hesitated only a second before following me.

It took us almost seven hours to reach New Orleans, a trip that should have taken three. Just a few people stopped to offer us a ride, so we had walked a good deal of the way. Once downtown, we discussed whom we should call first with the news of our arrival. I decided to call Nancy. I thought she might be able to handle the situation without panicking and without calling the police. We were on Canal Street, near the riverfront. An old gray stone wall lined the perimeter of a cemetery; the stone archway was forbidding in its contrast to the endless stream of traffic moving down the street. A public phone booth covered with graffiti stood nearby.

I dialed Nancy's number, filled with a strange excitement.

"Where are you?" she asked, incredulous, when she heard my voice.

A horn blared somewhere behind me, and an old woman in a faded blue dress walked toward the entrance to the cemetery. Suddenly I was happy, excited at the thought of seeing my family again. "I'm on Canal Street, near the cemetery, and Ray is with me. Will you pick us up and take us to Covington?"

"I don't think it's a very good idea to have Ray with you now," she cautioned me. "And Mama doesn't live in Covington anymore; she moved into an apartment near River Ridge a month or so after you left. Carol and Mike still live there."

"Will you take us to your house, then?"

"Of course. I'll come get you now. Stay where you are, don't leave."

I waited for her to pick us up. I was afraid that she might contact Daddy first, but a short while later she appeared in her Camaro. I was full of questions. It felt as if I'd been away for fifty years, not just three months.

"I guess Mama just wanted to get away from the memories," she explained when I asked about Mama's sudden move back to the city. "She gave up hope of ever finding you. Daddy hired a detective, but it didn't pan out. All of us were worried sick about you. Mama was devastated when you left."

I felt ashamed. "I'm sorry," I said. "I can't explain why I did it. I didn't want to hurt Mama, I just wanted to get away. Leaving was the only way to do it."

Nancy's expression softened. She loved me, and I could tell that her relief at having me home again outweighed any anger she might have felt. She wanted the best for me, I knew, and she probably sympathized a little. When we got to Nancy's, she asked, "Don't you think you should call Mama?"

Fear squeezed the breath from my chest. I did not want to face Mama. Nancy handed me the telephone. Her quiet insistence gave me the strength to dial the number.

After several rings Mama answered, her voice so warm and familiar that I almost started to cry.

"Mama?" I said, my voice barely a whisper. Finally I let the tears come. "I'm home."

After many an emotionally charged discussion about my future, Mama and Daddy decided that I would live with Mama in her apartment, a two-bedroom flat located near the Mississippi River. I attended Riverdale High, an all-girls' school, to make up for the time I'd missed by running away.

By the end of the summer Ray moved into an apartment nearby to be close to me and took a job in a clothing store. We saw each other often, and it wasn't long before we were a couple like we had been in Covington. By the fall of 1974 I had turned sixteen and started eleventh grade. Daddy allowed me to keep seeing Ray and even put him to work around the yard so he could earn some extra spending money. It was difficult for me to return to the life of a child after what I had done earlier in the year. I felt older than all the girls I met in my classes, unable to fit into their world of boyfriends, dates, and eleven o'clock curfews. I had seen too much of the adult world too soon, and for me there was no turning back. In October Ray joined the army, and I announced my plan to marry him as soon as he completed six weeks of basic training at Fort Polk, Louisiana.

Mama and Daddy were shocked to hear the news. We met at Daddy's house for a heated discussion about my plans, and both tried to dissuade me from what they obviously considered a serious mistake on my part. I would never have admitted it then, but marrying Ray was also a way to hurt my parents. I was now Daddy's fourth daughter in a row to forgo college, and I knew how important education was to him. Mama thought I was making a big mistake, but breaking away like this gave me an overwhelming sense of power over her. I knew what I wanted, and I was determined to get it. It was no longer necessary to spare her feelings. A coldness came over me.

"I've lived with Ray for three months," I said to them icily. "We've been seeing each other every day since I've been home. How can you expect me to return to school when I don't feel like a kid anymore? I'm different now. I've lived on my own, and I can't go back to being a little girl again."

In the end they agreed to the marriage. I think they felt that I might run away again if they didn't approve, but having accepted the situation, they decided to have the wedding at Daddy's house. I felt uneasy at the prospect of a large wedding. I was barely sixteen, and it was obvious that the event was considered more of a tragedy than a cause for celebration. I asked Daddy to invite as few people as possible, and he agreed.

On December 21, 1974, Ray and I were married by the same judge who had performed the wedding ceremony for Nancy and Gary. Despite Daddy's promise of a small wedding, over one hundred guests attended, many of them his associates.

Mama helped me dress in Carol's old bedroom. It seemed strange to be in Daddy's house after all that time, and I knew Mama felt a little uneasy, too. It must have been hard for her to accept that Marty now lived in the home she and Daddy had sweated and sacrificed to build, but she hid her feelings well.

We left the room and stood on the balcony that gave a full view of the living area and the dining room. My maid of honor and best friend, Sally Lincks, in a simple but elegant green silk dress, smiled at me and kissed me on the cheek before getting in line ahead of me at the top of the stairs. Mama hugged me, examined my lacy gown with inlaid cuffs of finer lace at the throat and sleeves, then slipped a strand of pearls around my neck. Nancy, Joanne, and Carol waited eagerly at the bottom of the stairs. I felt a pang of remorse at my decision to leave them and build a new life with Ray. Daddy stood by proudly as Ray and I exchanged vows on the patio. When it was over he took me aside and gave me a check for a thousand dollars as his wedding gift to us. He also told me that he had taken out a life insurance policy on Ray worth forty thousand dollars.

Despite my apprehension about a large wedding, I had a wonderful time. As the reception ended, the crowd of happy, drunk guests gathered on the front steps. Ray and I bent our heads against a deluge of rice as we made our way down the steps to our car. Ray opened the door, and I slid into the passenger seat. Mama stood on the top step, her eyes shining with tears. Daddy leaned into the vehicle, smelling of Old Spice cologne, his favorite scent.

"If you ever need anything, baby," he said, "don't hesitate to call me."

CHAPTER 17

CAROL

By late 1974 our smuggling ring had turned into a highly profitable business. Mike, John, and Mark had become experts in their chosen line of business. The money kept rolling in, thousands of dollars at a time. The problem was that since the money was not gained legally, it couldn't be deposited in a bank or any other financial institution. For lack of a better idea, Mike began burying large sums in coffee cans around the premises.

Easy money was what I called it. Easily come by and twice as easily spent. Mike bought a new Dodge pickup truck for himself, and several truly lavish gifts for me, one of which was a Thoroughbred gelding. The horse was incredibly beautiful, with a deep, glossy sheen to his coat and four white stockings. He had a long, aristocratic name that I completely ignored in favor of Lovie. In spite of the animal's blue-blooded pedigree, he became nothing more than a pet and followed me and the kids around like an overgrown puppy.

After Mama's departure from Covington, Mike and I had abandoned the mobile home and, with Mama's permission, moved into the house. Mike was often gone on trips, so as a hobby I began to breed Irish setters, captivated by their sweet temperament and red-coated beauty. Mike always teased me, since I couldn't bear to part with the pups that were born. He built a large multirun kennel to house the growing number of pups, but I couldn't bear to see them confined to a small run, so I let them roam about the acreage. All you had to do was look across the open fields in any direction to catch a red streak flashing by. Though I'm embarrassed to say it now, I was very happy to be smuggling.

About this time Mike began to talk about branching out in the pot smuggling business. Working on the theory that he would serve no more time in prison if busted for three hundred pounds of weed than he would if busted for half that amount, he came up with a new scheme. Mike built a camper on the back of his pickup truck, but it was no ordinary camper. It contained a hidden box that would easily store two hundred kilos, or approximately five hundred pounds, of marijuana. The box ran the width of the camper, and when the lid was raised there appeared to be a deep-well area of storage space that could easily be filled with camping paraphernalia. When the weed was picked up in Mexico, it came in small, compact packages weighing two kilos each. Mike planned to empty the box of camping equipment and squeeze his way into the narrow opening. Then he'd slide the packages into an open, hollow end of the box. When all the marijuana had been stashed, he would simply replace the camping equipment and close the lid.

Mike proudly announced his new plan of action to John and Mark—he planned to drive the pot through the border station, right under the noses of the United States Customs officials.

Mark and John stared at him.

"You've got brass balls, Mike," said John. "But you can count me out. The last thing I care to do is spend my life in prison."

Mike looked to Mark, but Mark shook his head no. "We've been through a lot, old buddy, but this time it's your funeral."

They decided to make another trip, with Mike driving his modified camper truck and John following in his own vehicle. They would do everything the way they always had, with one exception. This time they would part company in Nueva Laredo, with John and Mark going on to Beauquias, and Mike leaving Mexico at the Customs station.

Mike returned home after two weeks, grinning from ear to ear. Two days later John and Mark showed up, tired from their long trip and with only a quarter of the pot Mike had. That was the end of Mike's partnership with them. Neither John nor Mark possessed Mike's cold nerve. Though they wanted fear of getting busted by customs to look like the reason for the parting, it was envy. Mike had one-upped them both. He was now the clear leader, and they knew they couldn't keep up.

Three weeks later Mike took off for another run. One night while he was gone, my phone woke me from a deep sleep. At first I had trouble recognizing the voice on the other end of the line, because the words were so slurred.

Finally it dawned on me. The caller was Daddy.

"Daddy, are you alright? You sound weird; are you loaded or something?"

"I took a few pain pills. So what?" he mumbled.

"Quit taking them," I said, careful to enunciate each word. "You're becoming addicted to them."

"Maybe I'll just take them all, and who would care? I'm going broke, your mother no longer loves me, and my kids don't know I exist. I've spent a lifetime doing for my kids, and now it's come to this."

I could picture him in his chair, wallowing in self-pity. "Don't talk that way, Daddy. Please."

"Come see me, Carol. I need you."

I felt a deep pity for him, despite everything he'd done. He sounded so lost and miserable, and I was happy, free, I thought, from his dangerous games. "I can't drag the kids out of bed at this hour, but I promise you I'll be there first thing tomorrow morning. I love you, Daddy." I hung up the phone.

The following morning I went over to his house. He'd calmed down a bit, and he was slightly more lucid than he had been the night before. He was dressed in his pajamas and sitting in the library in his easy chair. I pulled up an ottoman and sat down at his feet.

I started gently.

"Okay. Now tell me what's bothering you."

His bleary eyes gazed into mine as if he were having trouble focusing them. "I'm going broke. I've spent all the money I got for the loss of my hand. I have no steady income other than my investments, now that I've quit practicing law. I'm up to my ass in debt, and I see no way out of it but to kill myself. I'll drive my Cadillac off the Mississippi River bridge. It'll look like an accident, and no one will know that it wasn't but you and me. I'll leave behind tons of insurance, so all of you will be taken care of for the rest of your lives. That's all that matters to me." He delivered the last sentence as if he were on stage: laced with self-pity and purely for effect. I didn't believe he'd kill himself, but he probably was in trouble.

I patted his hand. "Look, killing yourself is no answer. There must be another way out of this." Mike's business immediately came to mind. I could afford to help now. Maybe if Daddy had some money, he would calm down and we could get on with our lives. I took a deep breath and plunged in. "I don't think you know what Mike does for a living."

"He works for some oil company, doesn't he?"

"Not anymore," I said cautiously. "He smuggles marijuana from Mexico. I know you probably disapprove, but he's making a lot of money."

He sat up straight in the chair; his befuddled expression changed in a second to sudden interest. "How much money?"

"He makes an average of thirty grand a trip, depending on the going price per pound."

"How many trips has he made?"

"I don't know exactly. Probably six, maybe seven."

Daddy let out a low whistle. "Son of a bitch!" he exclaimed. "Do you think he'd cut me in for a piece of the pie?"

"I could ask him, but Mike doesn't like partners."

"I can certainly accept that. But, Jesus Christ, I'm desperate. Talk to him, baby. See if he's willing to go into a partnership."

"I'll see what I can do, but will you promise me—no more talk of suicide?"

He settled back down in the chair, and his expression once again became maudlin. "I can't promise you that. If Mike doesn't help me, I'll have no other choice."

I might have been onto all of Daddy's tricks, but I'd given him what he needed to create a new and deadly scheme.

Mike had been home from Mexico for three days before I could work up the nerve to approach him on Daddy's behalf. Although I hadn't expected him to be thrilled about the idea, I wasn't at all prepared for his violent reaction.

"No way!" he exploded. "Forget it. I don't need any partners. I've got enough problems of my own."

"I know it's a lot to ask, but I'm worried about Daddy. I know this isn't your problem, but it is mine. I've never seen him like this. He's so depressed, he's talking about killing himself."

I may have been overstating my case, but I had to make Mike understand how serious the situation was.

"Forget about it. He's probably just blowing smoke, trying to get some sympathy," Mike said, but his eyes refused to meet mine. I was getting through.

"But what if he's serious? I would never forgive myself. With all the money you've made, and as many times as you've been down there, would it be so hard for you to do this for him, just this once?"

His blue eyes were troubled as he sat beside me on the sofa. "You know, every time I go down there I wonder if I'll make it back. I try to put it out of my mind, but there's always the chance that I'll get caught and go to prison. If I had to be separated from you and the kids, I don't think I could handle it. It's one thing to take the risk for us because I want my family to have something in life, but it's another thing to risk it all for your father. He's not worth what I stand to lose."

All that he'd just said was true, and I knew it in my heart as surely as I knew my father had sent envelopes of money to me in Germany without being asked to when Bruce and I didn't have a nickel to our name. Now it was my turn to help. How could I turn my back on him?

Mike could sense the turmoil within me. He cupped my chin in his hand. "Now come on and smile for me, baby. I can't stand to see you sad. If it means this much to you, I'll do it. But not for him—for you. I'll make the run and give him all the money, but no partnerships. And I'm not going for him again."

Three weeks later I handed Daddy a thick stack of one hundred dollar bills totaling thirty-two thousand five hundred dollars.

For a long time he sat in the chair just gazing at the pile of money, lost in thought. Finally he broke the silence. "I owe Mike one. You know, the kid has style, no doubt about it. If Mike were to up the number of trips he makes, just imagine what we could make in a year."

His face grew thoughtful. I could only wonder what he meant by "we."

"Shit," he continued, "we'd be making over a quarter of a million dollars a year, tax-free!"

I didn't have the guts to tell him face-to-face that this was the first and last trip Mike would be making for him, so I just sat there in silence and let him ramble on.

"Think of it," he said. "If that much money can be made bringing the stuff in by truck, just imagine how much could be made using the sailboat to smuggle it in." His eyes were lit, his imagination off and running. "It's the perfect solution to my financial problems. Mike can continue to bring the stuff in by truck, and Bruce can hustle it in the sailboat."

Mike would never stand for it. "Daddy, you're getting carried away here. There's no way Bruce is going to involve himself in a crazy scheme like that. You'll probably send him over the edge just mentioning it to him."

He smiled. "Don't you worry. There are ways to ensure Bruce's cooperation." Whatever that meant.

I pondered that one as he dialed Bruce's number. I was running late and should have headed home, but after hearing Daddy tell Bruce he'd see him in a few minutes, I wasn't about to miss out on the show.

As soon as my ex arrived, Daddy ushered him straight into the library. Bruce glanced a question at me, but I just shrugged my shoulders—I had no idea what this was all about. Bruce had barely sat down on the sofa when Daddy let him have it with both barrels.

"How many pounds of marijuana could we fit into the *Stiletto*?"

Bruce gawked, first at Daddy, then at me. "What are you planning to do, smuggle dope or something?" He joked lightly, but with caution. He knew Daddy well enough to know he could be serious.

Daddy pinned him with his eyes. "Maybe."

Bruce pushed out a nervous laugh. "You've got to be kidding. You don't know the first thing about an operation like that. You've been watching too many movies, L.J." He gave me a pleading look. "He's kidding, right?"

"Believe me," Daddy said. "I couldn't be more serious. We could make a fortune." His eyes had that strange glow again.

Bruce half rose from the sofa. "What do you mean, *we?* Count me out. I have no intention of spending the rest of my life in prison."

Daddy stared him down. "You won't be spending any time in prison, not if you do it right."

"In the first place, I'd have to sail all the way to some place like Colombia. I don't have much sailing experience on the open seas, not to mention that I would need a top-notch crew. Then once I got there—provided, of course, that I got there at all—I'd have to find a contact. One I can be sure won't slit my throat the minute the deal was made. Last, but not least, pot is a very bulky commodity. It wouldn't be easy to hide enough on board to make the trip worthwhile. It's just a ridiculous idea, L.J."

"Why not hide something smaller, then?" suggested Daddy. "Like cocaine?"

"Jesus," said Bruce. "Now you're really talking trouble. Okay, coke would be a cinch to hide, but it's a dirty drug, and it carries bad karma with it. People die every day from overdoses of cocaine. It's bad news."

"How long do you think it would take to find a decent crew?" asked Daddy, completely unfazed by Bruce's objections.

"You're just not listening, are you? I won't do it."

Daddy leaned back in his chair, unperturbed by Bruce's declaration. "That's just too bad, then, Bruce, because now I have no alternative but to take the boat away from you. I'll find someone who'll be willing to do it, and if I can't, then I'll just sell the boat."

Bruce was near panic. "You can't be serious! You know how much that boat means to me."

"I do," said Daddy, nodding in agreement. "But I also know that I need money. So, in view of that, I suggest you go home and think about it. Who knows? Maybe you'll change your mind."

CHAPTER 18

CAROL

Several weeks after Daddy's conversation with Bruce, John Smith paid Mike and me a visit. We were sitting outdoors in lawn chairs reminiscing about old times when I happened to spot a shooting star in the sky.

"Look at that, a shooting star," I said. "Now we all get to make a wish."

John laughed, and the sound carried in the quiet night.

"What's so funny?" asked Mike. He popped the top on a fresh can of Budweiser.

"Nothing much. I'm just wishing that Bruce Applegarth is as good a sailor as he says he is."

"That's an unusual thing to wish for," I said.

He laughed again. "Not if you're about to set sail with him all the way to Colombia."

I thought my heart had stopped beating. "When are you sailing to Colombia? And what for?" I asked, but I knew already.

"We're leaving tomorrow to try and set up a big coke deal. Your old man really put Bruce's ass over a barrel, threatened to take his boat away."

"How do you know about that? I didn't think you and Bruce were such good friends."

"Yeah, we're pretty good friends. I run into him once in a while, and we have a beer and a few laughs. I've told him what I do for a living, and I guess that's why he called me. He told me what was going on, and I said I'd go with him. I'm not a half-bad sailor, and neither is

Mark. So when I passed on the news to him, he agreed to come along."

Why on earth would Bruce agree to do something that dangerously foolish? Surely it wasn't worth it just to keep the *Stiletto*. "When are you leaving?"

It was hard to make out John's features in the dark, and I caught only a quick glimpse of his eyes as he lit up a Marlboro, cupping his hand around the match. "Tomorrow at dawn," he said, and flicked the match into the grass. "The supplies are already loaded. Your old man sprang for some very sophisticated Loran equipment and a four-man lifeboat, along with enough food and booze to feed an army."

As he and Mike discussed sailing the open seas, I remembered Bruce's reaction to Daddy's suggestion that he smuggle cocaine. What in the world did Daddy say or do to change his mind?

I slipped into the house and dialed Bruce's number, determined to get to the bottom of it. The phone in his apartment rang several times, and I was about to hang up when Bruce picked up the receiver.

"Bruce," I said. "John's over here, and he says you're sailing tomorrow for Colombia. It's some kind of joke, right? You're not really going through with this, are you?"

His voice was husky. "I have no choice."

"What the hell is that supposed to mean? You could die out there," I shrieked. "That boat can't mean that much to you, can it?"

There was a dead silence on the other end of the line. Finally he said, "It isn't just the boat, and believe me when I tell you that my life is safer on the open seas than it would be in this town if I didn't go."

The hysteria in his voice set my pulse to pounding. "Bruce, did Daddy threaten you into going?"

"I never said that. Just do me a favor, Carol. Hang up the phone, and keep your nose out of this."

On that note he hung up. I paced the house, frustrated and anxious.

After a lot of thought I called Daddy. Maybe I could talk some sense into him. At the sound of his voice, though, all attempts at peacemaking flew right out the window, and I lit into him.

"You're forcing Bruce to sail to Colombia, aren't you? How did you twist his arm? What have you done to make him do this?"

His voice was casual and completely unmoved by my shrill outburst. "Just hold on a minute. I haven't forced Bruce to do anything. Now, I'll admit that I told him I'd have to sell the *Stiletto* because I need the money, but that's all I said. He made the choice to do this on his own. What do you think I am, anyway?" he said in his best aggrieved tone.

"Don't hand me all that crap, Daddy. I know Bruce Applegarth, and I'm telling you, you put the squeeze on him somehow. He would never have agreed to make this trip if you hadn't."

He sighed theatrically. "I don't know why you would say something like that to me. I've said it before, and I'll say it again: Bruce made the decision to go. I had nothing to do with it."

"In that case you'll have no objections if I convince him to change his mind, right?"

"You listen to me, young lady," he roared. "I call the shots around here, and I don't want to hear that you've tried to talk him out of it, you got that?"

"I got it," I said. I was unintimidated, but also smart enough to know when to quit.

"And you can remember one last thing while you're at it. If that boat doesn't set sail by dawn, Bruce Applegarth won't live to see sunset."

Daddy's words still rang in my ears as I sweated out the next few weeks. I got in touch with everyone I knew who might have heard from either Bruce, John, or Mark, but no one had had any word since they'd left. It seemed as though all three men had told the same tale to everyone—they were going to sail to the Bahamas for a little fun in the sun.

My nerves were frazzled when halfway into the third week of their absence, Mark Wright showed up on my doorstep. His hair was long and wild, and his face was badly in need of a shave. He looked terrible. Mike and I gaped at him as he stood in the doorway. I reached out to him.

"Jesus, Mark, I thought you were halfway to Colombia by now. I've been worried sick about all of you."

He grabbed me in a bear hug and planted a big smack on my cheek. "We never made it past Dauphin Island, Alabama." He grinned, happy to be alive. "Bruce ran her aground on a sandbar, and the boat had a lot of damage to her underbelly. It'll be another two to three weeks before she'll be seaworthy again."

"Thank God," I said. That was a relief.

"The only problem is, the damage came to a pretty penny, and Bruce is going to pay hell explaining that one to your father, because he used the money the old man put up to buy the dope with."

"Then the trip is off, right?"

"No question about it. I wouldn't try that again on a bet, and John feels the same way."

"L.J.'s going to love this one," said Mike. He handed Mark a beer.

"Yeah. Well, Bruce is scared shitless to tell him. He made me swear I'd lie low until he and John can get the boat back here. That's why I came up here—so I can keep out of sight. Mind if I bunk in the trailer for a few weeks?"

Mike said it was fine, so now we had another person hiding out from Daddy.

Within three weeks the *Stiletto* was repaired. Bruce and John Smith sailed her back home and docked her in her familiar slip at the New Orleans Lakefront Marina.

A couple of hours later Bruce called me. "Tell Mark he can come out of hiding. There's nothing left to do now but face the music." He sounded resigned to his fate. "None of this is my fault. If I could have helped your dad, I would have. I just never expected he'd ask me to do something like this."

I realized then that Bruce had never actually tried to make the trip at all. My instincts had been right all along. He was too smart and too clean to go along with Daddy's plan. He just left town and came back when the money ran out. No matter what actually happened, I knew how hard it was going to be for him to break the news to Daddy that he didn't have the drugs. Before I could stop myself, I volunteered to go with him to Daddy's house.

"You can come if you want to," he said, "but you know the shit's going to hit the fan. He'll probably be twice as pissed if you're there, because this whole thing is between him and me."

I didn't give a damn about how pissed Daddy got. I felt that Bruce needed support. Maybe my presence could help ease what was no doubt going to be an ugly scene. I drove the fifty miles to New Orleans, stopping to pick Bruce up at his apartment before heading for Citrus Road. Bruce sat beside me and drummed his fingers against the dash, his body poised tensely on the edge of the seat. I hated Daddy then for placing Bruce and me in this terrible situation just to satisfy his own selfish greed.

Daddy opened the door to our knock. Without a word he turned and headed for the library, with Bruce and me following him reluctantly. Once we were inside he closed the louvered doors behind us, to shut off our escape.

He whirled on Bruce. "You chickened out, didn't you?"

Bruce's voice faltered. "No, ah, the boat ran aground in Dauphin Island, and we had to use some of the money for repairs."

Daddy's mouth compressed in a thin, tight line, the surest sign of his anger. Bruce shrank before that ferocious face. "How much of the money is left, Bruce?"

"Five thousand," he answered in a whisper.

"Give it to me."

Bruce unhooked a money belt from around his waist and handed it to Daddy with shaking hands. Daddy crossed over to his desk and retrieved some papers from its cluttered surface. He gave them to Bruce.

"Read this," he said.

As Bruce, read his face grew ashen. "It's an insurance policy on the *Stiletto*. I don't understand."

"You don't understand?" Daddy said with mock patience. "Then let me spell it out for you. Your precious boat's about to be blown sky high."

The next day Mama called me. "What in the name of God is your father up to?" She plunged ahead. "Has he gone completely off his rocker? Do you know that he showed up on my doorstep late last night to demand that I sign over the title of the *Stiletto* to him? I told him point blank that I had no intention of doing any such thing, and that's when he said that it would be wise of me to sign the papers, unless I'd care to be a party to blowing it up. The last thing in the world I need is to be involved in insurance fraud."

"Well, of course," I agreed. "Listen, Mama, you don't even want to know the details that have led up to this craziness."

"I know what you mean. I lay in bed at night wondering where it's all going to end. With your father you barely have a chance to recover from one disaster before the next one rolls along. Oh, well. Who knows— maybe I'll get lucky and he'll blow himself up along with the boat."

I made up my mind to have as little to do with Daddy as possible. It was a decision I'd made before, and I guess I knew deep down that I'd make it again, but I'd had enough of his verbal abuse, his violent nature, and his craziness to last me a lifetime. I would have given anything in the world if things could have been different, but I tried to accept that they never would be. He'd grown progressively worse in the last few years, and the odds of his changing back into the father I once knew were slim to none. I still loved him dearly, in spite of the way I felt, but there were other people in my life I loved, too. And he had hurt too many of them.

The week before Christmas, a few days prior to Shirley's wedding, I was in the kitchen mixing eggnog in the blender. Through the open bar that separated the kitchen from the den, I watched Mike toss another log on the fire. Red-and-amber flames flickered brightly as he coaxed the dying embers back to life with a fireplace poker. It was a cozy, peaceful evening, and we were just getting ready to decorate the tree. I was finally re-creating the wonderful tree trimmings of my youth. I mixed up a final batch of eggnog, and above the whir of the blender I heard the telephone ring.

I picked it up. There was only a crackling noise coming across the wire. I was ready to hang up when I heard Daddy's voice, weak and far away over the long-distance connection.

"Carol, it's Daddy. I'm all alone. Can you come over here now?"

"Where's Marty?" I asked sharply.

"Gone to her parents. I'm sick and dizzy, and there's no one here."

Here we go, I thought. It's time to play on Carol's sympathy. "Why don't you call Nancy? She's right next door." The kids were tugging at my jeans, ready to decorate the tree, and I had no time for more of Daddy's theatrics.

"Not home," he said. On the other end of the line I heard a loud crack as the receiver apparently hit the floor. There was a series of muffled noises, then total silence.

"Daddy!" I screamed into the phone. When after several seconds no response came, I turned to Mike, panicked.

"Mike! Something's happened to Daddy! One minute

he was talking to me, and the next he was gone. I heard the phone drop; maybe he's fainted." I was shaking.

"Give me the phone." Mike grabbed the receiver and called Daddy's name.

"Hang up," I said. "I'm going to go over there and check on him. You stay here and decorate the tree with the kids. I'll call you as soon as I get there."

I grabbed my coat and rushed out to my car. I sped to River Ridge, guilt rising in me for having given Daddy such a hard time on the phone.

When I arrived the only car in the driveway was my father's gold Eldorado, and there was only a dim light on in the library. The front door was unlocked, so I burst into the living room foyer. There was no sign of Daddy anywhere. I made my way down the hall to the library, filled with a curious, sinking sensation. A vision of him lying on the floor came to mind, and I braced myself for the inevitable.

He was stretched out on the sofa, and he lay so still that I was sure he was dead. I reached out to feel his arm and found that he was warm to the touch. Up close I could easily see his chest rise and fall in rhythm to his shallow breathing.

After a moment he opened his eyes and stared at me in confusion. "Carol, I'm so glad you came. I must have passed out; I couldn't stand up anymore."

I kneeled down beside him.

"It's alright."

"I guess it's my heart," he said weakly. "I've been feeling ill for some time now. All this stress. I'm afraid I'm heading for another heart attack." He closed his eyes.

"What stress?"

His eyes fluttered open. "The same old story, money troubles. You know how severe my last heart attack was."

I knew no such thing, but that seemed neither here nor there at that point.

"I almost died from that heart attack, and my doctor

demanded that I quit practicing law. I have a little cash left from Mike's trip, but that's not enough to make a dent in my bills."

He covered his face with his hands and began to sob harshly. "I'm fifty-two years old, and my life is over."

It broke my heart to hear him say that. The sight of my big, strong father crying was more than I could bear. If he was acting, he was doing an amazing job. So amazing that I believed him. Daddy needed me. "Listen to me, Daddy. I'll do anything I can to help you. Only please pull yourself out of this depression—it's eating you up alive. Maybe Mike can help out again. I'll ask him, I promise."

I drove back across the Lake Pontchartrain Causeway with a heavy heart. I'd made a promise that would be very hard to keep. It was nearly three A.M. by the time I made it back to Covington. Mike had waited up for me, and as soon as I stepped through the doorway, he sensed what was up. The look on my face probably told him everything he needed to know.

"I can't go again," he said.

"You mean you won't go again. It comes out the same both ways." I walked over to the kitchen counter and slumped dejectedly down on one of the bar stools.

"Carol, please, be reasonable—"

I cut him off in midsentence. "It's easy for you to be reasonable. He's not your father." It was an unfair statement, and I knew it.

"That's not fair. I laid my ass on the line for your father once. Isn't that enough? It isn't going to end with just one more trip. You know that, and I know that."

"Yes, I do know that. But all of my life I've tried to earn my father's love, and that's probably hard for you to understand. Now the balance has shifted, and he needs me. For the first time he needs me."

Mike was exasperated. "But at what price, Carol? Don't you see how destructive all this has become? You aren't just compromising yourself, you're compromising everyone you love. It's not love you feel for him, Carol. It's a goddamned obsession."

His words cut me. They were so close to the truth that I had to turn against Mike. "Are you telling me there's something wrong with loving too much?"

He gazed at me intently. "Yes, if that love goes beyond all rational thought and loyalty. Listen to me, baby," he said, his eyes earnest and caring. "When are you going to realize that it's not your fault? How long do you think we can go on supporting your father? It's just not realistic. There's nothing in this world I wouldn't do for you, and it's not that I have anything against L.J. personally. It's just that things are changing in Mexico; things are happening that I haven't wanted to tell you about. For a long time now the odds have been in my favor, and God knows I'm a man that runs with the odds. But things have started to turn around. The *federales*, the border police, are cracking down; there are roadblocks and checkpoints everywhere."

He paused for a moment. "I guess what I'm trying to say is, it's just not a game anymore. It's not easy money. It's become a real, deadly business, and it's taken me a long time to face the truth."

"What truth?" I asked.

"I'm losing the most important thing I need to survive in this business: my confidence. It's time to get out."

I was ashamed of my selfishness. I had never seen the turmoil inside of Mike. He'd made those trips to Mexico seem so easy that I'd never once looked beneath his calm face. Our smuggling days were over.

The next morning I drove to Daddy's house to deliver the news that there was no way for Mike and me to help him. He was in the backyard spreading mulch over a bed of camellias when I arrived. Kim and Bruce streaked across the yard ahead of me and flung themselves on Daddy, almost knocking him down in their enthusiasm.

Leonard J. Fagot. 1941.

Daddy receiving the Silver Star. 1945.

Mama and Daddy on their wedding day. 1946.

*Joanne and
George Westerfield's
wedding. 1966.*

*Marta
Courtney Fagot,
as she appeared
in the Riverdale
High yearbook.
1967.*

Nancy's wedding. 1973. (left to right — Shirley, Joanne, Daddy, Mama, Nancy, and Carol)

Carol and Mike Holland. 1974.

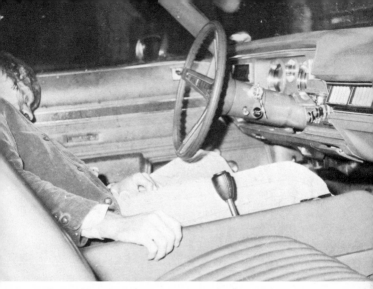

Mike Holland's body, as found by the police. (Courtesy of Jefferson Parish Sheriff's Office/Joseph Passalaqua)

The driveway where Daddy shot Mike. (Courtesy of Jefferson Parish Sheriff's Office/Joseph Passalaqua)

The house on Citrus Road. (Courtesy of Jefferson Parish Sheriff's Office/Don Carson)

Police photo of Daddy taken the night of Mike's murder. (Courtesy of Jefferson Parish Sheriff's Office/ Thomas Waguespack)

The .38 caliber Charter Arms Daddy used. Police found it in an envelope hidden behind a row of books in the library. (Courtesy of Jefferson Parish Sheriff's Office/ Thomas Waguespack)

Daddy's library. (Courtesy of Jefferson Parish Sheriff's Office/Thomas Waguespack)

A close-up showing the injury Daddy sustained during the murder. (Courtesy of Jefferson Parish Sheriff's Office/ Thomas Waguespack)

The Thunderbird which contained Daddy's body, as it was found March 18, 1978. (Courtesy of Jefferson Parish Sheriff's Office/J. Deidrich)

"Come on, kids. Take it easy," I said.

Daddy balanced one on each knee. "These little rascals are fine."

"Isn't it a little chilly for yard work?" I pushed my cold hands deeper into the pockets of my jacket.

"It doesn't bother me, and it's supposed to freeze tonight. I want to make sure some of the less hardy of the plants survive."

"I'd like to speak with you alone."

He slid the two squirming kids from his lap. "Why don't you two run inside? There's some chocolate pudding in the refrigerator, and I bet Marty will fix you both a bowl if you ask her."

"Thanks, Paw-Paw!" They dashed toward the house.

"Now, what's on your mind?" he asked me.

"Mike doesn't want to make any more trips to Mexico. I'm sorry."

"Sorry isn't good enough," he shot back. "You could insist that he go. I've seen you in action, and believe me, if you pushed him hard enough, he would go."

I could only stare at him. "Daddy, just think about what you're saying. I love Mike, and I don't want to push him. And there's no way I or anybody else can force Mike Holland to do what he doesn't want to do."

He stabbed the shovel he'd been leaning on into the ground beside him. "Well, you go back home—right now, right this minute—and convince him otherwise. You can do it. I know you can."

"I won't do that," I said. "Can't you see the position you've put me in?"

"What about the fucking position I'm in?"

"I have tried the best I know how to help you, Daddy. Now, I don't have to stand here and listen to you yell at me about something I have no control over." I began to walk away.

"That's right!" he yelled. "Walk out on me. Everyone else has. I counted on you, and you let me down. Just remember this: I don't have a daughter named Carol anymore, and don't you forget it!"

I continued walking, head down, hands jammed into my pockets. "Don't worry, I won't forget," I whispered softly.

CHAPTER 19

CAROL

One might wonder with just cause why I did not at this point, or even before, simply say "Enough is enough" and turn my back on my father once and for all. My only defense is that I had made a lifelong habit of loving him. He had said and done the cruelest of things to me and to others I loved, had made a mockery of all that I believed in, had committed the most vicious of crimes. And still I loved him. Maybe if he'd been a less strong willed and compelling presence in my life, I would not have become a victim of the power he wielded over me. I'd grown up with such devotion to him, admiring him so, it must have been easy for him to figure out that my need for him was much like the need of a heroin addict for a fix. This time, though, I told myself that I had to stay away. Everything Mike and I had built in Covington was threatening to collapse if Daddy got involved in my life again.

I wished I had the fortitude of my sister Joanne, who had by then completely alienated herself from him, or that I lived far away from this, as Shirley did. Only Nancy bore the full brunt of his sad decline and came close to understanding everything. In fact, I think she loved him even more than I did. Over and over again she would call me, begging me to make amends with Daddy. I had forsaken him at a time when he needed me the most, she would say, although he had said he was forgetting me. She refused to listen to my excuses for not seeing him and would eventually break down in tears at my insistence on not having anything to do with

him. Unfortunately, her persistence wore me down
over time. I knew that she should not have to deal with
Daddy single-handedly. His moods were too much for
anyone to cope with alone. And one visit wouldn't
break up Mike and me. Swallowing my pride, I went to
see him at the house on Citrus Road.

I found him sitting in the library in his old, familiar
leather recliner. I sensed instantly from his glassy-eyed,
heavy-lidded lethargy that he was drugged. He sat in
virtual darkness, save for a small desk lamp that cast a
halo of light in a far corner of the room. From the built-
in speakers set high above the bookcase Hank Williams
sang a song of loneliness and heartache. Daddy was
floating on pills and self-pity. His eyes were half-closed.
I nudged him gently on the shoulder and he peered at
me. I felt a sudden compassion for him, sad to think that
he found it necessary to resort to such self-inflicted misery.

"Daddy, what are you thinking about?"

"It's just like a jigsaw puzzle, and I have to put the
pieces together," he mumbled.

"What's like a jigsaw puzzle? Tell me what you
mean."

He leaned his head back. "My children have all
stabbed me in the back, and there's no remorse in any
of them."

"Daddy, we love you. We only want to help."

"All of them are greedy users, and they've married
men exactly like themselves." It unnerved me to hear
him speak in the third person like that, as if he didn't
know I was there or he were talking to some invisible
person. "What do they want from me? Blood?" He
laughed a low, insidious chuckle. "Well, I've already
sacrificed that for them once. Wasn't that good
enough?" He raised the stump of his arm, as if in salute
to me. "How many sacrifices am I supposed to make?
How many bits and pieces of me do they want?"

He stared at me, then bent forward. His eyes were

cold and flat, devoid of everything but Valium and codeine, the soulless eyes of a snake.

"Is it blood you want?" His question was absurd, undeserving of an answer. Was he asking me or his invisible guest? "Then blood you'll get."

It was a statement of fact, as flat and expressionless as his eyes. I did not know this man anymore, and the sense of loss crushed me. It was as if I'd never seen him before. I ran from that room and the madness within it, changed by what I had seen and what I now truly knew. On the endless ride back to Covington I came face-to-face with the knowledge that I had tried for so long to hide from: Daddy had crossed over the line between sanity and insanity. The father I once knew was lost forever to me, and I knew that nothing would bring him back. No drug or medical treatment could cure him. Can a doctor restore one's soul, or give one back a conscience?

"Then blood you'll get." I could only imagine what he'd been hinting at, but even my wildest imaginings did not prepare me for what it really meant.

I first heard the news from Nancy, who called my house at dawn one spring day to tell me that Daddy had been in an accident. She had heard it from Marty and didn't have many details. Apparently he'd been run off the road at the intersection of West Esplanade Avenue and Power Boulevard, in Metairie, ten miles from home. His heavy gold Cadillac had plunged through a ditch on the side of the road and run down a chain-link fence before slamming into a residence several yards away. He'd been wearing his prosthesis, an artificial forearm with two stainless steel pincers attached to the end that served as fingers. I'd seen him wear it only twice in the almost four years since he'd lost his arm. The hook had pierced his left eye, and he'd been rushed to the emergency room.

I got to the hospital at eight A.M. Joanne was in the tiny cubicle that served as a lobby for the intensive care unit. Dressed in a soft blue pantsuit, she sat in a chrome-and-vinyl chair, leafing through a *Time* magazine several months out of date. She acknowledged my presence with a grim nod, then went back to the magazine. Her brow was furrowed, and her eyes inscrutable. I was surprised she was there, but she didn't appear open to having that conversation.

"Where's Nancy?" I asked.

"She went to get a bite to eat," Joanne answered, not looking at me. "She'll be back soon."

I sat on the chair beside her with one foot curled under me, lost in thought, my other foot nervously tapping the highly polished surface of the tile floor.

"Will you please stop doing that?" snapped Joanne. "You're driving me nuts."

"I'm sorry," I said, uncurling my leg and placing both feet on the floor. "I just keep thinking of Daddy's accident, picturing that hook—" I glanced at my watch. "The nurse at the front desk said he's been in surgery for over an hour. Have you seen him yet?"

"No." Her eyes had gone dead. There was no emotion in their hazel depths. "I have no intention of going in there to see him. I only came here to make sure he's going to survive. As soon as he's out of danger I'm going home," she said curtly.

I knew she had made her break with Daddy, but I didn't think she had to be callous. "Oh, so you're just doing your duty, is that it?"

She didn't look up. "If you care to look at it that way."

"Look. I know you have every reason to be hurt and angry with him, but it surely has to end somewhere, doesn't it? He needs help."

"It will never end. He's taken too much from me." Her eyes were somber. I remembered the pretty girl who used to sparkle with life. There was no trace of her now in this silent woman.

"I agree. It was a rotten thing for him to do. He sold your house right out from under you."

"That and other things."

"What other things?"

"You don't want to get me started on that subject. You won't like the things I have to say, and I'll just end up wishing I'd never said them." She tossed the magazine onto the table and turned to me. "But since you've brought the subject up, we might as well get it out in the open." Searching through her purse, she pulled out a pack of cigarettes and lit one up. "For several months now I've known about the life insurance policy that Daddy collected when George died. Mama finally admitted the truth about it to me. Neither you nor Mama had the right to keep that from me."

"We didn't want to hurt you."

Her face softened slightly. "I hope that's the case, because I don't want to believe that either of you were hiding this from me to protect him."

"Protect him from what?"

"You add it up, Carol. He takes out a whopping life insurance policy on George and hides the fact from everyone. Six months later George dies on Daddy's property, doing one of Daddy's little jobs, and who benefits from his death? Daddy collects two hundred thousand dollars, and he turns over a check to me for twenty thousand. But even that wasn't enough for him, he had to steal most of that money, too."

She bent to crush out her cigarette in the ashtray. "He murdered George for the money. He's a purely evil man, as cold and selfish as they come. He would do anything, and I mean anything, to achieve his own ends. No one will ever make me believe otherwise." The strength in her voice backed up her words.

How had this happened to us? What had made our perfect family decay this way? "I had no idea you felt that way, Joanne. Mama and I discussed this very same thing a long time ago. We haven't talked about it since."

"Mama," said Joanne, "is lucky to be alive. The only reason she is, I guess, is because she backed off at the time of their separation. If she had pushed him, she wouldn't be here now."

"You honestly believe that?"

"From the bottom of my heart."

There it was, out in the open, and I had never dreamed she suspected any of this. It seemed I was not the only one who knew him well.

"He has to be crazy," I pointed out. "Mentally ill." Even now, I was still apologizing for him.

"I wouldn't know how to diagnose him. I'm not a psychiatrist, but I will tell you this. He is completely without conscience, and that makes him dangerous. Aside from that, he's exceptionally clever. Look at how he's manipulated all of us. He pulls the strings, and we dance. If he's having a hard time getting his way, all he has to do is fall down and fake an attack. It works every time."

"You think he fakes his attacks?" It hadn't occurred to me, but the idea didn't surprise me at all.

"I'm sure he does. Haven't you ever noticed how conveniently timed they are? Think about it. I'm sure he's used you the same way he has everyone else."

"I have thought about it," I admitted, "but then I start to feel like a rat, and I convince myself that I'm imagining things. It just seems so impossibly crazy."

Joanne moved closer to me. "Do you want to know what I think, Carol? I think he shot off his own hand. I think he probably staged this car wreck."

That was the last thing I wanted to hear. It only confirmed my own suspicions. "Jesus, why would anyone do such things?"

"To collect the insurance money."

"For God's sake, he would have had to rip his own eye out. What kind of person would deliberately maim himself that way? He could have died!"

"A sick and desperate one," Joanne answered. Her face was worn, like a sad old woman's. "One capable of murdering the man I loved and leaving my children fatherless."

*   *   *

Four hours later I learned that Daddy's left eye had been so severely damaged, it could not be saved. He was still unconscious from the anesthesia, but a nurse was kind enough to allow me a peek at him. He was deathly pale, almost as white as the pristine walls of the hospital room. A large bandage covered his left eye, and I suppressed a shudder at the sight of it. I tried not to think about the gaping hole beneath that bandage and what it meant. I looked down at the disfigured stump of his left arm, which lay limply atop the coverlet. A wave of sadness and horror coursed through me. *Bits and pieces. Sacrifices. For us.* I wondered if somewhere deep inside him, he believed that to be true. The thought that he might was a thousand times worse than the thought that he was twisted and sick enough to do such things for money.

We never wanted any of this from you, Daddy. All we ever wanted was for you to be happy, so you would stop draining the happiness from us. Now I know that we should have wanted happiness for ourselves, for our own sakes. You're drowning, Daddy, and I don't know why. I only know that every time I try to toss you a lifeline, you pull me under with you. You've pulled for so long and so hard that I'm struggling to keep my head above the water. If you have ever loved me, have ever loved any of us, please let go. Let go before you pull us so far under, we'll never find our way to the surface.

In a week Daddy was released from the hospital. Still the dutiful daughter, I visited him. I knew beforehand that I would live to regret it, but the ties were too thick and too old to cut quickly. My heart still believed that I could help him, even when I knew it was too late.

I found him surrounded by loved ones. My two aunts, Daddy's sisters, Lacey and Valerie, hovered over him, doing everything possible to comfort him. I had grown up very close to Aunt Lacey and Aunt Val, as had my sisters. They were like second mothers to me, and their children—my cousins Mary Ann, Judy, Jay, Beth, Susan, and Patrick—were like brothers and sisters. But since my parents' separation I'd seen little of them; family get-togethers had become a thing of the past.

Nanaine doted on Daddy. He had always seemed the favorite of her four sons and two daughters. A sweet, lovely, silver-haired lady, Nanaine had only one trait that often drove me crazy—she was totally incapable of seeing wrong in anyone. It was certainly an admirable quality, but Nanaine's refusal to face the unpleasant was extremely frustrating at times and dangerous then. She clearly considered Daddy, her Leonard, a victim of circumstances, as did Lacey and Valerie. This was, I'm sure, what Daddy wanted them to believe. And, of course, they blamed his children and Mama for his misery. He had managed to convince his family that my sisters and I were a bunch of greedy, selfish users.

Nanaine lectured me gravely on the necessity of building a stronger relationship with Daddy. Taking me aside, she confided that he felt his children had abandoned him and that he was no longer certain that we loved him. She went on to chastise my mother for leaving him and to praise Marty for all that she had done. I swallowed the gall that rose in me and reassured her that we did love Daddy, each and every one of us, and that we would never, never abandon him. What else could I say? That I believed my father was insane? That deep in my heart I suspected he was a murderer? She patted me on my shoulder in her sweet way, relieved to know that all was well on the home front. I could not look into her gentle blue eyes.

A couple of weeks later I subjected myself to visiting him again. Marty opened the door to me and immediately started complaining. Dressed in jeans and high heels, she had her black hair pulled into a tight bun on her head. Her yellow sweater, which should have brightened her dark skin, only made her complexion look sallow. "It's about time you came to see your father," she said imperiously.

I was not in the mood for her childishness. I pushed

by her and headed for the library, where he usually was when I came.

"He's in the sunroom," she said.

I changed direction and entered the sunroom. Marty pushed her way past me and stopped at the foot of the brick steps. Making an exaggerated curtsy, she announced, "Her highness is here to see you, Len."

Daddy was propped up on pillows, resting on the rattan sofa. His expression was serene as he stared out of the windows toward the pool, unconcerned by Marty's spiteful words.

"Get out of my way." I shoved Marty aside and went down the steps.

"You can't talk to me that way," she cried.

"I'll talk to you any way I like, you asshole." It was a crude thing to say, but I must admit I enjoyed saying it.

Her cheeks flamed. "You pampered, spoiled little brat. You should be grateful to me, you know. I'm the one who takes care of your father, and I'm the only one who has the slightest bit of concern for his welfare. You and your sisters are just alike. All you have ever done is take, take, take!"

"You'd love for it to be that way, wouldn't you, Marty? Then you would have succeeded in doing what you've tried to do all along."

She put her hands on her hips. "I have no idea what you're talking about!"

"Sure you do," I said smoothly. All I wanted to do was hurt her, to inflict the kind of pain she had brought with her into our lives. "Ever since you planted your ass right smack in the middle of our lives, all you've wanted was to be rid of all of us. You stand here on your high horse preaching to me, and it just drives you right up the wall to know you can't have it your way."

Her black eyes narrowed. "Oh, I will have it my way, alright. Make no mistake about that." To me, her voice seemed filled with menace.

"Maybe so," I conceded. I was shaking with fury. "But at best you'll always be second banana."

"What is that supposed to mean?"

"Figure it out." I turned my back on her and went to Daddy's side, but I couldn't shake her. She was right behind me.

"How long are you going to let this go on?" she demanded of Daddy. He just kept on staring out the window. "I'm the only one that gives a damn about you."

"My children love me. They care about my welfare," he answered groggily.

"Sure they do," Marty said. "Then why do they take advantage of you? Why doesn't Joanne let you see your grandchildren? Why won't your highness here help you out of your financial dilemma?"

Daddy's voice was husky. "Shut up! You don't know what you're talking about."

She looked as if she'd been slapped, lips parted in surprise. I was surprised, too. Maybe they weren't always such a happy couple. "Damn you, anyway!" She tore from the room. A door slammed.

I sat down in the chair opposite the sofa. Daddy looked pale and thin, the worst I'd ever seen him. A large white bandage covered his left eye, and the rest of his face was haggard and drawn. Even following his heart attack and the loss of his hand he'd been robust, his body lean and muscular, though his eyes were dead. Now he was a pale shadow of his former self. I felt a little sorry for him, even if this was his fault.

"You look like you've seen better days," I teased lightly, trying to cover my self-consciousness.

"I feel like someone beat me with a two-by-four. But that isn't important, baby. Would you do me a favor and get Bruce on the telephone for me? There's something I need to discuss with him."

I dialed and handed the phone to Daddy. Bruce must have been very hesitant about coming over. After what had happened with the "trip" to Colombia, no doubt he'd rather be drawn and quartered than confront Daddy again. Daddy all but had to beg him before he apparently gave in and agreed to come.

Bruce arrived thirty minutes later. Marty was no-where to be seen, so I let him in. He wore a hangdog look on his face as he took in Daddy's pathetic appear-ance. My heart went out to Bruce. I knew how much courage it had taken for him to walk through the front door.

Daddy did not even glance his way or move from his position on the sofa as he said, matter-of-factly, "I want you to blow up the boat this weekend." His face never lost its bland appearance.

Bruce stood there speechless. "Just like that, huh? After all the work I've done on that boat?"

"Screw the work you've done. The insurance is worth more than the boat will ever be," answered Daddy.

"Not to me. You might not be able to understand this, L.J., but I happen to care about that boat. It's the only thing I have left that means anything to me."

Daddy laughed. "What do you want me to do, bring out the violins? Understand me once and for all: That fucking boat's going to blow, and you're the one who's going to do it."

"Why me? Why don't you get someone else to do your dirty work this time."

"It's going to be you, because you ripped me off."

Bruce walked to the windows, his back to us. "How do you plan to do it?"

"Easy. You sail her out into the middle of Lake Pont-chartrain, spread some gasoline around, throw a torch to her, and bingo! Up she goes."

Now Bruce laughed, but his laughter had the ring of hysteria to it. "And what about me? Am I supposed to blow myself up along with the boat?"

Daddy sighed with exasperation. "Don't be stupid. All you have to do is dive over the side and swim away."

Bruce swung around and faced Daddy. "Just swim away, huh? Christ, you amaze me, L.J. You know, you've done plenty for me, I'll admit, and maybe I do owe you something. But no way do I owe you my life." He moved toward the door.

"Maybe not," Daddy called after him. "But I will tell you this. If that boat doesn't blow, your life won't be worth two cents."

Bruce stopped dead in his tracks. I think both men had forgotten that I was in the room. Bruce cast a resigned look over his shoulder at Daddy. "I'll think about it," he said, and hurried out the door.

I gathered my purse and car keys in utter disgust. I turned to Daddy. "What is it with you, anyway?"

He licked his lips. "A matter of survival."

CHAPTER 20

CAROL

Daddy wove fact and fiction so tightly that it was becoming increasingly difficult to separate the two. Any doubts I may have harbored about the notion that he'd once again deliberately maimed himself quickly dissipated when I heard his version of the most recent accident. It was as farfetched as anything else he'd ever said or done. He claimed that while he'd been driving aimlessly late one night, unable to sleep, two men in a black Ford Galaxie had rammed the side of his car and run him off the road. When I pointed out that there were no eyewitnesses to this, he merely pointed to his left eye, recently fitted with a glass eyeball that seemed chillingly real. "I don't need an eyewitness. The proof is right here."

There it was again, that old favorite standby of his, proof. And I was not at all surprised to learn that he had filed an insurance claim for the loss of his eye. He reveled in telling this latest tale of woe in great detail. He added new tidbits every time, embellishing his story in what was surely an effort to make it more credible.

"I wonder who the person is that wants to kill me," he mused.

Daddy told me all this when I stopped by on an impulse visit on my way to visit Mama. I could never rid myself of guilt if I ignored him for too long, and it was somehow easier to visit with him than it was to live with that depressing burden. I was able to recognize my feelings for what they were, but I thought I owed him something. Maybe my debt was only to the memory of the man and father he'd once been, but I owed it none-theless. Mike just let me do what I had to do. I wish he would have stopped me.

"Why would you think something like that, Daddy?" I asked. "Are you in trouble?"

"Obviously. Someone hired those two men who ran me off the road. I wonder who it could have been."

A figment of your imagination, I wanted to say. Instead I played his little game and gave him the attention he seemed to so desperately need. "I can't for the life of me figure out who wants to kill you, Daddy."

"How would you know?" he snapped.

"You don't have to bite my head off," I snapped back, tired of it all. "I'm only trying to help."

"If you want to help me, then believe me when I tell you that someone is out to get me."

I nodded in agreement. That seemed to appease him.

"I'm going to have to protect myself from now on. It's as simple as that," he said calmly.

"What do you mean, 'protect yourself'?"

"I've decided to build a fence around the property. I'll have infrared camera monitors with electronic eyes installed in the rear of the house. I'll set up electronic gates at both ends of the driveway. That way no one can get on or off the property without my knowledge."

Was this another of his paranoid delusions? Did he truly believe all this, or was he playing another deadly game. There was no way of telling anymore.

True to his word, in early summer of 1975, two or three months after his accident, he turned the property at 279 Citrus Road into a fortress. A huge iron barrier constructed of old brick, wrought-iron gates, and pickets were erected around my father's house. It was a forbidding contrast to the flowering plants and shrubs lining the drive. The steps leading to the front door were encased in glass. Along the sides of each pane were thin, almost undetectable wires connected to a highly sophisticated alarm system within the house. A small wrought-iron gate set with a brassy gold keyhole allowed entry only so far as the front door. To get inside one had to have a key.

Nancy, pregnant with her first child, still lived next door, in the home that I had occupied during my marriage to Bruce. One day as Mama, Joanne, and I were visiting her, we were startled by a loud banging at the back door.

Nancy opened it to a frantic, sobbing Daddy. He seemed on the verge of hysteria, his face ashen. "I knew they were out to get me!" He sobbed as he pushed his way into the kitchen. Tears streamed down his face, and he held one hand over his glass eye in what I imagined was an attempt to keep the eyeball in place. "Somebody fired two shots at me in the front yard. One of the bullets whizzed right past my head." He was a pitiful sight. You could almost smell his panic. His stalkers may have been delusions, but *he* believed in them. He was terrified.

Mama took command of the situation. "I think we should call the police."

"No," said Daddy quickly. "I don't want them involved."

"Don't be ridiculous, Len. If someone is trying to kill you, then you need police protection."

"*If* someone is out to kill me?" he exploded. The tears changed to anger in seconds. "What will it take to make you believe me? I tell you someone has a vendetta against me."

Suddenly he doubled over, clutching his chest. We'd seen many of these attacks, and now doubted their reality, so no one panicked anymore. Nancy and Mama supported him on either side and guided him down the narrow hallway to the living room. They settled him there on the rose-colored sofa beneath the large bay window.

"Just take it easy and try to relax, Len," said Mama. "Take a few deep breaths. You'll be alright."

"No one understands. I have every reason to believe they'll strike again."

"Why?" asked Nancy. "What's going on? Is there something you're not telling us?"

His face was secretive; his voice cryptic. "Well, I haven't mentioned this before, but I've seen those two men who ran me off the road again. They were lurking around in front of the house. They've been clever so far, though. I haven't been able to catch them. The other day they threw Molotov cocktails across the fence and burned two patches of grass in the front yard."

"Did you recognize the men?" I asked.

"Only as the same men who ran me off the road. I'd never laid eyes on them until that night."

"I still think we should call the police," said Nancy.

"No police." Daddy was adamant. "What I need is for my family to stand by me and offer their support. All of you have just been witness to this vicious attack on my life, and you all know who's responsible. I may very well need statements from you to that effect."

Joanne rolled her eyes. "Who will we be making these statements to?"

"To the insurance company—who else? With all of you as witnesses I have proof positive that these men exist."

"What does the insurance company have to do with this?" asked Mama, confused.

"Everything," he said, as if we had somehow missed the point. "I think now they'll be willing to settle my claim for the loss of my eye. After all, with the way I've suffered over all this, I think I deserve that much."

He left under his own steam several minutes later, apparently revived enough to make it across the yard. The door shut, and Joanne said, "That's the biggest pile of bullshit I've ever heard. He should have made acting a career."

"How can you say such a thing?" cried Nancy. "He was about to fall apart at the seams. I believe every word he said. Don't the rest of you?"

I just shrugged my shoulders.

"What do you think, Mama?" Nancy demanded.

Mama mumbled something noncommittal.

"I don't believe this! None of you believe him, do you?"

A trio of nos answered her question. She was on the verge of tears. "God, what's happening here?"

"I wish to God we knew, honey," said Mama softly.

Although he would not admit it to anyone, least of all to me, Bruce Applegarth had obviously gone into hiding. He'd packed up everything he owned and moved to an apartment on Jefferson Highway in Kenner, Louisiana, along the levee. He'd gotten a new unlisted phone number, which I wheedled out of a friend of his on the pretext that I needed to be able to reach Bruce should the kids ever have to see him. I was worried sick about him. I had no idea if Daddy really meant to blow up the boat, and it was impossible to say whether Daddy planned to carry out his threats against Bruce or whether he was just trying to rattle Bruce's cage. Once again, separating fact from fantasy where Daddy was concerned was no easy trick.

Trying to see Bruce was like living out an episode of *Mission: Impossible.* I finally persuaded him to give me his address, and he told me that when I came, I should knock in code—three loud raps followed by two light raps on his front door. He would not open the door to me otherwise. When I got there I knocked as I'd been told. I stood there for several long seconds, no doubt being given the once over through the peephole in the door, before I heard the sound of the lock being disengaged.

Bruce was alone in the apartment, and it was easy to see how edgy he was. He paced across the room, pausing every so often to part the living room drapes and peer out the window facing the levee. I watched his antics for some time, mystified by his odd behavior. I tried to make small talk—a thorough waste of time, because he seemed to be barely listening to me. I finally gave up and asked him outright, "What's with the window, Bruce? Is someone out there?"

He gave a low-pitched giggle, a sure indication that he was extremely nervous. "Uh, the last few nights, I, uh, thought I saw a man on the levee, right across from this apartment. It was probably just someone walking a dog, or something."

I tried to drag some more information out of him, but it was pointless. He'd clammed up. I left, frustrated and deeply afraid for Bruce. Something was going to happen to him, I felt certain. But how could I hope to prevent something from happening when I had no idea when or where or even *if* Daddy would strike?

As the summer of 1975 drew to a close, my worries about Daddy and Bruce were put on a back burner. I had much more important things to worry about. Mike had fallen into a depression and had turned to alcohol. My wonderful breath of life became silent and withdrawn. If I tried to draw him out to talk about what was bothering him, he ignored me and just stared at the television set. Most nights he would walk out of the house and disappear into the woods for hours at a time. Sometimes he stayed overnight. He would come back in the morning, haggard, with bloodshot eyes, more silent than ever. He had once been so considerate of the children, but now he ignored them, too. If he bothered to acknowledge them, it was only to bark at them. Mike's moods began to wear at Kim and Bruce. They became sullen and argumentative, displaying behaviors I'd never seen in them before. Each demanded my complete attention and whined that I was being partial to the other.

I could see my little family crumbling around me. My nerves were stretched to the breaking point as I tried to constantly placate the children and communicate with Mike. My whole life was now trying, trying, trying, but it all seemed in vain. Mike rejected my every attempt to change things. I was losing control of everything around me, living with the blind hope that all Mike needed was time to adjust. That one day my life would return to normal. That my children would survive this emotional onslaught and emerge as healthy and well balanced as they'd always been until now.

We'd been running out of money quickly since Mike's decision to give up smuggling marijuana. Just as he'd sacrificed a well-paying job with Shell Oil Company to run off in search of riches south of the border, so had he forfeited his secure position in life. Although he never admitted it to me, and maybe not even to himself, he'd become too used to being his own man. The thought of a nine-to-five job must have seemed to Mike like taking a giant step backward in life. It was easier for him to blame me for his lot in life than to accept any blame for himself. In fairness, the blame lay equally upon both our shoulders, and it seemed that the time had come to pay the piper for our previous indiscretions. I tried the best I could to help him overcome his troubles by maintaining a cheerful, loving nature. I blithely went about my everyday life as if I were as happy as I'd ever been. Underneath my cheerful facade lay the grim knowledge that we had two children to feed and clothe, and no money with which to do it.

Things came to a head in early September. In order to bring some money into the household I'd decided to sell the Thoroughbred gelding, Lovie. When I told Mike of my decision, he hit the roof.

"You'll do anything in this world to make me feel like less of a man, won't you?" he lashed out.

I tried to remain calm. "That is the last thing in the world I want to do, Mike."

"Don't hand me that bullshit. I know how much you love that horse. You're just trying to rub salt in an already open wound. I'm warning you, Carol, don't sell him."

But we desperately needed the money. Parting with Lovie was not as hard for me to do as Mike seemed to think it was. I knew I could get an easy three or four thousand for the horse, and there were things we needed, like food, and clothes for the kids, who were going back to school. As I watched the money in our checking account melt away, I began to see his reaction to the sale as selfish and childishly absurd. There were more pressing matters at hand than trying to salvage his wounded pride, so I sold the horse, without his permission and against his will. Mike refused to come outside the day the sale was made, and I was left to negotiate a price and deliver the horse to the man who'd bought him.

I pocketed the cash in my jeans and headed for the house. I opened the back door and sidetracked my way around Mike on my way to the kitchen. I poured myself a glass of iced tea.

Mike strode up to the kitchen counter and leaned across it. "How much did he rape you for?" he demanded, his voice laced with sarcasm.

"He gave me a fair price. I'm not going to go over all of this again," I warned. "We needed the money. It's over and done with. Can't you just let it ride?"

"Damn you!" He kicked viciously at the kitchen bar.

I decided to ignore him. I brushed past him out the door, slamming it shut behind me. I fed the dogs and filled their bowls with fresh water. Slumped in one of the patio chairs, I watched them eat. Not only was I burdened with my father's problems, but now Mike had turned into a drunken stranger. I had no more ideas how to make things better. I looked up to see Annie, the smallest of the setters and my favorite, watching me. She gazed at me with big brown eyes, a quizzical, almost comically concerned expression on her face. Abandoning her bowl of food, Annie walked up to me and laid her head on my lap. I stroked her silky red ears, happy to have her small, sweet face for company.

A moment later the back door opened, then slammed shut. Mike stomped across the carport with an ugly look on his face.

"Why don't you get rid of these fleabags? They're eating us out of house and home."

I stuck by my earlier decision to ignore him.

He hovered over my chair. "Why don't you answer me?"

"Because I don't want to fight with you."

"You don't, huh?" He kicked my chair soundly. Annie's head shot up, and she stared Mike down, a low growl rumbling in her throat.

"Who do you think you're growling at, bitch?" Mike's left foot shot upward, and he kicked the dog in the ribs with his steel-toed work boot. Annie let out a yelp of pain, then cowered nervously at my feet.

I jumped up. "Leave her alone!"

Mike grabbed me by the shoulder and pushed me aside. "I'm going to teach this bitch a lesson she won't ever forget!" In a mindless frenzy he kicked wildly at the dog, his boots slamming over and over again into her sides. I threw myself against him and tried to pull him away, but he shoved me aside. I fell sprawling to the ground. In a flash I was back on my feet, against him again in blind fury. I scratched and clawed at him, ripping his shirt down his back, screaming obscenities.

Suddenly Annie moaned, and her eyes rolled back in her head. She scrambled to her feet, her nails scrabbling for purchase on the concrete patio. Mike's boot came up again and smashed into the underside of her jaw. With a sickening crunch Annie's head flew back. She crumbled to the ground and lay still.

"Oh, God, no!" I flung myself across Annie's broken body. The dog exhaled, a long, wet, rattling sound, her tongue protruding through her teeth.

A terrible silence hung in the air. Mike stood beside me, his chest heaving as the anger drained from him. I wept as I hugged Annie's dead body. I looked up into Mike's face in anguish. His eyes were filled with shame.

The other dogs cut a wide path around him as he walked down the path that led to the woods.

I retrieved my son's wagon from the stable and maneuvered Annie's body into it, grateful that the kids had napped through this terrible violence. After grabbing a shovel from the storage room, I hauled the little red wagon to the back pasture. I spotted a mimosa tree in full bloom and made my way to the foot of it. I broke the ground and dug until the hole was deep enough to hold Annie's limp body. I gently rolled her out of the wagon and into the shallow grave, overcome with grief. As I shoveled the sandy soil over the body, I said a last good-bye to my pet, and a good-bye to much of the love and respect I ever had for Mike Holland.

Later that night as I sat curled in a ball on the sofa, Mike approached me. He was sober, for once. I wouldn't look at him as he spoke.

"I know that nothing I say or do will ever change this. I can't tell you how much I hate myself for what I've done. I love you more than anything, Carol. I have to make things right between us." He paused then. The silence lengthened between us. "I've made up my mind to go back down to Mexico for your father. Maybe it will help patch things up between the two of you. I owe you that much, after today. I'll make this up to you if it takes me the rest of my life."

He stood there, waiting, for something from me—approval, forgiveness, love. All I gave him was silence.

CHAPTER 21

CAROL

Though it no longer mattered to me whether or not Mike went to Mexico for Daddy, his desire to make amends for Annie's death really did touch me. It was Mike's first unselfish act in months, and I was reminded of how much he cared for me. Because I'd always overcompensated for my father's unforgiving nature by being too forgiving of others, it wasn't surprising that I found room to forgive Mike. Maybe I was wrong to do it, but he was the only strength in my life, and I couldn't forget the good things he'd done for me.

Although I had many misgivings about the impending trip, I decided to use it as an opportunity to bridge the widening distance between us. I made up my mind to go with him on the trip. My only thought was to spend time with my husband on the road and to try to recapture what we once had. I didn't even consider the dangers.

When we told Daddy, he couldn't contain his excitement. "I'm pleased you've had a change of heart," he said, as he extended his hand to Mike, grinning.

Mike shook it, but there was no smile on his face. "Let's get one thing straight, L.J. I want you to know up front that I'm not doing this for you, I'm doing it for Carol. She's had a hard time dealing with this guilt trip you've laid on her. I figure if doing this will get you off her back, it's worth it."

Daddy laughed. "You're a man who says what's on his mind. I like that. There's a lot about you I admire, Mike."

"I'm impressed," said Mike, sarcastically.

Daddy chuckled again. "Let's get down to business. If I put up the money, how much of a return can I expect to get?"

"Depends. The price per kilo fluctuates. But don't worry—you'll make out like a fat rat, considering I'll be doing all the work."

Daddy only rubbed his chin. "How long will you be gone?"

"Can't tell. A minimum of ten days, a maximum of two weeks. I won't know until I get there. Sometimes the weed's already packaged, other times it has yet to be cut."

Daddy handed Mike an envelope from the drawer of his desk with the five thousand dollars required to purchase the pot. "Good luck," he said.

"I'll be leaving first thing in the morning, but remember one thing: If I get caught, I'll need a good lawyer," said Mike.

Daddy shook his head. "Don't worry. I've got that one covered."

The drive to Guadalajara was a long one. During the first few hours of the trip we chitchatted happily, held hands, and sang along with old songs on the radio. But by the time we crossed the border into Mexico, Mike's mood had changed. He was silent and pensive, his thoughts a million miles away. We'd be getting down to the nitty-gritty of the situation soon, and no doubt that weighed heavily on his mind.

After eighteen hours of driving, we arrived in Guadalajara. I was surprised how easily the actual deal went down. Mike drove straight to the house of Rueben, his connection, where I was introduced to the Mexican's aging mother. She called herself Mamacita. His pretty teenage sister eyed my designer jeans so enviously that I gave her a spare pair I'd packed with me for the trip. She squealed with delight, and though I didn't understand a word of her broken English, I could tell that she was delighted by my gift.

We left Rueben's family behind and drove with him for endless hours deep into the mountains. I gazed with nervous excitement out of the darkened windows of the truck at the Mexican countryside flying by. Finally Mike turned off the main highway onto a narrow mountain road. The road was full of potholes, and the truck rattled and shook as it clambered noisily down the rutted lane. For a couple of miles I felt as if my insides had been mixed in a blender, and then Mike pulled off the narrow lane into a clump of scraggly bushes.

I waited in the darkness, pulse pounding. "What happens now?" I asked.

Rueben smiled at me, his teeth a white glow in the dark. "Now we wait for the burros."

Mike climbed from the cab of the truck. I was right on his heels. We sat side by side on a large, flat boulder. As Rueben and Mike exchanged small talk, my senses drank in the night around me. The sky seemed vast and infinite, as if it went on forever. Clusters of stars hung in the heavens, small iridescent chips of ice against a velvet background. A cool breeze blew in from the desert. A delicious sense of freedom soared through my being. I wanted to laugh out loud at the absurdity. Here I was, smuggling drugs with a husband I had doubts about, to get money for my probably insane and certainly criminal father. And I was happy about it.

About thirty minutes later Rueben tensed beside me and placed his finger against my lips. "Shh. No noise," he whispered. Then he made a series of odd little noises through his teeth that sounded something like "chit-chit."

A man moved out of the shadows. By the light of the moon I saw a small, slender Mexican, dressed in a white peasant shirt and pants. He entered the clearing, pulling a donkey on a rope behind him. There was another man behind him, and he, too, led a donkey by a rope.

Both animals were weighed down with several large burlap sacks slung across their backs.

There was a quickening in my pulse, and a thrill of excitement shot down my spine. It was all so clandestine, so illicit! So exciting! Then I realized why I was so happy—the fear and adventure made me forget all the painful aspects of my life and forced me to live purely for the moment. Rueben exchanged the money for the marijuana, then he and the other two Mexicans quickly unloaded the burlap sacks from the donkeys. In a matter of minutes the job was done, and the two men climbed atop the donkeys and disappeared from sight. Mike, Rueben, and I made a three-link chain to stash the marijuana in the camper's secret box. Rueben split open the burlap sacks and took out the kilos of pot, wrapped in brown paper, then passed them to me. I sat in the back of the camper and passed the kilos on to Mike, who was inside the stash box on his back, the only position in which he could fit inside the box's narrow confines. One by one the bags disappeared into the small aperture at the hollow end of the box. After an hour of steady work the job was done. We drove back down the narrow lane and once again reached the highway that led to Guadalajara. At Rueben's request, we dropped him off several miles from his home.

As he left the truck, Rueben shook Mike's hand. "Until the next time?" he said.

"No more next times," responded Mike, his voice husky.

"Maybe, maybe not." Rueben shrugged. The Mexican continued to clasp Mike's hand, his black eyes twinkling. These two men may have come from completely different worlds, but they respected and even cared for one another. Letting go of Mike's hand, Rueben turned to me. "At last you are a *contrabandista?*"

I smiled up at him. "What is that?"

He grinned widely. "In American words, a lady smuggler." He kissed me on the cheek, and a minute later he was gone.

Soon we were on the road again toward Nueva Laredo, where Mike planned to cross the border. As we made the exhausting eighteen-hour ride, Mike constantly scanned the sides of the winding Mexican roads for federalès checkpoints. There had recently been a lot of illegal gun trafficking across the border, along with the illegal smuggling of aliens into the United States, so the countryside would no doubt be crawling with federales.

The closer we got to Nueva Laredo, the more nervous Mike became. Twice he stopped to purchase a pint of Cuervo Gold in the hopes of calming his tightly stretched nerves, but the tequila only had the opposite effect. He was as jumpy as a cat. I suggested that we pull over for a few hours of sleep. Mike said no. The only thing he wanted was to get this trip over.

As we approached the town of Nueva Rosita, we spotted a checkpoint. Mike gripped the wheel. He quickly searched the sides of the road for a means of escape, but the narrow two-lane highway stretched endlessly before us, bordered on either side by desert scrub and mesquite. I could see the two jeeps blocking the road about a quarter of a mile ahead. Mike swallowed a long gulp of the tequila, his hands sweaty.

Suddenly he accelerated, and I thought for one wild second he was going to drive right through the barricade. I braced myself. Up ahead the federales stood in the road, waving their arms at us to stop the truck.

Mike touched the accelerator again. Then, to my immense relief, he braked to a stop. At least we had a chance to live, let alone get by, if we stopped. A tall, swarthy Mexican in uniform walked up to Mike's window. Three other uniformed men stood beside the jeeps. "May I see your papers, senor?"

Mike fumbled through his wallet for the pink visas and passed them through the window. The federales studied the papers closely. "You've been into the interior of Mexico, si?"

"Yeah. I've been to Guadalajara on business," said Mike.

Nodding, the Mexican official motioned for Mike and me to leave the truck. We obliged, my legs shaking as I fought to maintain my composure.

"What is your business in Guadalajara, senor?"

"I'm in the jewelry business. I've been pricing turquoise and silver."

The federale walked over to one of the two government jeeps. He pulled an overgrown German shepherd from the backseat. Mike's features froze.

The Mexican jerked his thumb toward the rear of the camper. "Open the camper."

Mike complied. The federales entered the camper, with the big shepherd leaping in beside him.

The seconds ticked away. I held my breath, unable to see into the camper from where I stood. Then the federales began rapidly firing words in Spanish to the three other men who still stood beside the jeeps.

The trio rushed over, two of them shouldering big, ugly rifles. Mike and I shrank back against the side of the truck as they pointed the rifles at our chests. The third man jumped into the camper and began tossing out camping gear, extra gasoline cans, and a variety of paraphernalia as Mike and I watched, both of us too terrified to move. They'd caught us.

Minutes later the two federales jumped from the camper. The one who'd ordered us from the truck swaggered over to us, shepherd in tow.

"Sancho here say you have marijuana in the truck," he said, patting the dog on the head. "And Sancho, he don't lie." He smiled at us, looking like a cat toying with a mouse.

"The dog's wrong," said Mike. "There's no weed in there."

The Mexican shoved his face close to Mike's. "I think there is, my friend. And I think if you don't tell me where it is, you goin' to be in very big trouble." He spat on the ground. His three compadres laughed.

Mike realized he had no choice in the matter. He got into the camper and began to unload the kilos from the stash box and into a heap beside the truck. When he finished he stood beside me, smoking a cigarette, as the federales conferred in Spanish. The little group soon broke, and a tall official approached us.

"How much money you got, my friend?" he asked.

"Two hundred dollars," Mike answered. I knew he had more than that stashed inside his boot.

"That's a lot of money." The Mexican's eyes gleamed. "Three hundred American dollars, and you can leave." I could tell he thought we were going to escape the bullet.

The Mexican eyed Mike, stroking his mustache thoughtfully. Mike took two hundred-dollar bills from his wallet and held the money out. I'd heard somewhere that the average Mexican's income was only about two thousand dollars a year. Two hundred dollars would seem like a fortune to the federales. He grabbed the money and stuffed it into his shirt pocket. *"Vamanos,"* he said. As we turned to leave and retrieve our pot, he put his hand on Mike's shoulder. "The weed stays here, my friend."

Back at Citrus Road we broke the news to Daddy.

His lips thin, nostrils flaring, Daddy roared, "You set me up, you miserable son of a bitch!"

Mike looked exhausted and defeated. His confidence had completely evaporated. "It wasn't like that, L.J. The trip was a bust."

"Oh, it was a bust alright. I lost money that I can't afford to lose, and I want it back, understand me?"

"Look," said Mike. "I used your five thousand dollars to buy weed, and they confiscated it. What do you want me to do, shit the money?"

Daddy's face was like stone. "How you get it is your problem."

"Screw you, L.J.," Mike exploded. "I laid my ass on the line for you, as well as your daughter's. We could both be rotting in some filthy Mexican jail right now, and all you care about is your fucking money. Do you know what it's like to have some stinking Mexican shove an M-16 in your face?"

"If that's the way it happened," said Daddy dryly.

Mike's eyes flashed. "You think I made this up to rip you off? Let me tell you something. I'll be damned if I'm going to sit here and listen to you accuse me of something I didn't do. You know what your problem is, old man? You think you can shove me around the way you shove everyone else around, but I'm wise to you. You sit here in your big house like some puppet master, pulling all the strings. You've browbeaten and bullied your wife and kids all their lives, and the sickening part is they've let you because they love you. You've taken that and twisted it to your own advantage. The name of the game is emotional blackmail, you son of a bitch, and you're an artist at it." He paused, glaring at Daddy defiantly. "I can't wait for the day your children see you for what you really are, and if I have anything to say about it, that day will be sooner than you think." Mike had summed the situation up perfectly. A new respect for him welled in me. In his defeat, he was becoming a man again.

I refused to meet Daddy's eyes. He laughed harshly. "My girls will never abandon me. They need me. Ask your wife—she'll tell you the same thing. If Bruce Applegarth wasn't man enough to take her away from me, you don't stand a shot!"

Mike looked at me and then at Daddy. His features twisted in disgust. "You're off your rocker, old man, gone over the edge. Now, you listen to me. I haven't seen my kids in two weeks because of you, so I'm going home now, and you can take your threats and stick them where the sun don't shine."

Though Mike burned with hatred for Daddy, I could only feel that the ill-fated trip to Mexico had been a blessing in disguise. Mike returned home with a resolve to make our lives work. He was kind and solicitous to the children, and as loving as he'd once always been to me.

Three weeks later Mike's cousin Gary casually mentioned a job opening at Tellepson Construction Company in Slidell, Louisiana. Mike signed on immediately. The job involved heavy physical labor and a one-hundred-mile round-trip drive every day, but Mike never complained. He seemed to welcome the physical exertion, but I'm sure that part of the reason he took the job was that it left him with little time to dwell on the resentment and bitterness he harbored for Daddy.

Although things had changed for the better between my husband and me, they had gone from bad to worse between me and Daddy. I refused to see him. He had put my marriage in jeopardy and called my husband a liar. If I were to see him, it would not only pose a threat to my relationship with Mike, but also prove to Daddy that I was every bit the spineless sucker he believed me to be. I stayed away from the big house on Citrus Road. Daddy dealt with my stubbornness in his usual fashion. He feigned grief at my abandoning him and accused me of siding with Mike against him.

One evening, while Mike and I were at home watching television, Daddy called. The litany of self-pity began again. He begged me to visit him. I was depriving him of his grandchildren. Knowing how angry Mike would be, yet unable to resist a sudden impulse to speak with Daddy, I turned my back on Mike. I spoke in muffled tones, trying to hide the identity of the caller from him.

It didn't work. Mike looked at me without a word and left the house. I heard his truck start up, then roar out of the driveway. I'd just walked over the very tender shoots of our new start. I hung up on Daddy. I felt worried about Mike and, as usual, unreasonably guilty about Daddy. I fed the kids, put them to bed, and settled down on the sofa in the den. I tried to read but couldn't concentrate on the words. I counted the minutes as they ticked by on the clock above the mantel.

It was midnight when I heard Mike's truck come down the winding driveway. The sour smell of liquor came in the room before Mike. I may have made the first mistake, but I sensed Mike was about to do something final.

"So, what did Daddy have to say?" he sneered, edging closer to where I stood then in the kitchen.

I tried to stay calm. "Nothing. He misses the kids."

"You're lying." He raised his hand and cuffed me across the head. "He's trying to poison your mind against me, isn't he?"

I braced myself against the kitchen counter to give myself a better position of defense. "Mike, please, let's talk about this in the morning," I said as calmly as I could. I thought that if I remained calm, I stood a better chance of reasoning with him, but reason doesn't work well against scotch.

"Like hell we will." He shoved me hard against the counter, and I felt the edge of it cutting into my back.

"Mike, please, stop this. I'm not going to stand here and let you throw me around."

He ignored me. "Your father's a crazy old fucker, you know that? He's as crazy as they come." With wild eyes, he swayed into me. I placed my hands against his chest, shoved him away from me, and edged my way along the kitchen counter, out of his reach.

"You're not afraid of me, are you?" he taunted. He slowly stalked me down the length of the counter, then lunged for me, moving so quickly I had no time to react. His open palm slammed across my face, and I felt a warm trickle of blood run from my bottom lip. Stunned, I slapped back at him, landing a blow on the bridge of his nose. He hit me with a glancing blow to the left of my face that sent rockets of pain shooting through my skull and nearly brought me to my knees.

Unsteadily, I pushed him and ran down the hallway to the bedroom, where I locked myself in. I grabbed a baseball bat and waited for what seemed like forever for another attack, but none came. Hours later, I fell into an exhausted sleep, still clutching the bat.

When I woke the next morning, he was gone. He stayed away for two days. He stared solemnly at my split lip and bruised cheek when he came back, then broke down and cried. "Forgive me," he said. "It will never happen again," he said. It was in my nature to forgive— almost a habit by now—so forgive him I did, but I did not forget. My emotions were all tangled by then, a knot of love and fear and need and hatred, for Mike, and Daddy. But I still didn't feel strong enough to cut through the knot and create my own life, free of their smothering force.

In the weeks to come Mike stayed sober during the days. He'd be the same old Mike I'd fallen in love with. Then he'd come home drunk and abusive, swearing at me, though he never tried to strike me again. Again and again, I made up my mind to leave him, but I could never bring myself to do it. There had been too much between us for me to just walk away. He'd given me my first taste of real happiness back in Covington. I told myself I owed him, just as I had convinced myself that I owed Daddy a dangerous trip to Mexico. I should have learned from that.

I was in the kitchen tossing a salad one evening in November, and the kids were on the carport playing. They were filling Bruce's toy dump truck with loose gravel from the driveway, totally engrossed in their play.

I heard Mike's truck pull up, and five minutes later I heard a loud, childish wail from outside. As I peered out the kitchen curtains I saw a streak of orange flame shoot up from the direction of the driveway.

I ran outside and found Bruce and Kim, their faces streaked with dirt and grime. Both children clung to me, sobbing. To the right of the carport Mike stood before a pile of smoke and flame.

"What's the matter?" I asked the kids, confused.

"Mike burned all our toys!" cried Kim. "He said we shouldn't a left 'em in the driveway. He burned my baby, and Bruce's wagon and dump truck. I loved my baby," she wailed.

"I know you did, sweetie, but now I want you both to go inside and wash your faces."

I nudged them in the direction of the back door, and they despondently dragged inside. I turned back to the pile of burning toys and saw Mike kick Bruce's little dump truck further into the flames. I approached his tall figure, silhouetted by the fire. It was one thing to hurt me, or even my dog. But Mike had gone after my children.

"Get out of here, you son of a bitch!" I screamed. "If you ever come around here again, I swear to God I'll kill you."

He pivoted and entered the cab of his truck. Shifting the truck into gear, he roared out of the driveway, spraying gravel as he went.

Back inside the house I packed suitcases with my clothing and basic essentials. I remained dry-eyed through the whole ordeal, incapable of feeling anything. After packing my bags I entered the kids' room and began to throw clothes randomly into another suitcase. "Gather your favorite toys together," I told them. "We're going to visit Nana."

Obediently the two youngsters began picking up their toys, all the while casting solemn looks in my direction. Pushing them ahead of me, I left the house. I tossed the bags in the truck of my Cougar, then threw pillows and blankets on the backseat, along with the hodgepodge of belongings the kids had dragged along. As I drove down the driveway the setters followed, a game they loved to play. I glanced at them once through the rearview mirror before turning onto the long blacktop road.

When we arrived at Mama's, she took one look at the tear-stained, bedraggled faces at her door and wisely remained silent. She bathed the kids, then tucked them gently into bed in the spare room. I sat at the kitchen table and nursed a cup of hot tea.

"Would you like to talk about it?" Mama asked. Her fingers brushed long blond strands of hair from my forehead.

"There's not much to say. It's over between us. Mike's not the man I used to know. He's become violent and abusive, and tonight was the last straw. He set fire to the kids' favorite toys because they left them in the driveway."

Mama looked at me in shock. "That doesn't sound like Mike. What's come over him?"

"The same thing that always comes over him. Alcohol. He drinks like a fish. It's the life-style we've led."

"You mean the drug smuggling?" she asked softly.

It didn't surprise me that she'd known. Nothing in our family remained a secret for very long. "Yes. The drugs and the easy money. They've destroyed everything we ever had between us. And this endless feud with Daddy. I've been pulled in so many directions at once by the two of them, I can't even think straight anymore. The problem is I still love them both."

The tears came then. Mama pulled me close and held me until there were no tears left.

CHAPTER 22

CAROL

The time had come for Carol Fagot Applegarth Holland to grow up and face life on her own. I acknowledged the bitter fact that I'd lived my entire life dependent on men. I found myself suddenly faced with responsibilities I'd never had to face before—things that growing tomatoes and poling through the bayou hadn't prepared me for. A few weeks after leaving Mike I found a job as a receptionist and assistant to two doctors whose practice was located in uptown New Orleans. I hunted down a small apartment in River Ridge, only two miles away from Mama's apartment and less than five miles away from Citrus Road. It took my entire paycheck for the first month's rent and the required utility deposits, but I would have gladly parted with twice that sum. The apartment on Jefferson Highway was a haven for me, a place for some serious reflection.

At almost twenty-five years of age I was left to cope with the knowledge that I had set quite a track record as far as marriage was concerned. In five years both of my marriages had failed, and I had nothing monetary to show for either one, except for the clothes on my back and a few pieces of furniture I'd salvaged from the house in Covington. I was not bitter; at least I'd walked away with my two children.

Mike had abandoned the house in Covington and moved most of our mutual possessions into an apartment in Metairie. He often called me late at night to beg my forgiveness and insist we make a go of it again.

I'd listen to him for a while, then slide the receiver back into the cradle. The depression would last for hours.

On Christmas Eve 1975, Shirley gave birth to a daughter, Holly Bronwen Tresch. Mama flew to Colorado to help her with the baby. She stayed for several weeks before returning home to await the arrival of Nancy's baby, due several weeks later. On February 17, Nancy's daughter was born. Kristen Gena Gonzales was a dark-haired, blue-eyed image of her father, Gary. The births of Daddy's sixth and seventh grandchildren were followed shortly by the finalization of his and Mama's divorce.

Daddy visited Nancy and her new baby one day while I was over. He oohed and aahed over his new granddaughter for a few minutes, then announced to Nancy and me that he planned to marry Marty. There was an oddly resigned air about him. He was not happy.

"You don't seem too thrilled by the idea of marriage, Daddy," I commented.

He laughed, but there was no joy in his laughter. "If I had any choice in the matter, I probably wouldn't marry her."

"Then why do it? I've never known you to do anything you didn't want to before."

"This is different."

"I don't understand what you mean."

"Don't you? It's really very simple. Marty knows too much for me to let her walk away."

In mid-May 1976 he and Marty exchanged vows in a lavish ceremony held in Daddy's home. I didn't want to go, but Daddy begged me to and I agreed. Nancy also attended, and I think she felt every bit as uneasy as I did at the thought of giving Daddy and Marty our blessings.

Aunt Lacey and Aunt Valerie were there, as was Nanaine, of course. They seemed to be delighted by Daddy's decision to marry. I resented the easy way they accepted Mama's substitute. After all, Lacey and Valerie had been like sisters to my mother during her twenty-five years of marriage to Daddy. I wondered how they could accept Marty, a girl twenty-seven years Daddy's junior, with such open arms.

Over one hundred people showed up, including several of Daddy's fellow attorneys and quite a few of his and Mama's old friends. Marty was dressed in an old-fashioned puff-sleeved gown with a wide hat and long train. I couldn't help noticing the smile of satisfaction on the bride's face as she posed for the photographers. A receiving line formed, and I took my place, smiling, hugging Daddy, offering my sincere congratulations to the newlyweds. Surely if ever any two people deserved each other, they were Leonard Fagot and Marta Jean Courtney.

In the weeks after the wedding my relationship with Daddy began to improve, if only slightly. The closeness I'd once felt with him, though, had become a thing of the past. We talked on the telephone now and then, and once in a while I'd drop over with Kim and Bruce to visit. Daddy seemed very grateful for my consideration. "Here, take this," he'd say, pushing some bills into my hand. Who knows where he got the money. "Buy yourself and the kids something nice." Then he'd pat my shoulder affectionately. An old, familiar feeling would come over me, and I would remember a time long ago, when our family was happy.

One day in August I paid a visit to Daddy. I found him brooding in the library, his thoughts apparently far away. I knew he was still popping pills, but by then his drug habit had become much like everything else in my life, an unquestioned fact. I stayed awhile, trying to cheer him up, but he remained silent and distracted. It was not until I rose to leave that he acknowledged me at all.

"Carol, do you still have that life insurance policy on Mike? The one I gave you on your wedding day?"

"Daddy, I've never had that policy. You said you

would hang on to it and make the payments. I'd forgotten all about it."

"That's right," he said vaguely. "I've been making the premium payments. I'll give the policy to you. I think you'd be wise to keep up the payments."

"I have no use for the policy, and I certainly don't have the money to spare for the premiums. Why don't you just have it canceled?"

"No. I'll hang on to it. You never know."

A week later, during another visit, he cornered me out by the pool, where I lay sunbathing. The kids splashed away in the water.

He squatted down beside my chaise lounge. "I was wondering, where does Mike live?"

An odd question. "On Harvard Street in Metairie. Why?"

"Just curious," he said casually.

I settled back on the chaise lounge to resume my tanning.

"Have you ever been to his apartment?"

"Whose?" I asked.

"Mike's," he said, exasperated.

"Once, to pick up some things of mine."

"Do you think you could get in there again?"

I sat up. "If I wanted to. Why?" What did he want with Mike?

"Why don't you do that for me, baby? And unlock some of the windows while you're there."

"Why would I want to do that?"

His lips curled in a faint smile. "So I can get into the apartment and kill him."

He said it in the same casual tone that he might have used if he had been talking about the weather. An icy chill washed over me. *Not again. Don't let him kill again.* The only response I could come up with was, "Don't be ridiculous, Daddy. Mike lives with a roommate."

"Well, then he'll just have to go, too."

I gathered my kids together and beat a hasty retreat.

* * *

On the Thursday following that conversation, Mike called me at my apartment. He seemed in unusually high spirits.

"I've found a couple of acres in Slidell. I'd like to build a house for us."

I started to protest, but he wouldn't hear it. "Please, just think about it, Carol. I haven't been drunk since you left me. Things will be different this time around. I promise."

"Don't start," I warned.

"Alright. But I'm about to come into some money. Your dad called me today and offered me a fair amount of money to get rid of some pot for him. I could use the cash as a down payment on the acreage."

"Daddy called and offered you money? You two haven't spoken since the incident over the trip to Mexico."

"I know," said Mike. "I still hate him for that, but I need the money, and he was apologetic. He suggested we let bygones be bygones."

Sure, I thought. There was about as much chance of that as there was of my moving to Slidell with Mike.

"Mike, when is this supposed to happen?"

"Tonight. I'm going over there at nine o'clock to pick up the weed. I'll turn the stuff over to my main man and be that much richer in a couple of days."

My heart was beating doubletime. "Listen to me, Mike. Do yourself a favor and stay away from Daddy. He'll kill you. I know he will. Please don't go over there."

"Bullshit, Carol. I can handle your father. Gotta go— I'm running late."

The phone went dead in my ear.

I paced the tiny apartment. There were bad vibes in the air; I could feel them in my bones. I could only pray that this once Daddy was bluffing. After all, Daddy had threatened Bruce and his boat. But Bruce Applegarth was still alive, and the *Stiletto* was in one piece at the Lakefront Marina.

There was a sudden knock at my door, and I ran to answer it. Mama stood on my doorstep. I stared at her a moment, expecting her to give me some bad news. She looked at me quizzically. "Aren't you going to let me in?"

I realized I'd invited her. "Mama, I forgot you were coming over."

"Would you like some tea?" I hurried into the kitchen without waiting for an answer. I filled the teapot with water, slammed it down on the stove, and turned the knob to the gas burner.

Mama eyed me. "You've got the wrong burner on."

"Oh." I flipped the burner off and began rummaging through the cabinets for tea bags. I was completely frayed. I knocked over spice bottles and dropped a teacup on the floor. I stared at the shattered pieces of the cup, then burst into tears.

"Carol, what is wrong with you?"

"Nothing," I answered. "I . . . oh shit, Mom. I'm scared."

"Tell me what this is all about."

"I know you'll think I'm crazy, I know you will. I think Daddy's planning to kill Mike tonight. Daddy tried to warn me days ago, and I should have taken him seriously. He's called Mike over tonight to set up some kind of pot deal. Daddy's going to kill him, I know it!"

Mama's face turned a dead white. "Where are the kids?"

"At Joanne's spending the night. Oh, God! Mama, I warned Mike not to go over there, but he wouldn't listen."

"It's a quarter of nine," said Mama after a glance at her watch. "Let's go over there now."

We cruised down Citrus Road and passed Daddy's house several times. Mike's gold pickup truck was parked in the side driveway. A dim light shone through the living room curtains. We had no plan of action; we pulled over to the front curb to wait for something to happen. Maybe nothing would, but I had a hunch. I was a jumble of nerves, and Mama lit one cigarette after another as we sat in the dark, watching the front of the silent house.

After an hour or so, the front door opened and Daddy came out wearing a white windbreaker. He made his way over to Mike's truck, his hand buried in the pocket of his jacket.

I clutched the steering wheel, my eyes glued to the side driveway.

Daddy disappeared around the side of the house. A few minutes later I heard an engine roar to life. Mike's truck backed slowly out of the driveway. As the Dodge neared the end of the driveway, I could clearly see Mike's familiar profile behind the wheel.

The relief nearly overwhelmed me. I turned to Mama. "I feel so foolish. I have this imagination that runs away from me at times."

Mama said nothing. In silence she watched the taillights of the pickup disappear down Citrus Road.

CHAPTER 23

CAROL

Two nights later, on Saturday, September 11, 1976, I took Kim and Bruce to the Applegarths' house to spend the night. At nine-forty-eight P.M., while I was having dinner at a Chinese restaurant with Steve Donahue, an old high school friend, a nightmare unfolded at the house on Citrus Road.

Eyewitnesses say this is what happened: The wrought-iron gate on the left side of Daddy's driveway was wide open. A car's engine raced. Seconds later, a brown-and-white Pontiac Le Mans shot backward out of the driveway. It tore clear across the paved road to the front yard of the house at 278 Citrus Road, directly across the street.

Andre Bellou, a twelve-year-old riding by on his bicycle, stared as the car crashed backward into a tree, where it spun around upon impact. At the sound of the crash, Rene "Dutch" LaBruyere, the owner of the house, ran out and rushed to the wrecked vehicle. In the front passenger seat he saw the silhouette of a man who seemed to be attempting to leave the car. Before Dutch could react, the man disentangled himself from the crushed Le Mans. By the muted glow of an overhead streetlight he watched as the man assumed a crouched position before suddenly sprinting across the street and disappearing into an empty lot next to Daddy's house.

For the first time Dutch LaBruyere noticed there was a second man inside the vehicle, hunched motionless over the steering wheel. Andre Bellou had just drawn abreast of the car on his bike when Dutch opened the car door to help the man out. Dutch later stated that from the amount of blood covering the front seat, he had known immediately that the man inside was beyond all aid.

Dutch called the police. Upon their arrival minutes later, Jefferson Parish police officers quickly cordoned off the 200 block of Citrus Road. Dutch and Andre told them that the car had seemed to come from Daddy's driveway and reported that a second man had fled from the vehicle shortly after impact. A cursory examination of the corpse, a white male in his mid-to-late twenties, revealed several bullet wounds in the man's head and chest. Blood soaked the dead man's brown corduroy jacket and blue jeans. A call was placed to the homicide division. Sergeant Walter Gorman, who had been with the sheriff's office for eight years, arrived. He put in a call for a police dog, in the hope of finding the man who had fled into the woods. When the shepherd arrived, it led the detectives along the fence bordering Daddy's property to the rear of his house.

I had just gotten home with Steve when the telephone rang. It was midnight. The voice on the other end was low and hesitant. "Carol? It's Bruce."

"Bruce! You scared me half to death calling this late. Is anything wrong?"

He hesitated. "I shouldn't have been the one to call you. You don't know what's happened, do you?"

Bruce's voice was low with emotion, and the sound of it sent a feeling of dread through me. "What are you talking about, Bruce? Has anything happened to the kids?"

"The kids are okay. I just don't know how to tell you this."

By then my heart was racing, my fingers clammy and numb as I gripped the receiver. "Just tell me, Bruce. What's wrong?" My voice had risen to hysteria.

"Your dad and Mike had a shootout on Citrus Road tonight."

"A shootout?" Wild, impossible images of old Western movies popped into my head; crazy scenes of them hiding behind the palm trees, shooting madly at each other.

"I don't know how to tell you this, Carol, but Mike's dead."

Mike's dead. Mike's dead. The words kept repeating in my head like a record with a stuck needle.

I remember only brief flashes of that night. The kindness of Steve Donahue, who stayed by my side throughout those impossibly long hours. Mama's face, a white mask of disbelief as I babbled nonsensically when she arrived. "Mike's dead, Mama, Mike's dead. I told you this would happen. Daddy killed him, Daddy killed him!"

The police arrived at my door. They asked questions about Mike, Daddy, and their relationship. Sergeant Gorman, bespectacled, brown hair parted neatly on the side, was considerate but intent on finding answers.

"Do you know of anyone who would have wanted to harm your husband? Did anyone have a grudge against him?"

"No," I answered. A thousand times no.

"Mrs. Holland, we have reason to believe your father is involved in this. Two eyewitnesses saw Mike's car race out of his driveway. Do you know anything at all that might help us get to the bottom of this?"

"No." One more lie, but who was counting?

Detective Sergeant Gus Claverie had warm, friendly eyes that looked right into my soul. "Take my card, Carol. Call me if there's anything you'd like to talk about."

At seven o'clock the following morning, September 12, Daddy called. He begged me to see him. Physically exhausted and emotionally drained, I was no match for his dogged insistence. Against Mama's advice I drove the few miles to Citrus Road. A light rain began to fall as I pulled into the driveway. I sat in the car a moment, watching the raindrops splatter on the windshield. A thousand little points of pain cut into the protective numb layer my mind had created in defense against what it could not accept. I could not look at the house across the street.

A figure loomed in front of my car. The passenger door was jerked open. Daddy climbed into the passenger seat and brushed the rain from his face and hair.

"Thank God you came. We need to talk." His words tumbled out. "Have you heard from the police yet?"

"Yes. They came by last night. Daddy, will you tell me what's happening?"

"I killed him, baby. I plugged him right through the heart."

I stared at him in shock.

"Don't look at me like that," he said sharply. "I did it for you."

"For me?"

"Well, who else would I have done it for? I don't want the insurance money, believe me. Every penny of it is yours. I don't expect anything out of this except your loyalty and your help."

I swallowed, found my voice. "Why do you need my help?"

His face was inches from mine. The car now smelled of Old Spice cologne. "Because I screwed up, baby. I was going to drive the son of a bitch at gunpoint to the shopping mall. I was going to shoot him there. It would have looked like a robbery, but the dumb bastard had to fight me for the gun. I had no choice but to shoot then and there, so I plugged him right through the heart. I still could have salvaged the whole thing if the asshole's foot hadn't jammed on the accelerator. The car sped backward out of the driveway and hit the damned tree. I was thrown forward and hit my head on the dash; I was lucky I didn't pass out. I ran inside, and Marty helped me into the shower with my clothes still on."

My eyes filled with tears as I pictured the final, brutal moments of Mike's life. Daddy grabbed my chin and forced my face around. I saw the undisguised cruelty in his eyes, and I fought the urge to gag.

"I can beat this with your help," he continued. "All you have to say is that you knew Mike hated me, that he planned to rob me, and that he always carried a gun."

I shook my head in mute denial; his fingers pinched my chin. "Listen to me, Carol. Everything I've ever done has been for you and for your sisters. I've sacrificed everything—even my blood—for you."

"The shooting accident," I said, "the car wreck. You did everything yourself, didn't you?" I watched, transfixed, as his lips curled in a smile.

"I do what I have to do to survive."

"And George?" I whispered.

The smile left his face. His features might have been carved from granite, so calm and stern. "George was a worthless little shit. Getting rid of him was the best thing for Joanne. She's happy now, isn't she? My kids owe me, and you owe me most of all."

A car pulled into the driveway behind us. Its headlights washed over us, and Daddy shifted moods. "That's Nancy. I called her over here to tell her in private what's happened. I want you to come inside and wait while I speak to her."

He got out of the car and strode up to Nancy's car. I sat behind the wheel, too shaken to move. I thought of starting the engine and speeding away, but he was walking back to my window by then. Escape was impossible.

Daddy ushered us through the front door. He led Nancy down the hallway to the library, and I sat in the living room on the sofa until they returned. My sister wore a closed, baffled look on her face, and I wondered if he'd been as explicit with the gory details as he'd been with me.

"I love you," he said, patting my back. "I'm counting on you."

For the first time in my life I cringed at the feel of my father's kiss upon my cheek.

Once outside I walked Nancy to her car. The rain had stopped, and a mild breeze cooled the air. Nancy was silent, but I needed to talk. I wanted her to assure me that this was a horrible dream, that I had imagined last night. Last night and the six years leading up to it.

"You don't seem very surprised by what Daddy did, Nancy."

She furrowed her brow. "Daddy only acted in self-defense, Carol. Anyone would have done the same thing. If I were in Daddy's shoes, and Mike pulled a gun on me, I would have grabbed for it, too. The way I see it, it's Mike's own fault that he's dead. I mean, I'm sorry that he's dead, but he should have known better than to pull a gun on Daddy."

Why had he told Nancy one thing and me another? Nancy believed him; it was there in her eyes. But I believed what he'd told me, too. What did it all mean? Was it possible he was trying to pit one of us against the other? And if he was, why?

I would not know the answers to these questions for some time to come. But before all was said and done, Daddy would tell too many versions of what happened that night. And I would always believe that the version he told me came as close to the truth as anyone would ever get.

CHAPTER 24

CAROL

The police began to collect evidence. After Nancy and I left Daddy's house, Sergeant Gorman showed up with a search warrant. A thirty-eight-caliber Charter Arms wrapped in a brown envelope was found hidden behind a row of books in the library. Beside it was an envelope containing four spent casings.

Four bullets were removed from Mike's body during the autopsy at the parish morgue. The medical examiner determined that the four shots had been fired at very close range, more than likely by someone sitting in the front passenger seat. Two shots had entered Mike's chest, and two more had been fired into his head. A lack of blood around the head wounds indicated they had been inflicted after Mike had already died.

The Pontiac Le Mans was registered to Mike's roommate, Manny. Mechanics inspected it and ascertained that it was in perfect working order. The accelerator was functional, and nothing turned up that would indicate any mechanical reason for the car's hasty departure from the driveway. They could only speculate that Mike's foot had turned rigid, slamming the gas pedal to the floor and causing the car to hurtle backward.

I became unable to sleep or eat, and I sank into my own world of fears. My mind crawled with vague and random horrors. I was locked into a private hell. Memories plagued me. Visions of a laughing, blond George Westerfield bending over to scoop his baby girls up into his arms before evaporating in a swirl of metallic blue, the color of his coffin as it was lowered into the cold ground. Mike Holland, tall, sunlight in his hair, blue eyes crinkling at the corners, his face as familiar and dear as my own children's. The image would begin to fade and blur into blood spilled across a car seat, his body torn by bullets. And always, at the end, the wild, laughing face of a man devoid of compassion. The same man who had given me life, my father. The same man I had respected and loved. A self-made man, a hero, a top-notch marine. Now, all these years later, that heroic marine had appointed himself executioner and claimed to have murdered for the love of his children.

Where did that leave the rest of us? Were we supposed to bury our heads in the sand and allow him to continue wreaking violence and death? That was exactly what I'd done all along. I had condoned his transgressions by burying them within myself and hiding them from the world. The cost of doing so had been dear—Mike Holland. Only it didn't end with Mike, any more than it had ended with George Westerfield. It included the suffering of a long line of people—the Westerfields and the Hollands, who'd lost their only sons; the sisters each young man had left behind; Kelly, Lori, and Kim, who would be denied the love of their fathers for the rest of their lives.

Mama made arrangements with the Applegarths to keep Kim and Bruce for several days, temporarily relieving me of the burden of caring for them. She stayed with me constantly, as did Steve Donahue. Their caring and reassurance helped to ease my pain and return me to life.

Daddy called and insisted that I meet with his attorney. Mama demanded that I not go, but like a dutiful robot I dressed myself and waited for him to pick me up. I just didn't know who was in control of my life.

On the way to the attorney's office Daddy was solicitous and condescending. He smiled at me tenderly. "You're a levelheaded kid, Carol. We can get through this together *if* you say the right things." I was silent for the whole ride.

When we arrived, Roy Price, a man in his mid-fifties with graying hair and a long, serious face, greeted me. He lived diagonally across the street from Daddy, but I had never had the occasion to meet him. He was soft-spoken and walked with his head tucked into his shoulders, an odd, shuffling gait that made him seem older than his years. There was another attorney present, Bob Broussard, the father of a former friend of mine. I'd spent many weekends at his home in my youth. He was a handsome, graying man with a warm smile and gentle manner.

Once we were seated at the conference table, with Daddy to my left and Price and Broussard across from us, Price cleared his throat and began his questions. "Carol, this is not a formal deposition, although Mr. Broussard and I will be taking notes. There are some things I'd like to ask you, in the hope that I'll be able to sort through all of this. Now, I understand that you were separated from your husband at the time of his death?"

"Yes, we were separated."

"Alright. And will you tell me why you were separated?"

I shifted in my seat, and Daddy nodded encouragingly in my direction.

"Well, for several reasons. We'd reached an impasse in our marriage. We weren't getting along anymore. We —" I hesitated, "we fought a lot."

"I see," said Price. "Was there any particular reason why you fought, or did you just fight about everything in general?"

I glanced sideways at Daddy, and he winked at me. I pulled my gaze straight ahead and answered, "Mike and my father didn't get along. They had a falling out, and it put a lot of pressure on my marriage because I was always in the middle. If I was sympathetic to Mike, then Daddy was hurt, or the other way around."

"Did Mike ever strike you during these fights?"

I wondered how he could have heard about that. "Yes, a couple of times, but only when he was drinking."

Price seemed to consider my answer for a moment. "So, when he drank, he beat you?"

"I didn't say that."

"But that's what you meant, isn't it?" Price looked serious as he leaned toward me.

"I don't know."

"Isn't it true that he beat you on several occasions, and at times he beat your children?" Price persisted.

"No, that's not true. He never beat those kids. He loved them," I answered defensively. Daddy was dragging me into this.

"Do you remember a time when Mike held a knife to your throat?"

I glanced at Daddy, and he once again nodded for me to go on. He obviously expected me to lie, to become an accomplice to my husband's murder. I felt warm with perspiration; all the air in the room seemed suddenly stale.

"I don't remember," I answered quickly, torn between allegiances.

"Did Mike own a gun?"

The question caught me by surprise. "Yes. He had a shotgun and a rifle he used for hunting."

"What about a handgun? Did you ever see him with a handgun?"

"He had a small twenty-five automatic when we first lived together, but I can't say what's become of the gun since."

"How did Mike feel about your father?"

I hesitated. "He despised him."

Price tapped his pencil on the tabletop. "I think that's enough for now. I appreciate your coming here, Carol. You've been very helpful. I thank you," he said with courtesy.

He rose from the desk and left the room with Daddy. I faced Bob Broussard across the table. He smiled at me and said, "I know this has been tough on you, but your father will need all the help you can give him. He may be facing a very serious charge."

"I know that, Mr. Broussard, but I can't help him. I can only make things worse for him," I said.

"I don't understand."

"There are too many things you don't know about."

Broussard was silent as Daddy and Price reentered the room. In front of both lawyers Daddy pulled me close and patted my back affectionately.

"Thank you, baby," he said. "It makes me feel good to know I can count on you."

Paul and Ruth Holland, Mike's parents, asked to bury their only son in their hometown of Natchez, Mississippi. I agreed. On the Monday following his death, while I was talking to Roy Price and Bob Broussard, Mike's body was released from the parish morgue to his parents. Mike's wake was held that night, but I did not attend, having heard from Ruth Holland that it was to be an open-casket affair. I knew that seeing Mike's dead face would send me into that sea of madness whose shores I'd been walking along these days.

He was to be laid to rest on Tuesday morning in Midway Cemetery in Natchez. The last thing in the world I wanted to do was attend Mike's funeral and face his loved ones, but his memory demanded it. Joanne, Mama, and I planned to ride to Natchez together. They were dressed in black and waiting for me so we could get moving. I searched through my closet, procrastinating some, but also looking for something that would buoy me through this. I spotted Mike's favorite, a blue-and-white summer dress, and hugged it close before putting it on. Joanne and Mama were a bit taken aback by my inappropriate attire, but they also sensed that it was right and fitting in its own way for me. They didn't say a word about it.

Mama led me by the hand toward the gathering of mourners clustered about Mike's casket. I clung to her for support. I had not slept or eaten in two days, and whether because of that, or simply because I was too distraught, I could barely focus my eyes. Mrs. Holland approached us and hugged us each tightly. Her pleasant, middle-aged features were ravaged by tears. Mike's father, Paul, pulled her away, his weather-beaten face mournful and bewildered by all this meaningless suffering. I looked once at the coffin, its gleaming surface covered with a blanket of flowers. The sky spun around me, and there was a roaring in my ears. My legs gave out, and strong hands gripped my arms. I stared into the face of John Smith, and it swam dizzily before my eyes before fading completely out of focus. The rest of the funeral is a blur to me, and I thank God for that.

We arrived back at my apartment two hours later. Mama and Joanne hovered over me. They knew that more than just grief had made me faint. They tried to draw me out, but I felt incapable of speech until eventually their loving concern and persistence broke through the terrible wall of silence within me. I told them what happened when I went to see Daddy's lawyers.

Joanne, never one to mince words, was the first to speak out. "You can't allow yourself to be put in the middle of all this. What if Daddy's arrested? He'll take you down with him. I know he will."

"Joanne's right, honey," agreed Mama. "Whatever happened that night will come out sooner or later. If you got caught in a tangle of lies, you could be charged as an accessory."

"I already know what happened that night. Daddy pulled a gun on Mike and shot him dead."

"He admitted that to you?" asked Joanne, wide-eyed.

"Yes, and now he wants me to help him cover it up. I think he plans to turn the whole thing around and claim that he killed Mike in self-defense. Daddy needs to prove that Mike drank, owned a gun, and had a reason for hating him, and I'm supposed to confirm all of this."

"He wants you to help him cover this up? What kind of father would ask his child to do something like that?

Never mind," Joanne added. "I know what kind would do that. Our kind."

Mama spoke up. "Carol, I know you, and you won't be able to live with a lie like that."

"Why not, Mama?" I lashed out. "Haven't we been living with lies for years now, all of us? What's one more lie, one more little lie on top of so many others?"

I'd hurt them both. I could see it in their eyes, and it was really the last thing I wanted to do.

"What could we have possibly done to change things? We had no way of knowing this would happen. It's not our fault," said Mama unhappily.

"You're right, Mama. We can't change what's already happened. But isn't it our responsibility to try and prevent anything else from happening? This compulsion in Daddy that drives him to do the things he does did not die along with Mike. It will always be there, inside of Daddy, and one day it will rise to the surface again. When it does, God help us all, because who can say what he'll do next?"

"Carol's right," Joanne said softly. "It's time for us to take our blinders off. The law can't stop him—at least, I don't think it will. I have no doubt that he'll walk away from this, just as he did with George. I, for one, will not sit back and wait to see who offends him next. Maybe it will be Gary or Ray, or Joe. Maybe it will be one of the children."

There was a lengthy silence after Joanne's words. Finally I spoke. "I know in my heart that I have loved Daddy as much as any daughter could love a father; and there have been times when loving him was damned hard to do. He's put my love for him on the line over and over again. And I have tried my best not to fail him. Now he's pushed me into a corner. If I speak up in defense of him, then I unjustly condemn Mike, not only in the eyes of the law, but in the eyes of those who loved him. If I do that, then I condemn myself, too, because I'll be as guilty of murder as Daddy, and in the long run it won't matter much who pulled the trigger."

"I love him, too, Carol," said Joanne, "right or wrong, and despite the things he's done. But I love Mama, and you, and the rest of my family even more. I have seen Daddy try to destroy everything that is good in our lives. I've seen my family torn to pieces because of him. A person must accept that there are limitations in this life, and Daddy has crossed that line one time too many. We have only two choices that I can see." Joanne paused, her eyes fastened on mine. "We can either continue to cover up for him for the rest of our lives, or put an end to it now."

"Are you suggesting that we go to the police?" asked Mama.

Joanne was silent a moment. "Yes," she said firmly.

Mama looked stricken. "Carol," she implored.

"We have no choice, Mom," I told her with as much conviction as I could muster. "It has to end somewhere. We have to stand by Joanne."

"But think about the position you're putting yourselves in. Have you given any thought to what your lives will be worth if we go to the police?" She glanced wildly back and forth at Joanne and me. "What guarantee do you have that he won't retaliate, that either of you won't become his next target? Do you think for one minute he'll draw the line at this point because you're his children?"

"It's a risk we'll have to take." Joanne's jaw was as set and stubborn as Daddy's had ever been. I wanted to hug her for the courage she displayed.

Mama dabbed at her eyes with a tissue. "Then you won't be going alone to the police. I'll go with you. If we stand together on this, maybe your father will have to think twice before taking any action against all of us. Besides," she added bravely, "I'd rather die than spend the rest of my life in fear."

It was an alliance that would lead to more bloodshed. An alliance that in the days to follow would blow life-long friendships and family relations so far apart that

God himself could not have picked up the pieces. Many would come to believe that ours was a conspiracy of vengeance formed between an embittered ex-wife and her jealous daughters. Not one of these so-called friends or relatives would come close to understanding that our decision to go to the police had nothing to do with vengeance, and everything to do with survival. It was Daddy's survival or ours.

During the drive to the police station, which seemed to last longer than a lifetime, I thought about breaking the law I had made the center of my life—Honor thy father and mother.

The officer on duty at the front desk at the Jefferson Parish police station gave us a once-over before saying, "Can I help you?"

I glanced briefly in Mama's direction before answering. "We have information regarding the death of Mike Holland on September eleventh."

We were immediately ushered into separate rooms. Officers were assigned to take our statements. Mama disappeared into a room at the end of the corridor with a Detective Thibodeaux. Joanne entered the room beside mine with a detective named Simmons, and I found myself face-to-face with a tall black detective named Joe Morton. Sergeant Walter Gorman, whom I'd last seen in my apartment the night of Mike's death would later join us.

Sergeant Gorman was every bit as kind as he'd been that night. I felt like a penitent who has finally decided to unburden herself of years of crushing doubt and suspicion. He kindly but firmly picked my brain. He prodded gently and when at times my voice faltered, he patted my hand, his brown eyes filled with compassion. I had intended to say no more than I had to in regard to Mike's death, only that my father had admitted to me that he'd shot him. To my surprise Sergeant Gorman questioned me closely concerning the death of George six years ago, as well as about Daddy's loss of his hand

and the automobile accident in which he'd lost his eye. Panic rose in me as his questions drew tighter and tighter around Daddy. Gorman had done his homework well. From the start, I said, I'd been suspicious about George's death and I'd seriously questioned Daddy's accidents; but even now I would not say that Daddy had told me in the car that he had committed these acts. It seemed too full a betrayal of Daddy. I told myself that if the police were going to call him down for those crimes, then they were going to have to do so on their own. I could claim at least that much loyalty.

I admitted freely to the smuggling of marijuana from Mexico, implicating myself as well as Mike. In light of all that had come to pass, the pot smuggling seemed like child's play, but it was certainly an integral part of the whys and wherefores that had led to Mike's death.

"Did your father force you to go to Mexico?" asked Gorman.

I was at a loss for an answer. "Force me? He didn't twist my arm. *Coerced* is a better word. He threatened to kill himself if I didn't, at least the last time. But force me? I can't truly say he did that. I sent my husband down there when he didn't want to go, and I went down there myself because I loved him—no more, no less."

I had been in that room for over four hours, and I didn't think I could stand much more of Gorman's questioning. My brain felt like mush.

"Is there anything else you'd care to add to this statement?" asked Gorman finally, rubbing his eyes.

I shook my head, and he passed me the deposition he had written in longhand. "Sign your name here, and fill out the bottom line please, Carol."

I signed my name in a scrawl that seemed a caricature of my normal penmanship. My eyes strayed to the bottom line he'd requested I fill out.

After making this statement, do you have reason to fear for your life?

Daddy wouldn't. He just wouldn't.

* * *

Daddy checked into East Jefferson General Hospital, where remedial surgery was performed on his left eye. Sergeant Gorman visited him at his bedside and questioned him again.

On September 23, about two weeks after Mike's murder, Daddy and Marty were both arrested by the Jefferson Parish sheriff's office for second-degree murder. They were taken before Judge Wallace C. LeBrun and pleaded innocent. Bond was set at the staggering amount of one million dollars each.

CHAPTER 25

CAROL

Tom Porteous, assistant district attorney, would be prosecuting Daddy's case. I met with him in his office in the town of Gretna on the west bank of the Mississippi River. Porteous, who insisted that I call him Tom, was in his early thirties with a round, boyish face, and brown hair that had already started to thin on top. He had a warm congeniality that immediately put me at least somewhat at ease. Tom explained that I would appear before the grand jury as a witness for the state and what I would have to do. I was to try and remain as calm as possible during the hearing, because the only thing expected of me was the truth.

Despite Tom's reassurance, I woke feeling queasy the day of the grand jury hearing. I was taken to the hearing by a uniformed officer in a patrol car, and I wondered if this was normal procedure for a witness or whether there had been threats. No. Daddy didn't work that way. Besides, he was in jail. My conflicted heart was reassured and saddened by the thought.

In the hushed session, twelve jurors sat around a long oval table. In front of each was a microphone attached to the tabletop. A judge, in black robes, presided over the hearing. The jurors, six men and six women, were a severe group, like a roomful of principals. My heart sank. Tom Porteous, who would do the questioning, gave me a tiny smile and tapped the underside of his chin with his right index finger, as if to say, "Chin up."

After being sworn in I sat down in the witness chair. I drew a long breath and prayed that no one else could hear my heart pounding. Tom gently led me into my account of my conversation with Daddy on the Sunday morning following Mike's death. My throat felt clogged, but I repeated the basic gist of that conversation. Tom asked very few questions, and I was left to flounder through my testimony, unsure of how much to say. I was equally unsure as to how much *not* to say, since I still wanted to protect Daddy. So I said as little as possible. I said that Daddy had confessed to murdering Mike, but I left out a vast majority of the incriminating details. It occurred to me that I was telling only a portion of the truth, but Tom seemed hesitant to extract the whole truth from me. During my testimony no mention of drugs ever surfaced. I couldn't understand why, because the drug dealing between Daddy and Mike lay at the very core of the matter.

The jurors had only two questions. First a mild looking, gray-haired woman asked, "How old are you, Carol?" I told her that I'd just recently turned twenty-six. A distinguished-looking, silver-haired gentleman asked the second question. "Why did you wait so long after your father's admission to go to the police?" What a question! How long had I waited? For a few seconds I couldn't remember, but then it came. Mike had died on Saturday. I'd gone to the police on Tuesday. I'd waited three whole days. That didn't seem like a long time to consider turning your father in to the police. I wondered how this man could be so insensitive. I hated him with all my heart those moments and wished that he could stand inside my shoes for just one minute.

"I waited so long because he is my father. And I love him."

Unlike some states, Louisiana requires the establishment of a motive for a charge of first-degree murder. No definite motive was apparent in Mike's death. Though revenge and the drug deal were at the core, neither defense nor prosecution gained by bringing the drug dealings into the case. It could undermine any murder charge brought by the state and, on the other side, would certainly cast Daddy in a very poor light. After much consideration the grand jury returned a true bill of indictment against Daddy, charging him with second-degree murder in the slaying of Mike. It also returned a true bill of indictment against Marty, charging her with being an accessory after the fact of second-degree murder. While Daddy had told me she'd helped him clean up after the shooting, she'd told the police that she had heard a car crash while he was in the shower.

I had known all along that it would come to this, but I'd still clung to the foolish hope that somehow Daddy would manage to get out of being charged for murder. I'd gone to the police with my eyes open. I'd known exactly what I was doing, but I'd refused to acknowledge the reality of what might occur beyond that point. Daddy's formal indictment for second-degree murder forced me to accept that reality. The thought of Daddy's spending the rest of his life in prison haunted me, but then another side of me screamed for justice. For Mike and George and all the lives wounded by Daddy's murderous actions. I never resolved that battle inside of me. Throughout the trial and everything that happened afterward, I remained torn by loyalties and a wavering sense of right, and I still am today.

Tom Porteous argued passionately against the reduction of Daddy's one-million-dollar bond on the grounds that certain key witnesses might be subjected to intimidation tactics. The judge deflected Tom's protests by stating that if intimidation tactics were used, another hearing would be called for.

After the hearing Daddy and Marty were confined in the Jefferson Parish lockup. But both had pleaded not guilty, and shortly thereafter Judge Fred S. Bowes reduced Daddy's bond to one hundred twenty-five thousand dollars, and Marty's to ten thousand. They posted bond and were released, and a trial date was set for June 1977.

Joanne, Mama, and I were called to Tom Porteous's

office several times in the next ten months to prepare for the trial. Despite Tom's affable manner, I sensed a burning ambition in him. It seemed to me that this young prosecutor was secretly delighted at being handed a case with a special blend of ingredients that made for great headlines—the ex-marine war hero and rich attorney turned killer; the bizarre nature of the crime itself; and, more important, the testimony of the killer's own children. The media had already made Daddy's arrest a lead story, and Tom Porteous, a rising legal star, appeared to revel in the attention.

He was always kind and solicitous to us and seemed pleased that we'd come forward voluntarily with information that helped to further his case. But that was the problem—it was "his" case. That we had come forward out of fear seemed lost on Tom. We understood that the case really wasn't just a domestic situation anymore. Murder, and therefore the state, was involved. But rarely were we treated like victims; instead, we were sources of information. It was hard to talk about our lives in terms of pure dates and places and events— nothing had ever been so cut-and-dried. No one seemed to care how we felt now, how we hurt. And if we had at first thought Tom would offer us the same kid-glove treatment we had received from Sergeant Gorman, we soon learned differently.

Though it was hard to adjust to a dispassionate approach to the case, we also knew that doing so was necessary.

It would require a tremendous amount of character and emotional fortitude to withstand all that lay ahead, and I felt certain that at our first meeting Tom found us wanting. We were traumatized and vulnerable. He grilled us relentlessly, firing apparently random questions, no doubt trying to get a feel for how we would react under pressure. The first time was harrowing, but as our meetings continued, we did not disappoint him. We responded to his rapid-fire questioning with alacrity, dignity, and conviction. I sensed a growing admiration for us on Tom's part. He was beginning to understand, I think, that beneath the soft, outer edges of our vulnerability lay a steely resolve.

Although he admitted there was strong physical evidence against Daddy, Tom did not go into detail with us. He seemed to feel that Daddy was a man who believed himself to be above the law. Oddly enough, Tom seemed almost disappointed that Daddy had allowed himself to be caught. He admitted to a certain grudging respect for Daddy's talent in the criminal arena, but seemed unable to fathom the inner workings of Daddy's mind.

What worried me more than anything else was that no one seemed to take our concern for each other's safety too seriously, despite our requests for protection. Maybe this was understandable. Tom had never experienced Daddy's wrath or Marty's hatred and hostility firsthand.

In truth, as the days passed, I came to fear Marty as much as I feared Daddy. My instincts told me she was more capable of rash behavior than he, and at least where Daddy was concerned, I knew he had once loved us. Maybe, I thought, the memory of that love, if nothing else, would spare us from harm.

CHAPTER 26

SHIRLEY

Light snow fell, visible in the headlights of cars as they passed by my window heading north toward Gold Camp Road. The outline of Pike's Peak, forbidding, bleak, was all but hidden by a blanket of gray that obscured the foothills of the mountains. Beside me, my daughter, Holly, slept, a quilt snugly tucked around her body. I leaned back into the smooth comfort of the brown leather sofa and the silence of my home, my thoughts peaceful for the first time since I'd heard of Mike's death.

The telephone rang. I could hear the hum of the long-distance wires when I answered it, and then Carol's voice, low and hesitant.

"Shirley?"

"Yes?"

"It's Carol."

I felt a current of tension. Her voice was restrained, almost a whisper.

"Is something wrong?" I asked.

"It's Daddy—he's been arrested."

"No!"

"I can't tell you any more right now. Just please come home."

I hung up the phone. Ray came into the living room and immediately saw that something had happened. "What's wrong?"

I thought my heart would break. The different emotions mixed up inside—pity for Mike, concern for

Daddy—drained me. In just a few weeks my peaceful life had fallen apart.

"Daddy's been arrested," I said woodenly.

Ray held out his arms. I went to him and buried my face in his chest. For the first time in my life I knew what real fear was. I was afraid for all of us.

"Baby, don't cry," he said.

I could not believe Daddy had been arrested, or that Mike was gone, wiped out as though he had never existed.

"Why?" I asked aloud. "Why did you do it, Daddy?"

"You've got to try to accept this," Ray said.

"But there's going to be a trial now. He might go to prison for life." I pictured Daddy being taken away and handcuffed by the police.

"There's nothing you can do."

"I can be there for him, and for the rest of my family."

As I prepared for my trip home I thought of Carol and tried to understand why she had turned Daddy in. I did not realize at that time that the police had found the gun in Daddy's library or that they had a case against him based on more than Carol's statements. I knew very little of what had occurred, so my imagination created story after story, and Carol was not the heroine in any of them.

When I arrived at Carol's apartment I was not ready for the sight of her. She was thin and pale, consumed with grief, her green eyes constantly filled with tears. She controlled herself only with obvious effort and reached out to hug me tightly. Her body trembled against mine, and when I released her, I could see the fine lines of anguish about her eyes.

"I didn't want to turn Daddy in." Her voice came in sobs. "But what else could I do?"

Mama, who was seated in an armchair by the sofa, began to weep. Their grief seemed to paralyze me.

"Why did Daddy kill Mike?" I asked.

Mama looked at Carol and then sighed. "Your father and Mike were dealing marijuana."

"Marijuana? Daddy was involved in selling drugs?"

"Mike had made a few runs to Mexico," Carol said softly. "And when Daddy found out how much money he was making, he asked for a piece of the action. Mike went for him once, but that wasn't enough for Daddy. He kept insisting he go again for him. I knew Daddy was under a lot of pressure—he was broke, depressed— so we decided to make one more trip for him."

"Let me get this straight," I said. I did not want to believe that my father would be involved in selling marijuana. "Daddy sold the pot?"

"No. Mike made the run and sold the pot, then brought Daddy the money. Daddy never actually fooled with the stuff."

I knew Carol and Mike had smoked marijuana. On occasion I had tried it myself. I wasn't even that surprised to hear they had been dealing it. After all, marijuana was no novelty item in the seventies. But to hear that Daddy had been involved in any way was a shock to me.

"On the last run we got stopped by the federales, and they found the weed in the back of the camper. They let us go, but kept the pot. Daddy swore he'd get Mike back."

"But you and Mike split up after that," I pointed out. "What was Mike doing at Daddy's house?"

"Daddy called Mike a few days before his death and said he had some weed he wanted Mike to sell for him. I told Mike to stay away from Daddy, that Daddy would kill him, but he wouldn't listen. He went over there, anyway. He went over there, and Daddy shot him, right in the heart."

"How did you know that Daddy was going to kill Mike?" It seemed ludicrous to me that Daddy would risk everything and murder Mike in the driveway of his own home.

"Because he told me. Not in so many words, but he was hinting, asking a lot of questions about Mike, warning me to keep up the payments on Mike's life insurance policy. The last time I spoke to him before it happened, he wanted me to go to Mike's apartment and unlock a window so he could get in and kill him."

I found it difficult to believe what she was saying. I could not see Daddy as a killer. He could be frightening, he could threaten, but never kill.

"Why did Mike go to Daddy's if he knew he was being set up?"

"Daddy apologized to Mike for everything. Mike simply couldn't believe that Daddy would kill him. Maybe it was his pride. He was pissed at Daddy to begin with, and I guess he believed that Daddy was bluffing."

"Have you talked to Daddy?" I asked.

Carol flinched at the accusation in my voice. "He called me the next day and said he wanted to talk to me. When I got there, he admitted to me that he killed Mike. He said he had intended to force Mike at gunpoint to the shopping mall, but that Mike struggled with him for the gun and it went off. He told me he needed me to make a statement to the police saying that Mike had a grudge against him and that he's been threatened in the past."

"Did Mike ever threaten him?"

"Mike was a burr in Daddy's side for a long time, but he never threatened to harm him. I don't think Mike was capable of anything like that. Daddy just needed the leverage so he could lay a foundation for his defense."

She started to cry. "I wanted to help Daddy, so I went to his lawyer's office and gave them a statement. Daddy wanted me to lie for him. But I couldn't live with that, and I don't know if I can live with this. Mike's death was no spur-of-the-moment thing on Daddy's part. It was planned revenge. He killed him in cold blood, without any conscience or remorse. That's when I realized that I couldn't lie for him anymore. I had to tell the truth. I had no choice. He's not the same man he used to be. He's changed, become all twisted inside. He has to be stopped, Shirley. None of us will be safe as long as he's free."

It didn't make sense. It wasn't true. Daddy would tell me the truth. "I'm going to see him."

"No!" Mama said. "Don't go over there."

"I have to. I need to talk to him."

"The police have advised us to stay away from him, Shirley. It's likely he already has a copy of the statements we gave to the police. He's dangerous. Believe me, it's for your own good that I'm telling you not to go."

"I'm sorry, but you can't change my mind. I'll be back in a little while."

I got to Daddy's house depressed and uneasy at the prospect of seeing him, despite my bold front. It had been almost seven months since I'd last been with him, and I gazed in awe at the huge wrought-iron fence protecting the property. I entered the left side of the gate and pushed a small button on an intercom set in a brick column near the entrance to the drive. After I announced my presence to Marty, the gate slowly opened, then closed behind me as I drove along the circular drive to the front of the house.

Marty unlocked the gate enclosing the front porch, gesturing for me to enter. "What are you doing here?" she asked angrily, bitterly.

"I came to see my father."

"Haven't all of you done enough to him?" Her dark eyes were filled with loathing. I could see how much she hated me. "None of you have ever cared for him; only I have. Now, because of your dear sister Carol, he has nothing. We might both go to jail."

I brushed past her and opened the front door. An alarm beeped—softly, but it caught my attention. I passed the kitchen and dining area and saw the alarm mounted on the wall. I wondered why Daddy felt the need for such an elaborate security system. When I opened the louvered doors to the library, I realized just how driven he was by paranoia. Half-inch-thick plywood boards covered the windows. The room was dark, gloomy. A single lamp shed light on my father's profile as he sat erect in the easy chair.

I took a few steps into the room. He turned his head at my approach, then closed his eyes. A single tear rolled from the corner of his right eye.

"I knew you would come," he said.

Pity for him overcame my doubts. I rushed to his side, kneeled down, and laid my head upon his shoulder. "It's alright," I said, knowing it would never be alright again.

"You've got to listen to me, baby," he pleaded. "No one else will. Mike came her to rob me; he demanded two thousand dollars in cash. He pulled a gun on me, and I struggled with him. The gun went off; it struck him in the chest. I don't know—in all the confusion the car flew backward out of the driveway and into a tree across the street. I hit my head on the dash; I don't remember very much after that. I know I ran across the street and came in the house by the back door. It all seems like a blur."

Marty, who had just entered the room, made a sound of disgust. "It's all your sister Carol's fault, because she knew your father was going to kill Mike. She was hoping to collect the insurance money, and now that things have turned out this way, she's turning him in to the police—her own father, her own flesh and blood. She was the only chance he had, and she turned her back on him."

I had come to my father's house hoping to find some shred of proof that he was somehow innocent of Mike's death, but I was now forced to accept the fact that Carol and my mother had not lied. Daddy had deliberately planned to murder Mike. It sickened me to see him place himself in the role of executioner, or God.

He held his hand out, pleading. "You've got to help me, baby. Tell them how violent Mike was. Tell them he'd threatened me in the past and that you know it. That's why I had to build the fence, to protect myself from him. He was always harassing me, but I never called the police because he was family."

They both looked at me as though waiting for my cooperation. I backed away, afraid to tell them the truth —that I couldn't help, that I wouldn't lie, not even for Daddy.

"All you have to do is say what I tell you to," he persisted.

For the first time in my life my father repulsed me. I took another step back and bumped into a corner of his desk. I closed my eyes, and when I opened them, I noticed a picture of Carol, who looked about seventeen years old, prominently displayed on the desktop. Her face had been cut out of the picture, although the blond hair around her face remained untouched. Her body, clad in a T-shirt and blue jeans, was intact. Other family pictures were also mutilated, and as I gazed at my own faceless picture, I was overcome with horror.

Marty must have noticed my look of fear, because her laughter was loud and mocking. She laughed so hard, she began to cry, and through her tears her eyes were frightening.

"She sold me out, you know," Daddy slurred. "She could have lied to the police, but she didn't, and now I have to depend on you."

He staggered to his feet. The brass floor lamp beside the chair crashed to the floor, and I ran to help him.

"Out of the way," he said, pushing me aside. I watched him stumble down the hallway and into the dining room. Charging forward, he smashed headfirst into the sliding glass door leading to the sunroom. As if in slow motion he fell, his head thumping on the terrazzo floor. Then he lay motionless, face down, arms limp at his side.

"Daddy!" I yelled. Reaching his side, I rolled him over. A large bruise was already beginning to form on his forehead. Sitting cross-legged, I placed his head in my lap, and began to stroke his hair softly.

He blinked in delirium. "Private," he said, looking at

me, "can't you smell the smoke?" My heart ached for him. "Advance," he continued. "That's an order."

Marty came into the room. We managed to get him on his feet, and slowly, his body a deadweight in our arms, we led him upstairs to bed.

I arranged the covers neatly and placed a pillow under his head. Tears streamed down his face as he turned to me. "We've all got to die someday, private." He closed his eyes, grasped the sheet tightly with his fist, then relaxed.

I felt like Judas when I left there: He betrayed someone he loved, too. But is it wrong to betray a person you love if he's evil? What I do know is that right or wrong, it hurts just as much. I stared through the oval windows of the plane on my way back to Colorado, thinking of Daddy, dying a little inside.

CHAPTER 27

CAROL

It was now November. We were advised by Tom Porteous that Daddy had received, in accordance with the law, a copy of the statements we had made to the police. Since I'd stayed away from Daddy after making the statement to his lawyers, I knew he was certainly aware that I would not be cooperating with him as he'd expected me to do. I cringed at the thought of his reading the words that would help put him in prison. I'd severed forever the ties between us by making that second statement. There would be no going back. Daddy would never forgive me, and I would never have the courage to face him again.

The trial was scheduled for June 1977, seven months away and almost eleven years after this all started with Joanne and George's marriage. Daddy had entered his plea of not guilty in September, and Roy Price and Bob Broussard had not, to my knowledge, been granted a continuance for the trial. The next few months would seem an endless time of waiting, and I hoped that we'd make it through safely.

I'd learned from Bruce, who continued to visit Citrus Road despite his fear, that Daddy had become a virtual recluse, buried within the cocoon of safety his study offered. Shirley told me about what Marty had said, and Bruce agreed, when pressed, that Marty had been making less than flattering comments about Mama, Joanne, Nancy, Shirley, and me.

One day in late December, three months after Mike's death, Gary returned home from Daddy's house white-faced and panicky. He'd insisted that Nancy pack everything they owned immediately. In Gary's words, they were "getting the shit out of Dodge." Nancy, bewildered and frightened, questioned him. His answer had been cryptic and unsatisfying. "Believe me, Nancy, you don't want to know."

They soon moved into an apartment in Metairie, not far from Mama's complex. Their relationship began to take a turn for the worse, and for months they argued and snapped at each other. Since I knew little about Nancy's private affairs, I wasn't certain what was causing the problem, but I knew that she was desperately unhappy. And every time she attempted to draw Gary out and question him about what had happened prior to their sudden move, he refused to discuss it. To this day he has never really explained what happened to scare him so badly.

His refusal to discuss whatever he may have seen or heard still bugs me. Though I can't be certain, I feel that it's likely Daddy may have tried to strong-arm Gary into testifying for him in court, maybe even going so far as to threaten his life if he didn't. If that's true, Gary was not alone in receiving death threats. We began receiving phone calls in the dead of night. "You bitches are going to die," the voice would say. "I'll see to that."

One night a phone call came through that was particularly chilling. A deep, throaty female voice chanted eerily into the receiver, "One little piggie knew too much. One little piggie talked too much. And one little piggie went bang! bang!"

The next morning Joanne and I went to Tom's office to tell him about the calls. Not only were they aggravating but they were making us even edgier than we already were. We never knew if or when the voice would appear at our door. Tom Porteous seemed sympathetic enough, but there was little he could say to reassure us. "You have no proof it's Marty making those calls. I suggest you either change your telephone numbers or quit answering the phone at night."

"Why do we have to put up with this, Tom? We don't have any proof that it's Marty, but we know it's her." Joanne looked irritated by Tom's casual attitude.

"Even if it is Marty, you can't prove it is. Without proof you've got nothing. Just stop answering the phone at night, and she'll tire of her little game." He smiled.

Frustrated, we left his office and reported the discouraging news to the others. We would just have to grin and bear the nightly disruptions, for lack of proof. *Proof* was a word with which in time we would all become intimately, painfully familiar.

Steve Donahue had become a very large part of my life during these months. He was twenty-seven years old, tall, dark-haired, and green-eyed. He'd served a stint in Vietnam and now owned one-half interest in a local hot spot called the Red Knight. Aware of all that had happened since Mike's death, Steve had remained a steadfast friend and confidant during those days when I so desperately needed a friend. Kim and Bruce adored him, and Steve seemed to love them back.

But while I thought I might have found a new companion for my life, Nancy was losing hers. One night in February of 1977, Nancy called me in a fit of depression. Her marriage to Gary was over. And I knew that the situation with Daddy had only served to deepen her depression. Nancy had been neither for nor against Daddy and would remain that way throughout the trial. Although in time she came to accept that he had killed Mike, she would not accept that Joanne and I had gone to the police. Like so many others, she felt we had betrayed him. I was desperately sorry for her. She'd been caught in the middle through no fault of her own. Nancy had not gone to the police, but Daddy had persecuted her every bit as much as he had us. We had all pressured her to see our own sides of the story, and right now I felt very guilty for having done that.

In an effort to lift her spirits, I invited her to go with Steve and me to the Red Knight for a drink. She accepted right away. Once we got there, she started to have a marvelous time, dancing and chatting with people her age. I had to laugh as I watched her enjoy herself. It felt so good to relax and feel normal again.

I'd promised to pick Mama up at Joanne's at midnight. Joanne and Joe were in the process of moving to Houma, Louisiana, where Joe, a salesman, had recently been transferred. Although she had offered to watch Kim and Bruce for me, I knew Joanne had many things to take care of the following day, and I wanted to pick up the kids early.

It was getting close to midnight, so with Steve's help, I managed to drag a somewhat inebriated Nancy from the dance floor.

"I think she's had one too many." Steve laughed.

"I think you're right," I agreed. Nancy's face was flushed, and her eyes were sparkling.

We settled Nancy in the backseat of my car. At Joanne's, Steve and I bundled up the two sleepy kids and put them in the backseat between Mama and Nancy. When we got to my apartment, I pushed open the door with one hand and tried to hold Nancy up with the other. I led her over to the sofa, then let her flop down, giggling, on the cushions.

She was worth a laugh. I said to Steve, "I think we'd better get some coffee in her. She's going to have one hell of a hangover in the morning."

Mama steered Kim and Bruce toward the bedroom and got them into their pajamas. In the kitchen I measured teaspoons of instant coffee into mugs while Steve got out the cream and sugar.

From the living room Nancy called loudly. "Hey, Carol, how come there's no faces in the pictures?"

I smiled at Steve. She really had had too much to drink. "What?" I yelled to Nancy, just to humor her.

"The pictures in the frames," she insisted. "How come there's no faces in them?"

I went to the living room just as Mama came down the hallway. Nancy was now in a spasm of giggles.

"What's so funny?" Mama asked, laughing a little herself because of Nancy.

"Looks like someone wants us out of the picture!" Nancy pointed toward an end table beside the sofa, where I kept several photographs in frames. The photos were of myself and the kids, and in each picture the faces had been cut out in perfectly formed little circles. Only the hair framing the faces and the torsos were still intact, making a hideous parody of the pleasant family scenes in the background.

Mama's face was ashen. Steve's eyes were serious as he studied the mutilated photos. Finally he spoke. "Whoever did this is one sick individual. I wonder how they got in here."

Nothing else in the apartment was touched, so it wasn't some random burglary. I checked the windows in the kitchen and living room, but neither room showed any evidence of a break-in. In my bedroom I spotted a broken pane in the upper righthand corner of the window. Small slivers of glass lay on the floor beneath the windowsill.

Mama came up behind me. "I think we should call the police. Whoever did this isn't playing with a full deck."

"We both know who did this," I said angrily. "She might as well have left a calling card."

Steve entered the room. "Maybe you should call the police and let them handle this, Carol."

"No. First thing tomorrow morning I'm going straight to Tom Porteous. He can handle it. Let him figure out what to do."

The next morning I confronted Tom in his office.

"Tom, when we first came to you after making our statements to Sergeant Gorman and the others, you reassured us that Daddy and Marty would never be released from jail because bond would be set too high. Once they were released, you said you would protect us if they tried to intimidate us. Now, I realize there's nothing we can do about the phone calls, but last night my apartment was broken into, and pictures of my family were vandalized. All of the heads in the photos were cut out; it was a gruesome sight. Only one person would do that, and you know who that is as well as I do."

He smiled tolerantly. "Listen, Carol. I don't know how to say this any more plainly. Even if it is Marty, she's just out to get your goat. Apparently she derives great pleasure out of childish pranks. That's all this was, a childish prank. I don't believe she poses any serious harm to you or anyone else."

"You sound just like my father, Tom. He thought it was just a childish prank when Marty bashed my mother in the head with a rock and tried to strangle her. She had no right to invade the privacy of my home, and since when is breaking and entering not a criminal offense?"

"It certainly is a criminal offense." He was trying to placate me now. "But what proof do you have that Marty is the perpetrator? We can't go around arresting everyone accused of committing a crime. There are certain ground rules we must abide by. Acceptable evidence must be presented in order to issue an arrest warrant. You have no evidence, no witnesses, no proof. Until such proof is presented, there is nothing the law can or will do to help you. I'm sorry, but that's the way it is. You must bear the burden of proof," he said with finality.

"What proof do you need, Tom—a dead body? As you've pointed out, I'm a key witness in this case. This isn't your run-of-the-mill break-in. It was a malicious act designed to intimidate me. The trial is still seven months away. How am I supposed to protect myself?"

He pursed his lips. "Any way you can. Just make sure you stay within the boundaries of the law."

"That's a good one, coming from you, Tom. Do you know that every day we ask ourselves, 'Why us?' We didn't ask for any of this. We could have kept the truth about Mike's death to ourselves. We're suffering no less for telling the truth, and it doesn't seem that we're any safer. The only difference is that now you have a big case to make your name with. Where would your case be without us? You sit here, nothing touches you, and we're the ones caught in the crossfire. I guess winning is the only thing that matters in this game."

CHAPTER 28

CAROL

The terror had only started. One night several weeks later I went with Steve to the Red Knight. The bar was crowded, and I offered to run a tray of drinks upstairs to the Golden Dragon restaurant, which was located above the Red Knight. Occasionally a customer would order a drink not on the restaurant's menu, and the waiter would call the order down to the bar.

After delivering the drinks I passed through the upstairs foyer, heading for the stairwell that led to the bar below. Halfway to the bottom of the stairs I froze in midstep. In the entrance foyer below me stood Marty, a gun in her hand. The barrel of the gun pointed right at my stomach.

"I've come to reason with you, Carol. To make you understand how you've broken your father's heart."

I inched my way to the bottom of the stairs, my eyes never leaving the weapon. Mustering every ounce of courage I had, I pried my tongue off the roof of my mouth and said, "If you want to talk, Marty, why don't we go into the office, where we'll have more privacy?"

"I can say what I have to say right here." Her eyes darted about. "If you don't go to the police and retract your statement, I can't be responsible for what happens to you, or to your family."

Her naturally ruddy complexion was mottled with rage. "All of you had better be prepared for what happens. You've brought it down on your own heads."

Her pure malice was mesmerizing. The door to the bar opened, and Steve stepped into the foyer. At the sight of the gun in Marty's hand he cut his eyes to me, and I flashed him a look of warning.

Marty backed slowly toward the door. "I warned you, but you wouldn't listen. Now you'll pay." As her back came to rest upon the exit door, she pushed it open and slipped outside, disappearing into the shadows beside the building.

Steve was right on her heels, and I screamed at him, "Let her go!" He swung around. I clung to him, my body trembling violently. He held me close, his breath ragged in my ears.

"Did you see the look in her eyes?" he asked, amazed. "My God, she looked like a rabid animal. I had no idea. From now on I'm not letting you out of my sight."

Two days after the incident at the Red Knight, Joanne drove past the house on Citrus Road on her way to the bank. She'd just gotten to a side street beside a wooded lot when something whizzed past her head and shattered the safety glass of the back window. Kelly, Lori, Jamie, and two neighborhood children were in the car with her. Before she could react amid the screaming, hysterical wails of the children, another projectile whizzed past her head, missing her only by inches before exiting the passenger side of the car through the open front window.

In a panic she swung the car around in a wide loop and back down Citrus Road, where she pulled into the driveway of a neighbor, a Jefferson Parish police officer. The officer called the sheriff's office, and a patrol car arrived minutes later. In her statement to the police Joanne said she had made a damaging statement against Daddy and Marty, and was certain that one of them had therefore fired the shots at her. Both officers appeared skeptical, but at Joanne's insistence they agreed to have the car impounded and examined. Although one window was clearly shattered by a bullet, no bullets were found inside the vehicle, so it was impossible for the police to determine the caliber of the weapon. One officer speculated that it may have been kids in the woods shooting a rifle. Joanne only shook her head in disgust. No one was listening. It seemed too much of a coincidence that of all the cars passing down Citrus Road daily, hers had to be the one that was targeted for two bullets. Before all was said and done, we were to hear the word *coincidence* more times than I care to remember, and I'm sure the word *paranoid* almost popped out a few times, too. But those who thought it weren't living our lives.

Marty had apparently taken up her old sport of following Nancy around town. Nancy complained constantly of being followed to work, to the shopping center, to anywhere that she was going on a given day.

Time dragged on. It seemed as if the trial would never take place. Meanwhile, the harassment continued. Joanne received a phone call warning her that her children would be killed. It was the same muffled voice that we'd all come to know and despise on the other end of the line. Kelly and Lori, now school-age, caught the bus at the corner of St. Paul Avenue each morning and returned each afternoon, walking the half-block to and from the bus stop. After the phone call, that changed. Joanne drove them to school in the morning and picked them up every afternoon. She couldn't afford to take chances.

I received a similar phone call right on the heels of Joanne's. The voice told me that my children would die. I felt bruised and humiliated, but I did what I had to do. I confined my kids to the backyard of my apartment when they weren't in school. Bruce and Kim, in the way of the very young, became restless and bored at the restrictions. They were used to playing with the other children, riding their bikes along the sidewalks and pathways of the apartment complex. Kim was barely six, and Bruce only seven and a half. They were completely defenseless, yet both sensed that their familiar, secure world was falling apart around them. With her child's naivete, Kim questioned me often. "Is there a bad man that wants to hurt us, Mommy? Is that why we have to stay in the yard? Is the bad man going to get us?"

I lied over and over again. "Of course not, honey. It's just easier to keep an eye on you in the backyard. That way I don't have to chase you around, trying to keep up with you."

Lies. But I was afraid the truth would hurt them. A part of me wanted to gather my children close to me. To say to them, "Listen up, kids. The bogeyman is real. He does exist. He has a name you know well and a face you love and trust. He's as vicious as a cornered rat and capable of damned near anything. And even if I'm wrong, even if he wouldn't hurt a hair on your heads, you still have to be very careful. Because there is some-one else out there, too, someone you know all too well, someone who might be willing to do it for him." I couldn't tell them that. So I continued to make up ex-cuses. Before long the excuses began to wear thin. Any mother can tell you that kids aren't stupid. Bruce and Kim knew I was lying. Every day became a battle of wits between me and my two children, each scene leav-ing me drained and the kids understandably resentful.

Finally Joanne and Joe moved to Houma, as they had planned to do months earlier. Mama, terrified of living alone and worried about the threats to the children, moved back to St. Paul Avenue and insisted that Nancy, Kristen, my children, and I move in with her. The idea was a sound one. Alone, we were sitting ducks. To-gether, maybe, just maybe, we stood a chance.

The house on St. Paul Avenue became a war zone. We devised a plan we dubbed the buddy system. We be-lieved there was safety in numbers, so we left the house at night only if accompanied by another family mem-ber. We had no choice but to look out for our safety and the safety of our children. No one was going to do this for us; we were on our own, with only Steve helping. Without his ever saying so, Steve Donahue kept an eye on the premises. He narrowed his work down to three nights to be around for us. At night he took to bunking on the sofa in the den, and all of us were deeply grateful for and appreciative of his presence.

One evening in May Steve suggested that we all go out to dinner at Middendorf's restaurant, a comfortable seafood restaurant overlooking Bayou Manchac, near Hammond, Louisiana. Enjoying a delicious dinner of crawfish, shrimp, boiled crabs, and oysters on the half shell, we began to shake off the dread that seemed constantly to shadow us. We could draw out the time for only so long, though. With great reluctance we piled into the car and drove the forty miles back to the house on St. Paul Avenue. I wished that we could drive on forever to parts unknown, to a place where fear did not exist. A few hours of freedom were too tantalizing for me.

As we entered the house, I froze. The house had been viciously, systematically trashed. Pillows from the sofa had been torn to shreds and covered the floor like so much confetti. Spray-painted across the walls in bold red letters was the message "Fucking bitches!" In the kitchen, garbage had been overturned on the shiny tile floor. Sugar and coffee had been dumped across the counters and packed into the gas burners on the stove. In the living room, record albums had been taken from their jackets and crushed into thousands of tiny black pieces. Once again bold red letters on the walls read, "Fucking bitches!"

The police were called. We were questioned. None of us was really surprised when the officers theorized that in all likelihood the damage had been caused by kids in the neighborhood.

After the police had gone, the telephone rang. I answered it. A familiar voice spoke into the wire. "You had your chance. Time's up!" There was a loud ringing, like an alarm clock's. Above the ringing I heard the sound of mocking laughter.

* * *

In the darkest hours of the night, alone in my bed, I murdered Marty in a thousand ways. I killed her over and over again for the things she had done to my family. She deserved to die, I reasoned. First she had helped my father destroy himself, then she had been killing us all a little bit at a time. In my heart I knew I lacked the courage to kill her, and I wondered what kind of person I was that I could sit back and allow her to reduce my family to something less than human.

One night Mama entered my room and seated herself at the foot of my bed. "Sleep is hard to come by anymore," she whispered softly. "I want to say that I have never been prouder of my children than I am now."

"I don't know why," I said sadly. "I feel like a coward."

She smiled then. A soft smile. "A coward runs from life, Carol. You, all of you, have faced it head-on. All that's happened, and never once have you backed down. Real courage is the moral strength to resist hardship, to hold one's own, to persevere in the face of danger and fear. These last few months have made me realize what my kids are made of. Each and every one of you has shown me the real meaning of courage. We have love, we have each other, and I've never known that more clearly than I do now."

CHAPTER 29

CAROL

In June 1977, nine months after Mike's death, Daddy was finally brought to trial. Although I was not allowed to enter the courtroom—I was a witness for the prosecution—Mama, Joanne, and Nancy were present for the first day of trial. Shortly after proceedings had begun, Daddy collapsed in the courtroom. From what I understand, all eyes were on him as paramedics rushed to his side to administer oxygen. A silence fell over the courtroom as emergency technicians placed Daddy on a stretcher and wheeled him from the room. Certainly the stress on Daddy was great, but knowing his history, I don't rule out his having faked it.

Feeling the jurors had been unduly influenced by Daddy's alleged angina attack, the judge had no choice but to declare a mistrial. Tom Porteous was now left in the unenviable position of bringing Daddy to trial without causing him any undue stress that might kill him in the process. Several cardiologists were called in to examine Daddy, and each concluded that he could withstand the rigors of a trial, providing the state supplied the necessary medical equipment and emergency personnel qualified to care for him in the event of another attack.

Tom also found himself faced with a problem of another sort. It was necessary that Daddy be convicted of murder in Mike's death before prosecutors could set a trial date for Marty. Since Marty had been charged as an accessory after the fact of second-degree murder, Tom was forced to prove that murder had been committed by Daddy. If Daddy's new trial ended in a mistrial, it was unlikely he would be tried yet a third time, in which case both he and Marty would get off scot-free. It was a gamble that Tom would have to take.

Bob Broussard and Roy Price appealed on Daddy's behalf to the state supreme court, moving for a dismissal of the charges because of their client's poor health. The appeal was denied. A new trial date was scheduled for mid-December 1977. We all dreaded another six months like the last seven.

Feelings were mixed, gossip at an all-time high around us. Daddy had told many people a half-dozen versions of what had occurred the night of September 11, 1976. The only consistencies in his stories were that Mike had been the aggressor and he the innocent victim. Many people believed him. I ran into an old friend of the family, a young man named Danny. Danny had dated Nancy during her last two years of high school. He had continued to visit Daddy with surprising regularity over the years. He said to me, rather nastily, "Your dad tells me you and your sisters have turned your backs on him. What in the hell's the matter with all of you?"

I stared at him, surprised by his fierceness. "All we've done is tell the truth, Danny."

He snorted. "The truth, huh? Fuck the truth. Let's talk about loyalty. If *my* father had lined up ten nuns in a row and shot every one of the motherfuckers dead, I'd defend him, anyway. I'd tell any fuckin' lie I had to to keep him out of jail."

Danny wasn't alone in his opinion. Friends and neighbors alike spoke openly of how "unnatural" we were. Evidently Daddy's magnetism and charm had been deeply entrenched in a wide majority of those who knew him. Daddy's sisters, Lacey and Valerie, as well as their children, refused to speak with any of us. The only cousin who continued to visit us at all was Jay Schanzbach, Valerie's son. Jay seemed embarrassed by the treatment our relatives were dishing out to us. He'd always loved Daddy, whom he called Uncle Len, but he was perceptive enough to understand that we'd had very sound reasons for betraying him. His mother's comment had been, "With relatives like *them,* who the hell needs enemies?"

We did have our share of staunch defenders. Mama's friend Joy Whitlow believed without a doubt that Daddy was guilty. "I always did believe that Len was a cruel, selfish man, capable of almost anything," she told me. "The only thing that surprises me," she said, "is that he finally got caught."

My grandmother Mom-Mom said to Mama and me, "I've always felt that something was wrong with him. He had a cruel streak in him. I sensed it from the very beginning. When he kissed that poor boy George on the lips that night at the wake, I felt the evil inside him. I've been afraid for all of you ever since."

Dutch LaBruyere, who'd always openly admired Daddy, had this to say. "I believed Leonard for a long time, but not anymore. He lied to me. I have no respect for him now."

Meanwhile, a friend of Daddy's had mixed feelings. "It seems impossible that Len could have done this. If he did, then I blame it on the rotten young bitch he married. Everything started to go bad when he met her. He hadn't been seeing her but a few months when George died. Then the hand, the eye. Now this. The Len I knew doesn't exist anymore."

CHAPTER 30

SHIRLEY

In October of 1977 Ray was discharged from the army, and we returned to New Orleans. We moved in with Mama in the house on St. Paul Avenue, with plans of staying until we found jobs. Fortunately, it was only a few weeks later that Ray started school at Oschsner Hospital to study radiological technology.

I visited Daddy often, bound to him by a sense of loyalty. I still loved him for the sense of security his presence gave me. Seeing him was, for me, a time of coming home, an affirmation of who and what I was. I knew my mother and sisters did not approve of my visits, but I went nonetheless. Sometimes when I got home they would ask me questions about how Daddy was, and if he had any plans I knew of to harm them. Eventually they came to understand that I went to see Daddy because I loved him, not because I had taken his side.

Because he was taking drugs, Daddy often seemed unaware of my presence during visits, but it was comforting for me to be able to show him that I cared. He was a broken man, hardly the same father I had loved all these years, content to hide from the world in the library of his home in self-imposed exile.

"I'm innocent," he'd tell me. "You believe me, don't you?"

I'd lie, unable to comfort him in any other way. "Yes, Daddy."

During one visit he was particularly depressed. "My children have deserted me. I'm all alone, except for Marty. What have I done to deserve this hell? I'm sorry."

"We love you, Daddy," I said, trying to ease his pain.

His appearance had changed drastically. He had lost a great deal of weight and now looked wasted, almost exposed. His skin was pale and dry to the touch, his eyes unfocused. He started taking more and more pills— Valium and codeine—in an attempt to ease his fear of the upcoming trial. He was often unaware of his surroundings now. His paranoia grew in stages, little by little, until he became far removed from the events around him.

Marty was more bitter and sarcastic than ever, so I came to dread my visits. Her snide comments and threats became commonplace, and often I stormed from the house, returning only after she was gone. Her hostility seemed to grow as time went by. It was only two more months until the trial, and the pressure was apparently getting to her, too.

The last time I saw Daddy he was lucid and calm, more clearheaded than I had seen him since my return. His face lit with pleasure as I seated myself on the ottoman beside his chair in the library. I was relieved to see him looking better. His cheeks were rosy; his eyes were bright, though there were tears in them.

"I think you should know," he said, "that I've decided what I must do."

I felt a sense of foreboding. "What's that, Daddy?" I asked lightly.

"Nothing can change what has come to pass. You're the only daughter who's stood by me, you deserve to know the truth. I killed Mike. He deserved to die— Carol should be grateful that I got rid of him for her. Your sister is a viper. Never turn your back on her; she'll strike so fast, you won't know what hit you. She's just like Judas, only instead of getting thirty pieces of silver, she sold me out to collect the insurance money. Mike's insurance. She could have lied for me, but she knew that if she did, the insurance company would never have paid her the double indemnity. They don't do that when a person dies during the commission of a crime, and that's just what they would have believed if she had told them that Mike had come here to rob me."

"But, Daddy—" I protested.

He cut me off. "And George, well he was just another useless bastard. Joanne is better off without him, too. I've always protected and cared for my children; when will they realize that I know best?"

I closed my eyes, sick inside.

"My own daughter," he said mournfully. "My own flesh and blood. What does she expect me to do? Go to prison for life? Never. If she takes the stand against me, I might as well be dead. And there's Marty's welfare to consider. If I'm convicted, she'll be tried as an accessory, and I can't allow that to happen."

He gestured dramatically about the room. "All of these things will go to Marty when I die. As she's pointed out, I must have my affairs in order, so I'm making her executrix of my estate. My girls are dead, you are dead, there have never been any children named Joanne or Carol or Nancy. As soon as you leave this house, there will be no more Shirley; that's the way it's got to be. But I want you to know that I did love you, all of you. I've always done my best to see to it that you were taken care of. If I'm convicted, I'll have to die; there's no other way out for Marty. All of you will be gone forever, and my life will be over, too. But I'm leaving my insurance money. It's enough to last for the rest of your lives. That's all that matters to me."

I began to sob, my face in my hands. He continued, his voice light, as though he cared little for the terrible impact of what he had to say. "Ever since Marty came into my life, things have turned around on me. I lost your mother, my girls turned away. Now Marty is my life; nothing else matters. I have to die so she can go free."

Tears were streaming down my face, but I didn't care. He looked at me, and his expression softened. "Now, don't be so sad, baby. It's really for the best, because my life is over. Let Marty run things now."

CHAPTER 31

CAROL

As the date for the trial grew nearer, Tom Porteous asked me and Joanne and Mama to meet with him again on several occasions. These meetings gave Tom the opportunity to bolster my flagging self-confidence and allay my fears of the upcoming trial. We also had the chance to discuss our grievances and to air our disgust with what we viewed as the law's inability to control Marty's actions. Tom remained outwardly sympathetic to our plight, but I sensed that he secretly felt we were overreacting to the situation, that perhaps we had allowed ourselves to be caught up in a form of mass hysteria.

I liked Tom Porteous. He was stubborn and gritty, and he did his job well. It was just that he didn't seem to care enough for what became of us. We felt as though we were being used as pawns in a high-stakes game. We'd bared our souls to the law, and in return it had left us to flounder along. Some of our fears may well have hinged on insecurity, or perhaps sprung from the terrible well of guilt inside us. But the vast majority of those fears were well founded. I came to truly believe that the police fancied they'd caught the big fish, Daddy, while Marty was nothing more than a minnow, hardly worthy of their consideration. Even if the minnow proved to be a killer shark in disguise, it wouldn't be *their* fault. After all, their hands were tied, and such was the law in all its definitive glory.

All in all, though, Tom worked very hard to prepare us for the trial. At one session he prepped me a little for

Price and Broussard. Tom said, "Look, the important thing for you to remember, Carol, is to tell the truth. Tell it in as straightforward a manner as you possibly can. I'm not going to lie to you. Price and Broussard will try their damnedest to shake you on that stand. Their main objective will be to impeach you as a witness, to destroy your credibility. It's the only effective weapon they have against you, and unless I miss my guess, they're going to come after you with both barrels. They'll try to rattle you and twist your words into an entirely different context. Remember, they want to win." His brown eyes were intense.

"Do you think Price and Broussard believe he's innocent?" Bless Joanne. She always had a knack for asking blunt questions.

Tom leaned back in his chair and lit a fresh cigarette from the butt of the one he'd just finished smoking. "I don't know. I know that Roy Price has a personal interest in this case. He is, after all, a friend of your father's. Personally I have no objection to Roy Price. He seems a fine man. But I do wonder about your dad's choosing him to represent him. Roy Price is not a criminal lawyer. In fact, if I'm not mistaken, this will be Roy's first shot at a criminal defense."

I was surprised. "Why didn't he hire someone better qualified?"

Tom shrugged. "I couldn't say. But that's where Bob Broussard enters the picture. He'll probably do a fine job of defending your dad. So whether they believe he's innocent or not is beside the point. Their job is to defend him, and I don't envy them that."

"So, you think they're up against a brick wall?" asked Mama.

"I think it's too early in the game to call the shots, Shirley. But if Leonard behaves true to form, and I believe he will, he'll be the one running his own defense. From behind the scenes, of course, but running it nonetheless."

I tended to agree with Tom. Daddy believed himself

to be far too clever to turn over the reins of his fate to someone else's hands.

Meanwhile, Nancy continued to mope nonstop. In the end it came down to her having to choose sides, just as I'd known it would. On December 10, 1977, the evening before the trial was to begin, she was tense and preoccupied. I wasn't particularly mindful of her distraction, since we were all in pretty much the same mood. We sat around the dinner table picking listlessly at our meal. Suddenly Nancy crumpled up her napkin and threw it in the middle of the table. "How can all of you just sit here?"

"What would you like us to do?" asked Joanne. She calmly buttered a dinner roll.

"What if he gets the death penalty? Would any of you even care?" Tears were rolling down Nancy's cheeks, smudging her mascara.

Mama said, "There is no death penalty for second-degree murder, honey."

"What we're doing goes against everything I feel. If he deserves to be punished, then let the law do it. Why do we have to be a party to it?"

Joanne laid her fork down on her plate. I winced, waiting for her to explode, but her face was almost serene. "Because he made Carol a party to it. When he did that, he made all of us a party to it."

Nancy collapsed then, and her crying lasted into the early hours of dawn. I tried putting a pillow over my ears to drown it out, but I could still plainly hear her. I was torn in two, and though I craved sleep, I was still awake by the time dawn greeted the horizon. Today, fifteen months after Mike's death, Daddy's trial would begin.

CHAPTER 32

SHIRLEY

The morning of the trial, December 11, dawned cold, gray, and misty. I hadn't been able to sleep all night. I tossed and turned, and every time I was about to slip off, I'd picture Daddy in the courtroom. Once I did fall asleep, I had a series of dreams in which he forced me to acknowledge him before the judge and jury, and I was unable to speak. The sadness in his eyes when he looked at me then broke my heart.

The lack of sleep and the bruising emotions had me groggy as we gathered in the kitchen, coffee cups in hand. No one spoke much; all of us were preparing for the trauma in our private ways. It felt like the eve of a battle: still and full of silent prayers. We rode to the courthouse in Gretna engrossed in our own thoughts. Mama sat beside Carol in the front seat as Steve drove slowly across the Mississippi River Bridge. The muddy brown water beneath us matched my grim mood. I felt stained inside, though I knew we were doing the right thing.

The Jefferson Parish Courthouse, where the trial was to be held, was an imposing structure, and the buzz inside only built up my sense of reverence and awe. Lawyers hustled down the gleaming corridors carrying briefcases and legal pads. Uniformed policemen lounged outside the courtroom doors. Steve and Joe led the way past several courtrooms, then rounded a bend in the corridor. They came to an abrupt stop in front of a large, noisy crowd. This was the place.

Outside the courtroom doors paramedics had created

a virtual emergency room, including an oxygen tank, a stretcher, and cardiovascular monitors, which would be used to gauge the severity of any attacks of angina Daddy might experience. Apparently Judge Patrick Carr, who would be presiding over the case, determined that the State of Louisiana would bring its man to trial no matter what. He was taking no chances with Daddy's health. When the slated time for the trial's start drew near, members of the press surged into the courtroom. Then the throng of people milling about followed and filed in, some heading boldly for the front rows, others slipping quietly into the benches at the rear of the room.

I clung to Ray and Mama, frightened and confused. My worst fear had become reality, and I wasn't sure if I could handle it. Deep inside I found myself hoping that Daddy would be proven innocent, that everything would turn out to be some mistake and he would walk away a free man. The thought of his spending the rest of his life in prison, a sure bet if he was convicted, was more than I could bear. I pictured him as he had been years before, his jaw square, his face strong as he'd worked so hard for a better life for us all. And I wondered how this proud man, who had once been a pillar of his community, would react to the public scrutiny and outrage that he now faced. Then his words the last time I had seen him at the house on Citrus Road returned to me. *If I'm convicted, I'll have to die; there's no other way out for Marty.* I was helping to kill a part of myself.

By the time the courtroom was filled, the battle lines were clearly drawn. Joanne and Joe, Nancy, Steve, Ray, and I seated ourselves on the left of the courtroom, behind the prosecution's table. Mama's friend of twenty years, Joy Whitlow, sat in the row behind us, along with Ruth and Paul Holland, Mike's parents, and several members of their family. I felt acutely sorry for the Hollands, who had suffered so much, and I had only to look into Ruth Holland's eyes to see the pain she suffered. Yet she held her head high and her chin firm as she conversed in low tones with her sister, Naomi. Ruth's dignity and pain were counterweights to my pity for Daddy. He'd killed this woman's son, and I knew justice had to be done.

Seated behind the defense table, to the right, was Daddy's band of supporters. In the first two rows were Daddy's sisters, Valerie Schanzbach and Lacey Bayard; Lacey's twenty-one-year-old daughter Beth; and Beth's husband, Mel, a man in his twenties with brown hair and a slight build. Lacey, a blond, hazel-eyed woman in her mid-forties, glowered in our direction. Her husband, Ralph, a heavy-set man with dark eyes and olive skin, did not even look our way. The rancor hung in the air, clear evidence that this case had divided an entire family right down the middle. Marty would not be allowed in the courtroom during the proceedings, because she would be tried as an accessory after the fact of Mike's murder if Daddy was convicted.

Carol was sequestered down the hallway from the proceedings. As a witness for the prosecution she would not be allowed into the courtroom, either, until after she had taken the stand. It was necessary, however, that she be present every day, since no one knew when her name would be called. In the meantime we all agreed to take turns visiting with her to keep up her morale and reassure her that she was not alone.

Mama joined us a few minutes after we'd taken our seats. She wore a somber navy blue outfit that might have been more suitable for a funeral. But sitting in that courtroom, a cold, formidable place full of lawyers, former friends, and a man who was once her husband, must have seemed to her a death of sorts. For years she had basked in the glow of Daddy's accomplishments in the courtroom, and now the courtroom would be a place of embarrassment, for all of us.

The hushed, expectant murmuring in the room stopped abruptly as Tom Porteous entered, followed by his assistant, Bill Hall, a young assistant district attorney with thick, dark blond hair and a handsome, youthful face. After acknowledging Mama's presence, Porteous winked at his wife, Mel, a pert brunet seated several rows behind us, and sat down at the prosecution's table. He began shuffling through a thick sheaf of papers, then leaned over to whisper with Bill Hall. Within minutes a third attorney joined them, Danny Martini, a blond, handsome research assistant and the righthand man of Tom Porteous.

Then Daddy entered, flanked by Roy Price and Robert Broussard. Dressed in a dove gray suit, white shirt, and patterned tie, Daddy cut a tall and elegant figure. His sandy-colored hair and dark-rimmed glasses made him look every bit the wealthy and distinguished attorney most believed him to be. The one odd touch was the stainless steel prosthesis protruding from the left sleeve of his suit jacket. A thrilled murmur shot through the crowded courtroom when it became visible. It made him look injured and wronged. Porteous smiled, a little amused at Daddy's clever ploy for extracting sympathy from the many onlookers who were seeing him for the first time.

The whole first day was spent on *voir dire*, the jury selection, and the panel was completed the second morning of the process. Court took a noon recess, then reconvened. I volunteered to stay behind and keep Carol company, but Steve had already said he'd spend the afternoon with her, so very reluctantly I went with the others back into the courtroom. I sat again on the long bench a couple of rows from the front of the courtroom. The room was modern, completely without distinction, as sterile and austere as a hospital room. At the very front of the room Judge Carr sat at his bench, which was slightly elevated and so made him appear almost kingly. To the right of Judge Carr and to the left of the spectators, the jury members filed in and took their designated chairs in the jury box. Ray sat beside me, silent and pensive, his eyes roving over the room as if seeking a familiar face in the midst of all those strangers. People continued to come into the courtroom, and the room soon filled to overflowing. Those without seats, mostly reporters, stood to the rear.

As Judge Carr called the court to order, I stole a glance at Daddy. I could see only his profile, face bleached of color, the silvery hair at his temples exaggerating the paleness of his features. He retrieved something from the breast pocket of his tweed suit, then popped whatever it was into his mouth and washed it down quickly with a glass of water. Valium, no doubt. The pills were most likely what gave him the tremendous amount of calmness and composure he'd displayed thus far.

Tom Porteous began his opening statement by describing the murder of Mike Holland—who was often referred to during the trial by his given name, George —and the chain of events leading to the arrest of Leonard John Fagot. Taken link by link, he stated, that same chain of events would prove beyond any doubt that on September 11, 1976, Leonard John Fagot had committed cold-blooded murder, an act that belied his professional and moral values. Tom pointed out that Daddy was an attorney, a professional who represented the law, and stressed the need for the judicial system to police its own. He also warned the jury not to be intimidated by Daddy's distinguished position in the community or by his personal wealth. Daddy should be treated, Tom told the jury, as any other man or woman who had violated the laws of the State of Louisiana. He advised them to disregard any reference made to the defendant's state of health. The defendant would attempt to gain the sympathy of the court, he argued, and the jury must not be swayed by any unfounded sympathy. The defendant had not shown a shred of pity for the deceased, Mike Holland, as he'd held a thirty-eight pistol to his heart and pulled the trigger.

I was jarred by the passion in Tom's oratory. Clearly he would be a formidable adversary. Somewhere inside

I prayed Daddy's lawyers were well prepared to do battle with him. Tom's statement had undoubtedly unsettled the others present in the courtroom as well. It caused a distinct change in the overall mood. Where there had been a cough here, a whisper there, now total silence and a tense air of high drama reigned. I felt suddenly clammy. My eyes strayed once again to Daddy. I still could not see his face, since he sat toward the front of the court, his back to the courtroom. Daddy's reaction to Tom's damning words was not visible to me. I watched as his hand again fumbled in his breast pocket. I hoped he would not suddenly turn his head around and make eye contact with me. I wanted to observe him without his knowing. To face him seemed too much to bear. It would be like looking at myself.

The first witness to take the stand was the officer who had been first to arrive at the death scene. He made a credible witness as Porteous ran him briefly through a description of the car and the condition of the vehicle. The uniformed officer set out the facts of what he had observed the night of September 11, pointing out that two eyewitnesses had been at the scene and that both had observed a second man fleeing from the wrecked vehicle.

A medical examiner was called upon to verify that Mike had been shot four times and that the cause of death had been from a single bullet that had entered the chest and then struck him in the heart and lung. A second shot had been fired into Mike's right arm, lodging in the upper chest cavity. Two more shots had been fired into his head postmortem.

Mama stiffened beside me. I tried to put visions of Mike lying hunched over the steering wheel from my mind.

An expert in forensics stated that although the blood found on the thirty-eight in question, the murder weapon, had been too scanty to type, the hairs embedded on the cylinder of the gun matched the victim's closely.

Then Sergeant Gorman was sworn in and calmly took the stand. If he had any idea of how important his testimony was, he didn't show it. Dressed in a conservative dark suit, white shirt, and black tie, he looked respectable and dignified.

After establishing Gorman's active role in the investigation with a series of short questions, Porteous faced Judge Carr and said, "I believe it is going to be necessary to lay a predicate at this point, Your Honor, outside the presence of the jury."

"Alright. The jury will be excused. As you were advised, ladies and gentlemen, there are certain things that must be taken up outside your presence."

As the jury filed out, I squeezed Mama's hand. What was so important that the jury had to be excused? She returned the pressure of my hand in hers, a gesture of support that I desperately needed.

I could not take my eyes off Daddy. He was seated beside Roy Price, his eyes now hidden behind dark glasses.

"Sergeant Gorman," Porteous said, "you went to 279 Citrus Road on the night of September eleventh, correct?"

"Yes."

"Did you meet anyone at that address?"

"I met a Mr. and Mrs. Fagot."

"Is Mr. Fagot in this courtroom today?"

"Yes, he is."

"Would you point him out to me, please?"

"The gentlemen sitting next to Mr. Price."

Speaking to the court reporter, an older woman with graying hair, Porteous said, "Let the record reflect that the witness has identified the defendant. Now, Sergeant Gorman, at that time, how long had you been at the scene, when you first went to Mr. Fagot's residence?"

"Approximately a half-hour."

"Was he a suspect?"

"No, sir."

"Did you advise him of any rights when you talked to him?"

"No, sir, I did not."

"Did you ask him if you could talk to him?"

"Yes, I did."

"He didn't show any hesitancy to talk to you?"

"No, sir. In fact, we had a gate separating us, and he opened the gate and invited me into the residence."

Under Porteous's questioning Gorman went on to describe how Daddy and Marty had brought him into the house that night. According to Gorman, after some general conversation with both of them, he took a statement from Daddy, which Daddy signed.

Porteous ended with a few more questions. "Did you handle him as a suspect at that time?"

"No, sir. He was not a suspect."

"When you left, did you tell him not to leave town, or anything like that that would indicate he was a suspect?"

"No."

"No further questions right now," said Porteous, "as far as the predicate is concerned."

I shifted uneasily in my seat as Broussard approached the witness stand. He addressed Gorman almost casually.

"Mr. Gorman, this was about eleven o'clock at night?"

"Yeah."

"You say you rang the bell and you waved to Mr. Fagot, and he told you to come on in?"

"He didn't tell me to come in from where he was waving. He waved, indicating, I assumed, he saw me. He proceeded over to the fence area. I told him who I was at that time, and he invited me in, yes."

"Isn't it a matter of fact that when they found out you didn't have a typewriter, didn't they offer you a typewriter to do your report at the house?"

"I believe they may have offered an electric, in fact, I

even made a statement, if I'm not mistaken, that I wasn't used to an electric typewriter. So it's quite possible, sir."

Broussard looked surprised. "You didn't find this behavior unusual when you interrogated these people?"

"I wasn't interrogating. I found Mr. Fagot very cooperative, very polite, and a personable gentleman, somebody whom, you know, was very easy to speak with."

"In your experience didn't you find him unusually cooperative against other people you may have interviewed or interrogated?"

"I can't really say that because I talk to many people in many surroundings and find people on both sides, either very personable or very objectionable to me."

"But you didn't find it unusual that you were invited into the house, that you would be offered a typewriter, at least you were offered a typewriter?"

"I was offered a typewriter, a cup of coffee. Yes, sir. There is no question about that."

Broussard turned toward the defense table. "That's all."

Porteous rose and approached the bench. "Your Honor, during the course of Sergeant Gorman's testimony there is going to be at least one other occasion where it is going to be necessary to lay a predicate. Unless the Court would object, or Mr. Broussard or Mr. Price, I see no reason why not to do it now, even though it is not in sequence, at least establish the predicate as long as we have the jury removed from the courtroom, subject to any objection they may have, of course."

Mr. Broussard and Mr. Price conferred for a few minutes, then conceded.

"Let the record show that the defense has no objection," said Porteous, with authority.

Porteous then took Sergeant Gorman through brief descriptions of the two other interviews Gorman had had with Daddy. The first was later the night of the murder, after their initial talk. The second was on September 14, while Daddy was in the hospital for reme-

dial eye surgery. Gorman testified that both times
Daddy was lucid and cooperative, but by the second
interview he was a suspect and had been read his rights.
Gorman said that in the hospital he had asked Daddy if
he was on any medication. Daddy had said that he was,
but it was nothing that would inhibit his thinking.

After Porteous finished, Broussard rose to his feet,
ready to cross-examine the witness. As he did so, Mama
signaled to me that she was leaving the room to visit
with Carol. I watched her go, then turned my attention
to the proceedings.

"Sergeant Gorman, I believe when Mr. Porteous began questioning you again, you referred to some other
oral statement? He asked you something about an oral
statement, not at the hospital, but between the one you
said was the written statement at the house and that
same night."

"Yes, sir. Following the written statement is when we
learned the identity, when we were leaving the residence, when he was walking me to the exterior of the
residence, of the identity of the victim. Once we
learned the identity of the victim and he recognized
the name and everything, I assisted him back into the
residence. At that time we engaged in an interview at
that point, separate and above the written statement
that was obtained."

"My purpose in asking that," explained Broussard, "is
that I've got a notice of intent to introduce statements.
It does not refer to any such statement. It says a written
statement given to Sergeant Gorman, September 11,
1976. Oral statement to Gorman, September 14, 1976. I
don't know if the state plans to have him testify in front
of the jury as to this now, the so-called oral statement, or
as he has testified. If so, I would object to him testifying
because we have not been furnished such notice of intention."

The two attorneys did some verbal sparring, although
their manner was curt and to the point. Finally Judge
Carr determined that the state had indeed given suffi-

cient notice of intent to defense counsel prior to the proceedings. Gorman's testimony as to Daddy's oral statement on September 11 would be heard by the jury. His testimony in the predicate was just to explain the circumstances of the acquisition of the statements. We hadn't heard the statements yet, so we had no idea then just how important Judge Carr's decision was.

CHAPTER 33

SHIRLEY

During the short recess I visited with Carol where she was sequestered. She was doing her best to remain composed while waiting for her name to be called. My sister looked a tragic sight as she absentmindedly twined her fingers in her lap, her eyes as haunted as I have ever seen them. Mama took a seat beside Carol and tried to distract her as Daddy and his entourage disappeared into a small room across the hall from the courtroom that contained medical equipment and personnel.

"Everything will be fine, honey." Mama squeezed Carol's hand. "Just hang in there. I know this isn't easy for you, and I want you to know that you're not alone. We're all pulling for you."

Carol's quick view of Daddy broke her composure. She was getting agitated. "How am I supposed to face him in the courtroom? What if I can't do it?"

"Take it easy," I said. "Take it one step at a time. He won't be sitting right beside you; you don't even have to look at him if you don't want to. We'll be there; all of us will."

"I'm afraid," she said.

So was I. I thought of Valerie's and Lacey's hate-filled faces when they had appeared in the courtroom, and I felt a stab of guilt. There was a part of me that still needed Daddy, that still *was* Daddy. And that part wanted to go and tell him that I wanted to stand by him. But another part of me had grown, because of the pain and because of my time away from Daddy with Ray. I was an adult now, and though I longed for what was, I couldn't desert my mother and Carol. I had already made my choice, though I regretted that choice many times.

Tom Porteous appeared. He nodded once in our direction and continued down the hallway. The sight of him seemed to bolster Carol's courage, and she held her head slightly higher.

Carol accompanied Mama to the restroom, and Ray and I waited in the hallway. Suddenly Daddy entered the hallway, cold, nearly stuporous. Marty stood to one side of him, and Lacey and Valerie the other. I longed so badly to hear his voice, to touch him, to reassure myself somehow that he was still my Daddy and I was still his girl. Leaving Ray's side, I walked up to him and brushed his shoulder with my fingertips. He didn't look at me, didn't move, as though he were frozen.

I wanted to slap him, to do anything to wipe that glazed look from his eyes. I shook his arm. "Daddy! Please!" If only he would talk to me, I thought, I could break through his wall of pain. We could go back again: He'd realize what he'd done wrong, and we'd forgive him. All he had to do was ask. Instead he ignored me, just staring ahead at the white walls of the hallway. I was suddenly consumed by anger. How dare he ignore me, when he knew how much I loved him? It had taken every bit of courage I'd possessed to face him, and he apparently didn't care! *My girls are dead, you are dead, there have never been any children named Joanne or Carol or Nancy. As soon as you leave this house, there will be no more Shirley.* I remembered his words to me as I'd sat beside his chair at the house on Citrus Road, sobbing. We do exist! I thought, filled with this new rage. It's not our fault! You're to blame! And you don't have the courage to end our suffering.

Through a red haze I became aware of Valerie angrily hovering over me. Marty slapped my hand away from my father's arm. "Stay away from him," she hissed, her eyes black with anger. "Leave him alone."

"Go back to your mother's side," Valerie added bitterly. Her face was twisted. "You've done enough to him already, you and your sisters."

"That's not true," I said heatedly. "What about Carol? What about Mike?"

I looked at Daddy, hoping to catch some flicker of interest in his eyes, but he stood mutely by, his face fixed and closed. In that moment I hated him.

Ray suddenly appeared at my side. "Shirley, I've been waiting for you. Come on."

He led me gently down the hallway, but I kept peering at Daddy over my shoulder, not wanting to leave him. I had the sinking feeling that I might never see him again, except maybe across the crowded courtroom. The thought was a crushing stone upon my heart. I knew that until I let go of my love for him, I would always feel this pain. But I couldn't do that without saying good-bye. Until I had that final confrontation with him, I could not turn completely away. And I wasn't ready for that yet.

Ray and I returned to the courtroom. Joanne and Joe were already seated in the second row of benches, and we took our place beside them. Nancy sat in silent grief. I knew she still felt close to Daddy, and in my heart I prayed that she would find some way of exorcising her love for him, as I would.

Sergeant Gorman was on the stand, his quiet voice a reminder that the ordeal had barely started. Gorman was repeating much of what he had said in the predicate, but now with the jury present.

"Now, Sergeant Gorman," Porteous was saying. "How did you gain entry to Mr. Fagot's residence on the night of September 11, 1976?"

"The residence is surrounded by a brick and wrought-iron fence. There is an electronic gate with a doorbell. I rang the bell a couple of times, but received no immediate answer. Then a few moments later I observed a white male, about fifty-five, clad in pajamas, and a young woman in her late twenties coming toward the front of the residence. I yelled the name Mr. Fagot, motioning with my hand, having obtained the name from the mailbox. And I observed the gentleman wave back to me and come in my direction."

"Was the gate opened for you?"

"The gate, when I got there, was closed and when the two people approached me, I advised them who I was and that I was investigating an apparent homicide, and I asked them if they would answer some questions. At that time Mr. Fagot opened the gate by way of an electronic device. The gate automatically opened and he walked with me to the residence."

"Where was this device he used to open the gate?"

"In his right hand."

"Now, when you walked into the residence, were you alone with Mr. and Mrs. Fagot, or was there another officer with you?"

"No. The public information officer, Lieutenant Robert Lindsay, was with me at the time I was at the gate and at the time I entered the Fagot residence."

"When you entered the residence, where did you proceed to?"

"We were invited to sit down in what I would imagine would have been the front room, what have you. Lieutenant Lindsay had a seat, and I had a seat."

"Was there any casual conversation at that time?"

"There was some casual conversation. We talked about Mr. Fagot's family. We talked about the fact that Mrs. Fagot and I had some mutual acquaintances. And there was some discussion about a small abrasion, about three-quarters of an inch, Mr. Fagot had right about here"—he touched his forehead—"on the left side of his forehead. I noticed some scratches on Mr. Fagot's hand, and I asked him how that had happened. He indicated that he'd been moving some furniture, which was kind of difficult with one arm, and it had fallen back on him."

"Did you take a typed statement from Mr. Fagot?"

"Yes, I did."

"I have a copy of that statement right here. Let's proceed through the statement, and if you have no objection, I'll read the question and you read the answers."

Mr. Broussard protested. "We are going to reurge our objection to the admissibility of this statement on the same grounds."

Again Daddy's attorneys were claiming that this portion of Gorman's testimony shouldn't be allowed because they had not been informed of it. Broussard, and therefore Daddy, must have known how incriminating the statement was.

"Objection is overruled, and it will be noted," said Judge Carr.

Porteous began to read from the typed statement. "'When did you first learn of what had happened?'"

Sergeant Gorman read Daddy's answer aloud. "'I was in the shower downstairs, and my wife came in and told me that something had happened outside. She said there was a lot of noise and asked me to go out and see what was going on. I got out of the shower, dried off, got dressed. It was about ten minutes before I got outside. Both of us were in our bed clothing. When I got outside, I checked the yard and observed a man with a German shepherd looking around the north side of my property. I walked around and asked a few questions and wasn't given any answers. There were about two dozen people milling about.'"

"'Was the fence closed when you came outside?'"
"'Yes.'"

"'Have you had any company since you returned home at six P.M.?'"

"'No. I had company last night until around four A.M., with six cars.'"

"'Was anyone over earlier today?'"

"'Just my two garden boys. They were here around nine A.M. to around five P.M.'"

"'Is there anything else you can add to this statement?'"

"'Nothing occurred that I knew anything about. The first information I had was that someone got killed in a car accident, and then Rene, he's Dutch LaBruyere's boy, told me that a man was shot twice.' "

Porteous nodded his head curtly. "Is that the end of the statement, Sergeant Gorman?"

"Yes, sir."

"After you took the statement, what did you do next?"

"We engaged in some general conversation for a few minutes, after which I exited the residence and went back to where the other officers were."

"You took another statement from Mr. Fagot that evening. What did you talk about that time?"

"I asked him about his son-in-law George Holland, and he told me that George Holland had been married to his daughter Carol, and that they had broken up about a year and a half before. He believed his son-in-law to be involved in some narcotics trafficking. And he indicated that his daughter had broken up the marriage because of mistreatment from her husband."

Mama's eyes met mine. There was a flicker of emotion in their clear depths, and I sensed her anger. Daddy had seen fit to expose Carol's private life to Sergeant Gorman to cover his own butt. He was such a hypocrite. He'd demanded loyalty from others as if it were his due yet he'd never been loyal to anyone but himself.

"Did he tell you what type of narcotics Mr. Holland was involved in?"

"There was an indication of marijuana at one point during our interview. He advised me that his son-in-law had contacted him about three days prior to this incident, trying to obtain one hundred dollars, and he had mentioned—"

"I'm going to have to register an objection at this point. I'd ask that the jury be removed from the room before I state the reasons," interrupted Mr. Broussard.

"All right," agreed Judge Carr.

I couldn't believe Mike would ever go over there and ask for money. He was too proud and too smart. It took a few minutes for the jury box to be cleared. I paid little attention to Mr. Broussard's loud oratory as he addressed the court, but I knew it had to do with Gorman's mention of narcotics. I looked at Daddy, who had a worried expression on his face. It was the first time in the past three days that I had seen him display any emotion. Every now and then Mr. Price would converse with Daddy in low tones and nod his head, as if agreeing with something Daddy said. It appeared that Daddy really was orchestrating his own defense, as we thought he would.

Broussard finished, and the jury was brought in. Porteous started up again. "Sergeant Gorman, I believe you said Mr. Fagot indicated he had talked to his son-in-law a few days prior to this?"

"Yes, sir. He indicated he wanted to borrow a hundred dollars."

"Did he indicate whether or not he lent this money?"

"The indication was no."

"Did he indicate whether Mr. Holland had been to his residence before?"

"Yes. He advised me that several months prior to this incident he had come over to borrow tools. In fact, he made reference to the fact that George Holland was not unliked at the house, and he said that he often saw him passing in his truck."

"Had Mr. Fagot ever seen this particular vehicle before?"

"No. He stated in his original interview he had never seen the vehicle before."

"Did you ask him whether or not he had any weapons of any type?"

"I asked him if he or if anyone else in his family, to his knowledge, had any weapons and at that time he told me that four years or so ago he had purchased a weapon from Quality Guns, a thirty-eight-caliber pistol, which he described as not a long-barrel, and he advised that he had given it to his first wife, that allegedly his first wife lent it to George Holland, and that Holland had lost it or had it stolen in Mexico."

"Did he indicate whether he owned any other weapons?"

"No, sir, he indicated that was the only weapon he owned."

"Did you question him as to why the incident may have occurred in front of his residence?"

"Yes, sir, I did. And at that time he gave me some additional information. He advised me that prior to his going down to the shower and what have you, he was alone with his wife and that he heard a bell, the gate bell ringing and that he had looked out the window and seen headlights, but that the trees had obstructed any real view, and he had declined to answer the bell. This is the information that he hadn't given me originally."

Daddy hadn't mentioned the bell before, or the headlights. He'd said nothing was unusual.

"Did he say anything else about Holland or anyone else, other son-in-laws?"

"That's pretty general," commented Mr. Broussard. "I'm going to object to it."

"Can you phrase it more specifically, Mr. Porteous?" asked Judge Carr.

"Yes, sir. I can probably lead him," Porteous said lightly.

"Without leading," Judge Carr replied, sounding annoyed.

"Did he say anything in reference to any thefts?" asked Porteous.

"He indicated that he had recently installed a burglar alarm in his residence and he indicated that the reason was he'd suspected his in-laws of stealing from him over the last three years or so."

"Did you observe the system at all?"

"If I'm not mistaken, it was a Saxon. As you opened the front door, there would be a beep tone."

"Now, on September 14, 1976, did you have occasion to see Mr. Fagot again?"

"Yes, sir, I did."

"Where was that?"

"At East Jefferson Hospital."

"Did you ask him then about any weapons he owned?"

"Yes, sir. I asked him specifically about the thirty-eight Charter Arms at that time. I asked him where he had purchased it. He said he bought it some time back from a friend of his, a cabbie, but he couldn't give me any additional information. He said he had purchased the weapon while having a sandwich at Tranchina's restaurant on St. Charles Avenue. He said at the time he purchased it he also purchased a handful of ammunition for it."

At the first questioning, Daddy had said he'd bought the gun at Quality Guns and that it was lost.

"Okay. Did he indicate whether he had ever fired the weapon?"

"I asked him, and he said the last time he had fired it was several days before the incident—that it was on Wednesday or Thursday of that same week."

"Did he tell you where he had fired it?"

"He indicated that he had fired the weapon in La Place near some pumps and a cane field—the same general area where he'd had a shooting accident that caused the loss of his arm."

"Did he indicate if anyone else had fired the weapon?"

"No, sir. He said he had fired it religiously since he'd become the victim of some suspicious persons. He also told me that he had had an incident where somebody had thrown a makeshift kerosene bomb at his residence, and since that time he had fired it religiously."

"Did you ask him how he maintained it or what he did with the spent casings or anything?"

"I asked him how he normally maintained the weapon, and he told me that the weapon was kept a couple of shelves below where he kept his Ruger. He indicated that when he was finished firing the weapon, he normally kept it loaded with what he described as hollow-point bullets—they were hard on the bottom and soft on top. He said he normally kept it loaded and that he kept the weapon in an envelope. And that on the last occasion that he had fired it he had packed it the same way but he had also taken the spent casings, four spent casings which he had used, and he had placed them in a second envelope. I asked him for what reason he would maintain the casings. He indicated to me that he received *American Riflemen's Association* magazine and that he was anticipating his wife purchasing him a reloading device for Christmas.''

"Did you ask him about any other type weapons he owned?"

"Yes, sir, I did. He told me he kept a forty-five Byer, or whatever, in his nightstand, and he did own a Ruger, here again that he kept several shelves above where he kept the Charter Arms, in the same section of bookshelves."

Why hadn't he mentioned them before, when Gorman had asked him at the house? Why had he lied?

"With respect to the thirty-eight Charter Arms, did you bring up the condition of it, with the blood?"

"I had asked Mr. Fagot if he had any explanation for the blood on the barrel, and he said he didn't. And he made a comment, he said something relative to, 'Walter, I feel like I'm going to be the patsy.' "

"Now, did you ask him or go into the alarm system at his house?"

"Yes. We were discussing as to how the weapon could have gotten in there and if anybody could have gotten into his house without his knowing, so we went—I asked him about the alarm system. He said it had three general settings."

"Did he say anything about anyone gaining entry?"

"We talked about the possibility and, in fact, I talked the possibility of anybody opening the gates, having a car in the driveway, getting the weapon out of the house, firing the weapon, getting back into the house, placing the weapon in the same type of wrapping, what have you, and then exiting the house without him or anybody knowing it. And he advised me he had no other explanation for it."

"Other than the occasion on the 14th, have you spoken to Mr. Fagot at any time since that date?"

"I did speak with him, well, I had occasion to speak with him that same afternoon. After our conversation at the hospital I had asked him if it would be possible for me to talk to his wife again, and he told me to come to his residence at about four o'clock. That Mr. Price, a friend of his, was trying to obtain the services of another lawyer."

"Did you go to his residence at that time?"

"Yes, I did."

"Did you speak with him?"

"Yes, sir, briefly. He told me that he would have to put off any more conversations until he spoke with Mr. Broussard. That Mr. Broussard had advised him not to speak with me until the he had had a chance to speak with Mr. Fagot."

"You didn't take any other statements after that?"

"I did ask him one or two other questions at that second statement. I asked him again about having seen Holland or contacts with Holland, and he had advised me that approximately three weeks prior to the incident, that Holland and a dark-haired, dark-complected individual had come to his residence, again trying to solicit several thousand dollars from him and that he had told them both to leave. He also made reference to the fact that either the day of or the day before the incident, that Mr. Holland had called him, wanting to borrow a thousand dollars to make a killing."

Now Daddy had Mike saying he wanted a thousand dollars. Before it was a hundred. I didn't believe it, in either case. Anyway, Broussard was right on top of the "killing" reference.

"I object, Your Honor."

"Objection sustained," said Judge Carr.

Even without understanding all the legal terminology, I could see that Daddy had slipped up in those statements. The entry of Gorman's testimony had put Daddy in a very tough spot.

Sergeant Gorman stepped down from the stand. Mr. Broussard rose to his feet. "Mr. Leonard Fagot, for the limited purpose of traverse."

Carr said, "Let him take the stand outside the presence of the jury, and it will be for the limited purpose of traversing the voluntariness of the statements."

Daddy was going to take the stand. The Court would determine if he had voluntarily given the three statements to Gorman or if there had been extenuating circumstances that showed Daddy had been under duress or not of sound mind. Maybe now he'd explain why he'd given Sergeant Gorman conflicting information and made up stories about Mike and Carol. Why he had the murder weapon in his house. He was less and less the man I knew every moment that went by. And I was sure he had something up his sleeve.

CHAPTER 34

SHIRLEY

The courtroom was very bright, with shiny walls reflecting painfully against my eyes. It was warm. The heaters seemed to stifle what little air was circulating. Judge Carr, in his black robes, looked to me like some avenging angel, ready to strike Daddy down in the name of justice. Although I respected Judge Carr and the bailiff, I wondered how these men of the law would have felt if their father stood before them, waiting to be judged. Would they consider the law to be just as important, or would part of them be as resentful of it as I was? I closed my eyes, wishing it all away, but the sound of whispering made me realize I couldn't. Daddy was making his way, cocky and emotionless, to the witness stand.

He was sworn in. His face was expressionless, his eyes still hidden behind dark lenses. He seemed unusually calm and composed, and my heart went out to him.

Mr. Broussard approached the stand. "Mr. Fagot, did you sustain an injury on September 11, 1976?"

"Yes, I did." Daddy's voice sounded unnaturally deep and somber over the microphone.

"Where did you sustain the injury?"

"On my forehead. It was about the size of a half-dollar, a contusion."

"Where were you at the time the injury occurred?"

"I was in a car in my driveway."

This sounded closer to the truth than his story to Sergeant Gorman about hurting himself moving furniture.

"Did the vehicle do anything when you were in it?"

"It accelerated backward and crashed into a tree at a very fast speed."

"You sustained an injury to your head?" Broussard's voice was very sympathetic.

"I sustained an injury to my head."

"Was there any contusion or abrasion at the time?"

"Yes, there was."

"Your Honor," said Broussard with respect. "I don't know how we segment this. I only want him on the stand one time."

There was a quick conference between the men, and then Broussard, apparently satisfied, began questioning Daddy again.

"Did you suffer any unconsciousness, momentarily or otherwise?"

"Yes, I did."

"Now, you heard Sergeant Gorman testify on the predicate about some statements or questions and answers at the hospital. You were in the hospital for surgery, is that correct?"

"Yes, surgery to my left eye. It's an artificial eye."

"The purpose was what?"

"Remedial surgery to it."

"Was it necessary to take sutures in what I refer to as the socket of your eye?"

"Yes, although I don't know exactly what they did."

"Do you know what medication you were given in the hospital on that Monday after surgery and that Tuesday morning?"

"No, I don't. But I was pretty groggy."

Gorman had testified that Daddy said the medication hadn't affected him.

"That's all."

Mr. Porteous walked up to the stand. "Mr. Fagot, do you recall having a photograph taken of your injury about September twelfth, a color photograph?"

"Where was that?" asked Daddy.

"At your residence?"

"Yes."

"I'm going to show you a photograph marked state exhibit thirty-five. I'll ask you whether you can identify that photograph."

"Yes, I can."

"Does the photograph indicate this abrasion you have made reference to?"

"Yes."

"Is that photograph a very accurate representation of the condition at that time?"

"Yes."

"You said you were knocked unconscious?"

"Yes."

"For how long?"

"I don't know."

"Well," said Porteous, sounding a bit more gruff. "What time were you in the car?"

"When?"

"When you hurt your head, Mr. Fagot."

"I was thrown out of the car. I would suppose that was when I struck my head, that was at the moment of impact with the tree. I was thrown into another tree, and that's what I think saved me."

"This impact—maybe I can do it this way—was the impact in your driveway or across the street?"

"There were several impacts," Daddy replied vaguely.

"The one where you were thrown out?"

"That was at the very last instance when it struck the big tree, and I was thrown out, into another shrub, bush, tree."

"Is this across the street from your house?"

"Across the street from my house, across the street."

"Do you recall what time you got in that car?"

"No, I don't."

Broussard rose to his feet. "I'm going to object," he stated.

"Objection is sustained."

"I'm trying to establish a time of unconsciousness,"

said Mr. Porteous. "He said he was unconscious; I'm trying to see how long he was out. We are going to have some issues as to whether or not he could understand what was going on. I need to determine how long he was unconscious; that's why I'm pursuing what time he got into the car, what's the next thing he remembers." He turned to Daddy. "After you hit your head, what is the very first thing you remember after that?"

"I don't know. I came to, I was groggy, I didn't know what was going on."

"Do you recall being in your house at any time that night?"

"I left from where I had been thrown and I walked across the street to my home."

"So you recall that?"

"I could not recall it until several days afterwards."

Daddy was now claiming he had amnesia the night of the murder! That was his excuse for the conflicting statements.

"When you got home, did you lie down?"

"I do not know."

"I object, Your Honor. We are getting into the case here," Broussard said earnestly.

"I'm trying to find out how seriously this man was hurt as far as his memory," Porteous insisted.

"Why don't you ask him the truth of what transpired with reference to Sergeant Gorman's testimony first?" suggested Judge Carr.

Porteous nodded and turned to Daddy. "Do you recall talking to Sergeant Gorman that night?" he asked.

"It was almost three or four days later before I recalled it."

"I'm going to show you an exhibit marked state thirty-three. Do you recall signing that?"

"I repeat what I said before. I recalled nothing for three or four days after the accident. After that I did recall it."

I didn't believe any of this.

"You don't recall being admitted to the hospital?"

"No, I do not."

"You don't recall being on medication at the hospital?" Porteous's voice did not disguise his sarcasm.

"No."

"You don't recall seeing Sergeant Gorman at the hospital?"

Daddy's face remained blank. His voice never faltered as he answered. "There was a period of time when flashes of recollection would come back."

"Was that one of those periods of time when recollection came back?"

"I'm not sure."

"When did you regain your senses so that you could recall things again?"

This time Mr. Price rose to his feet to object. "He's asked that question three or four times already."

"I want to know a date," Porteous replied evenly.

"I do not know a date," answered Daddy. "Three or four days after the accident."

"Were you home at the time?"

"I must have been."

"No more questions right now, Your Honor," said Mr. Porteous respectfully.

"You may step down, Mr. Fagot," said Judge Carr.

There was no way this would change Carr's ruling. Daddy's testimony had sounded like exactly what it was —the excuses of a desperate man. Lies.

CHAPTER 35

SHIRLEY

In the two days that followed, the prosecution called more witnesses. Among them was Ferdinand Marsolan, Daddy's partner in Investment Returns, the company that had been the source of Daddy's income for the last several years. A nervous, gaunt man with a pencil-thin mustache, Mr. Marsolan told the court that Daddy had obtained the thirty-eight-caliber Charter Arms from a cab driver who had placed the weapon, along with a color TV, up for collateral on a five-hundred-dollar loan. According to Marsolan, the cab driver had defaulted on the loan and had been forced to turn over the gun and color TV. He also testified that Daddy had taken posses-sion of the gun, saying that he needed it for protection. Mr. Marsolan then identified the weapon, which Mr. Porteous had introduced into evidence.

After Marsolan, Dutch LaBruyere was sworn in and took the stand. Looking distinguished in a gray suit, his silvery hair neatly groomed, he related the events of the night of September 11 for the court in a controlled manner. His testimony was simple. On the night in question, at approximately nine-forty, he'd heard a commotion outside his home. He'd gone outside and had observed a car racing backward, heading directly for his front yard. At the same time, he'd noticed a youth on a bicycle pull up beside him. He and the boy had watched in amazement as the speeding car had crashed into a large tree located near the end of his front lawn, by the street curb. He'd quickly approached the wrecked car, which he identified as a brown-and-white Pontiac. He'd noted that the headlights were on and the engine still running. He added that, to his surprise, a man had darted from the passenger side of the car and run across the street. Dutch had then approached the car to offer help and had noticed to his dismay that a second man was inside the vehicle, slumped over the steering wheel. It had taken only a split second for him to determine that the man behind the wheel was dead. He had then gone inside his home to contact the police.

Mr. Broussard tried his hardest to muddy the waters during cross-examination by raising questions about what LaBruyere actually saw that night. Mr. LaBruyere was a believable witness, though, and Broussard's attempt to undermine his testimony had most likely been in vain.

Porteous later led Andre Bellou through a telling of what he had witnessed the night of Mike's death. Andre told basically the same story as Dutch LaBruyere, with only one exception. Porteous was able to pull from Andre the fact that he had seen the Pontiac Le Mans before it exited the driveway at 279 Citrus Road. The engine had raced loudly, and the car had been, in Andre's words, "really laying rubber." Andre then went on to state that he had seen two men inside the car. After the crash one of the men had run from the vehicle directly across the street to an empty lot beside Daddy's house.

The evidence was piling up against Daddy, and Carol hadn't even testified yet.

CHAPTER 36

CAROL

I was condemned to an agonizing limbo. I spent hours in anguished contemplation of facing Daddy across a crowded courtroom and repeating his admission of guilt for all to hear. A part of me was filled with solemn resolve that I would walk into that courtroom with my head held high and do what was expected of me. Another, less rational part of me wanted to run screaming.

By the sixth day of the trial, my nerves were stretched to the breaking point. I wandered a short distance down the corridor alone for a drink from the water fountain. As I approached the drinking fountain, I caught a flicker of movement out of the corner of my eye.

Directly across from me was a recessed alcove, and I gaped in horror at the sight of Daddy surrounded by a small cluster of his supporters. I was so overwhelmed by the sight of my father that all reasonable thought flew from my mind. I was trapped, and Daddy's eyes bored into me. I could feel them somehow commanding me to look at him. I was powerless. My Daddy was angry with me, and I had to make him happy again, just like when I was a little girl. The stern, loving eyes I had lived to please. Daddy.

The coldness of his gaze made me flinch. It seemed impossible that this tall, grim stranger in the hallway could be the same man who'd sired and raised me. He'd fed me, bathed me, come to me when my fear of the dark had overwhelmed me in the night. He'd made all the bad things disappear.

Blind panic engulfed me. The easy thing would have been to run to him, to hold him close to me, to beg him to make all the bad things disappear, as he had before. But that was impossible now. Through sheer willpower I forced my legs to move and began to walk back in the direction I'd come from. As I neared Daddy, I gathered what small amount of composure was left me and did the only thing I could. I squared my shoulders, inhaled deeply, and kept on walking. With each step, I moved a little further from my past.

When I made it back to the sequester room, I collapsed in a spasm of tears. I couldn't stop trembling. For the rest of the morning and long into the afternoon, my stomach twisted into knots. Someone had set up a small artificial Christmas tree on a table beside the room's only window. The tree was bedraggled, scruffy-looking, its artificial branches drooping sadly. There was a single, ratty strand of lights wound haphazardly around the limbs, and as I stared at the colorful bulbs, a flood of memories came rushing to me. Christmases and birthday parties; getting tucked into bed. Long talks and getting dressed up nice for Daddy. So many sweet memories.

Tom Porteous wrested me from my thoughts. He entered the room and sat on the desk before me. "Today's the day, Carol. We have a ten-minute recess. Then I'm going to call you to the stand."

Despite all the pretrial sessions with Tom, his hours of advice and encouragement and calming, I felt totally unprepared. I was sure I would not be able to go through with it. Not after just seeing Daddy. But I didn't have a choice anymore. I followed Tom from the room, feeling like a prisoner taking his final steps to the gallows.

I entered the courtroom to a sea of faces. I have never felt so naked and exposed and utterly alone.

The witness chair loomed before me. Tom Porteous had warned me that I would sit before a roomful of people who would be judging not only Daddy but also

the truth of my words. I had known before that some
would find me wanting, but now I really understood
that I, too, was on trial, in a way. I stepped up, raised my
right hand, and was sworn in by a uniformed officer of
the court.

I sat down in the chair, and pandemonium broke out.
To the left of me at the defense table, Daddy grabbed
an oxygen mask and clamped it to his face. Bob Broussard and Roy Price made a fruitless grab for Daddy as he
collapsed heavily to the floor. People gasped.

My eyes flew to the jury box. Most of the jurors were
leaning forward in their seats, necks craned to get a
better look. One young man actually stood up. A nurse
whipped a stretcher into the room. Paramedics lifted
Daddy's limp form onto the stretcher and wheeled him
to the side of the courtroom.

I clenched the arms of the witness chair, feeling as if
I'd just been slapped in the face. It had taken every
ounce of courage I possessed to enter the courtroom,
and in a matter of seconds Daddy had succeeded in
reducing my morale to shreds.

Judge Carr instructed me to step down from the
stand and to take a seat in the courtroom. I did as I was
told and slid into the first available bench. In the midst
of all the confusion I didn't realize that I was seating
myself directly behind the stretcher that still bore
Daddy. I stole a quick glance at his face. His eyes were
closed, but I'd seen his attacks too many times in the
past. I knew he was conscious. He wore the same mask
of suffering martyrdom that he'd always worn when
trying to gain our sympathy. The upturned corners of
his lips gave him the slightest suggestion of smugness.

It dawned on me as I watched him lie there, surrounded by nurses and friends, that he was actually
enjoying himself. He was a superb strategist, a great
actor, and at that moment he was playing to an audience of many. He relished the attention. In truth, I
don't think he could have done anything else at that
point. I'm certain Daddy knew in his heart that this

time he would not win and this was his last play. With a little luck and a damned good lawyer, he might have been able to repair the damage done by the three contradictory statements he had given Sergeant Gorman. He might even have found a way to get around the fact that the murder weapon was found in his possession. But there was no way he would ever get around, over, or under the one fact that stood out more clearly than any other: He was a man who stood before a court of law without the support of his own flesh and blood. His own children, who surely loved him, sat opposed to him, literally, and he could have no possible defense in the face of such intimate denial. I knew that when it came down to the wire, he would try to destroy me on the stand, and he had just tried. By his admission of guilt, he had made me his worst enemy.

CHAPTER 37

CAROL

Daddy recovered from his attack in short order. He was wheeled back to his place in the courtroom on a litter by a uniformed nurse. She parked Daddy almost directly in front of the witness stand, where I had taken my place again. He lay on his back, with a pillow under his head and an oxygen mask on his face. I kept my eyes from him as best I could, looking straight out over the courtroom to a spot on the far wall. I was denied the comfort of seeing my family, because I would have had to look right at Daddy to do so.

Tom approached the stand, a manila folder in his right hand. I stared uneasily at the folder, wondering what it might contain. He opened it and pulled out an eight-by-ten glossy photo, which he passed to me.

"Will you identify the person in the picture, Carol?" His eyes bore into mine, never flinching.

I drew in a deep breath and forced myself to look at the picture. It was like gazing into hell. Believe me, a picture is surely worth a thousand words, because no words could ever adequately describe the anguish that raged then through my mind and heart. The photo was an enlarged head shot of Mike Holland, obviously taken at the morgue. His pale blue eyes were open, glazed, *filled* with excruciating pain. Worse even than the pain was the utter disbelief frozen for all eternity in those blue depths.

Time ceased to exist. The people around me ceased to exist. The only thing that existed for me was the face in the photograph. The face that I'd once loved more than life itself. The face of my friend, my lover, the father of my daughter. Gone forever. Murdered by another man I'd also loved more than life itself. And that man had murdered so much more than Mike. He'd murdered the very essence of me. Murdered my dreams, my values, my happiness. Murdered my terrible need for roots and unity. Murdered my children's God-given right to a good and decent legacy. Murdered the closest thing I have ever had to a brother, George Westerfield. And here, at last, he'd murdered my love for him, the one thing that had sustained me all these days.

I was dimly aware that Tom had removed the photograph from my hand, dimly aware that he'd asked me a question.

"Carol," his tone was firm.

"It's Mike."

Judge Carr leaned forward and spoke into the microphone. "Will the witness please speak louder so the court may hear?"

Why couldn't he understand that I could barely breathe? That I was afraid if I opened my mouth, I would scream and keep on screaming till I was locked away?

"It's Mike—Mike Holland."

Porteous again. "Carol, are you related to the defendant in this case?"

"Yes. He's my father." Someone sniffed to the right of me. I turned sideways. It was a lady on the jury. A sweet, kind-faced lady. But all the tears in the world couldn't save me.

"Were you also related to the deceased, Mike Holland?"

"Yes. He was my husband."

"Were you legally married to the deceased at the time of his death?"

"We were legally married, but we had been separated for several months."

"Carol, will you tell the court about a conversation

you had with your father on the morning following your husband's death?"

His question flustered me for a second. I hadn't been prepared for it to come so soon. "My father called me to his home that morning. He met me in my car and sat in the front seat beside me."

Porteous prompted me. "Did your father say anything to you at this point in time?"

I gazed down at the litter, where Daddy still lay. He quickly covered his face with the oxygen mask.

"He said he'd called Mike over to his house, then waited for him outside. When Mike arrived, Daddy said, he'd entered the passenger side of the car. Then he told me . . ."

"He told you what?" urged Tom.

"He told me he shot Mike. He said he plugged him right through the heart."

There was utter silence in the courtroom. The air in the room had become as dead and lifeless as my own heart. A low moan escaped Daddy's lips. It echoed the moaning in my soul.

"Did he say anything else?" There was an urgent pleading in Tom's eyes.

"Yes. He said Mike's foot hit the gas pedal, and the car shot backward out of the driveway and hit a tree."

"I have no more questions for this witness." Tom walked back to the prosecution's table.

Roy Price rose from his seat at the defense table and strode over to the stand.

"How old are you, Carol?" There was undisguised loathing in his eyes.

"I'm twenty-six."

"You've stated under oath that you were estranged from your husband at the time of his death, is that correct?"

"Yes."

"Was this your first marriage?"

"No. I was married before."

"To whom?"

"Bruce Applegarth."

"Were you faithful to your first husband?"

Time for dirty tricks. Please, God, help me be ready for them.

"I was seeing Mike during my marriage to Bruce."

Price nodded his head as if to say, "Yes, you certainly were." Then he asked, "How many children do you have?"

"I have a son and a daughter."

Price nodded again. What was he leading up to?

"Who is the father of your daughter?"

I felt an intense flicker of hatred for Roy Price, and it was wonderfully refreshing. For the first time since taking the stand I felt alive. I would not give this man the satisfaction of knowing that he'd struck a terrible wound to my heart. Porteous's face registered a brief shock, but he did not object.

I was not about to make it easy for Price. "Bruce Applegarth is the legal father." I felt I was locked in mortal combat with this man in front of me.

Price moved in for the kill. "I will ask you once again, Mrs. Holland, and remind you that you are under oath. Who is the natural father of your daughter?"

I looked him right in the eye and spoke as calmly as I could. "Mike Holland."

There was a stirring in the courtroom. A woman in the third row leaned over and whispered something to the woman beside her. It didn't matter, because in the row in front of these two women sat the people I cared about. I took in their faces one by one, absorbing the love reflected there. *You can't hurt me now, Mr. Price. You don't know the meaning of hurt.*

"Are you dating a man by the name of Steve Donahue?"

"Yes." *And I love him dearly, Mr. Price, because his love comes without a price tag.*

"Does Mr. Donahue ever stay overnight at your house?"

"Yes." *And I'm grateful for that much, because without him I'm desperately alone.*

"In other words, Mrs. Holland, you were married to one man, and during this time you became pregnant with another man's child. Within a few short months of your second husband's death you were living with yet another man, am I right?"

"Yes." *He was trying to break me. But I had been broken before in ways he'd never dreamed of. And I wasn't ashamed of my love for Steve.*

"Do you know a John Smith?"

"Yes. He's my friend."

"Your friend." Price smiled tightly. "Did you ever have dinner with this friend of yours? Was there any romantic involvement between you and John Smith?"

"Absolutely not."

"What about Mark Wright? Is he also a friend?" Price made the word *friend* sound like something dirty.

"Yes."

"Did you ever have dinner with him?"

"No. I did not."

Price sighed heavily. "Carol, you have stated under oath that the defendant told you he entered the passenger side of Mike's car. Do you recall stating previously that the defendant leaned into the window, rather than actually having entered the car?"

Price's eyes measured me. "I don't believe I ever said that."

He shuffled some papers in his hand. "Are you willing to swear to that under oath?"

Was I? "Yes, I am."

He turned away from me as if disgusted. "I have no further questions."

I'm glad, I thought, because I have no more answers.

I was allowed to step down. The state rested.

Tom Porteous stopped me in the hallway just after I exited the courtroom. He seemed angry. "Why didn't you tell me about your daughter? I don't like surprises, Carol."

My own anger was hot in my throat—anger with him, with Daddy, with Roy Price, with the world. "I didn't tell you about my daughter because I never dreamed that my father would allow her name to be dragged through the court. And you allowed Roy Price to turn me into a tramp on the stand while you did nothing about it. And you had to show me that picture of Mike. What was that for? So I could carry around the memory of his dead face the rest of my life?"

"I showed you that picture for one reason, Carol. To remind you of why you took that stand in the first place."

"I don't need you to remind me of why I took the stand. But once I did, you could have at least allowed me to defend myself."

Tom smiled sweetly at me. "But you did, Carol, and better than I could have hoped you would."

I was reminded of my testimony late that evening, when all I wanted to do was to forget it. Nancy walked in the door at Mama's house and gravely handed me a newspaper.

Across the front page in bold black letters were my own words, forever immortalized in print: "He told me he shot Mike." The writer had called my testimony "the highlight of the courtroom drama." It may have been a highlight to some, but to me it had seemed a slow death.

CHAPTER 38

SHIRLEY

It was Friday, the seventh day of trial, when Daddy took the stand. It was a complete surprise to everyone in the courtroom. The defense began with drama. Elegantly dressed in a pewter suit and patterned tie, Daddy admitted for the first time in the presence of the jury that he had been inside the Pontiac Le Mans the night of September 11, 1976. In a low monotone he stated that Mike had shown up at his house uninvited, but that he'd agreed to speak with him in the privacy of his car.

"Upon entering the car," Daddy explained, his voice low, "Mike pulled a gun from the pocket of his sports coat and pointed it in my face. He demanded two thousand dollars from me, telling me that he wasn't asking for the money, he had to have it. I made a grab for the gun, there was a struggle. In the confusion of noise and motion the gun went off. I'm not sure how many times it fired, it happened so fast. The next thing I remember, the car was careening backward at a tremendous speed. I recall its crashing into a tree across the street. Upon impact I flew forward, cracking my head on the dash. At that point I was confused, disoriented, and on the verge of passing out. I suppose in a state of shock I ran from the car to the safety of my home. I can dimly recall showering, but beyond that I just don't know."

"Mr. Fagot," said Porteous smoothly in the cross-examination, "you're an attorney. You were certainly aware of the seriousness of what had occurred. Why didn't you go inside, pick up the phone, and call the police if you were indeed acting in defense of your life?"

"I don't know," Daddy replied, then hesitated. "I was in a state of confusion."

"Do you recall making a statement to Sergeant Gorman on the night of your son-in-law's death?"

"No, I do not."

"Do you recall making a statement to Sergeant Gorman three days later, while you were in the hospital for surgery on your eye?"

"No. I vaguely recall making a statement to Sergeant Gorman, but I have no idea what that conversation was about."

"Do you recall making a statement to Sergeant Gorman the day the thirty-eight used to kill Mike Holland was found in your home?"

"No."

"Do you have any idea why two bullets were fired into Mike Holland's head after he had already died?"

"No, I do not."

"How did you feel about your son-in-law, Mr. Fagot?"

"He was a no-good user." His voice was hard, flat.

"Did you kill your son-in-law?"

"I won't dignify that with an answer."

Roy Price called next Dr. Pallato, a psychiatrist who had examined Daddy. Neatly groomed, with dark hair and brown eyes, Dr. Pallato said that in his opinion Daddy had suffered from temporary amnesia brought on by the blow to his head. During cross-examination Porteous questioned the doctor as to whether or not temporary amnesia was common. Dr. Pallato allowed as to how it was fairly common, but not tremendously so. After much beating around the bush, Porteous got Dr. Pallato to admit that temporary amnesia occurred as the exception to the rule, rather than as the norm.

Perhaps the most interesting question Porteous asked the psychiatrist was whether he thought it possible to detect if someone was faking temporary amnesia. The doctor was unruffled. "Mr. Prosecutor, in my profession anything is possible. However, I would like to think that all my years of professional training have not been in vain."

Court was recessed for noon break. We returned to Carol's room, too tired to even consider going to lunch. Steve, Joe, and Ray offered to run out for hamburgers and coffee.

Carol seemed calm, almost tranquil for a change. I was glad that the worst seemed to be over for her. Or was it?

Joanne let out a long, weary sigh and said, "How much longer can this go on? I feel like I was born in this courthouse."

Nancy yawned, covering her mouth daintily with her hand. "Who knows? Maybe we're in hell. It feels like it, anyway." There were dark smudges under her eyes.

"How are you holding up, Nance?" I asked, concerned.

She shrugged her shoulders. "I'm hanging in there, I guess."

Joanne lit a cigarette, coughing as she puffed. She was smoking very heavily. But then, so was I by that point. "I wish they'd just get on with it. Find him guilty and stick his ass in prison, where it belongs." Joanne took another vigorous drag.

Nancy got testy. "I wish you wouldn't say things like that, Joanne."

"Why not?" Joanne was just as brittle. "That's how I feel."

Nancy shot daggers at her. "You know, Joanne, I'm sick of this big brave act of yours. You're not fooling anyone but yourself. You don't want Daddy to go to prison any more than I do."

"Speak for yourself," snapped Joanne.

Nancy's voice grew louder. "And you don't know how *I* feel."

"Please, girls," begged Mama, sitting between them.

"Well, what right does she have saying such things?

Does it ever cross her mind that it hurts me when she does that?" Nancy rose from her seat and crossed to the window by the Christmas tree.

Joanne picked at some imaginary piece of lint on her black pants. "And I'm tired of your whining and defending him, Nancy. He deserves everything he gets, and then some."

"Lay off, Joanne. You're upsetting her," said Carol, going to Nancy's side. "It's going to be okay, Nancy." She hugged Nancy.

"Humph," was all Joanne said to that.

I felt sorry for Joanne, despite her tough treatment of Nancy. I knew she had a right to feel bitter, and I also knew she would continue doing her best to pretend she had no feelings left for Daddy. If she had cut out all her emotions toward him, she wouldn't have been so bitter.

Nancy whirled on her, coming to stand before Joanne. "Look, I've had enough of you. I'm having a hard enough time accepting all of this."

Joanne's eyes blazed. "Accepting what? Tell me what you've accepted, Nancy, if anything."

She might as well have slapped her. Nancy's lips quivered. "You're right," she said. "I can't accept sitting in a courtroom watching my father's life go down the drain. I'm not made of stone like you are." She collapsed in her chair and buried her face in her hands.

I gave Joanne a cutting look. "I hope you're happy now."

"Well, I have feelings, too, Shirley. Just because I don't wear them on my sleeve doesn't mean they're not there. You want to know how *I* feel?" Her hazel eyes were dark with emotion. "You want me to tell you how I feel every time I look at Kelly and Lori and try to think of the day that I'll have to explain to them why their Daddy's dead. Do you want me to tell you how I feel every time I go to George's grave? I feel like it's *my* fault. *That's* how I feel. And every time I look at Daddy in that courtroom, I hate him more. I wish that he had died when he had his heart attack. I could have at least lived with that. I hope they sentence him to death. At least it would be quick—not like the slow dying, the inch-by-inch dying, he's sentenced me to."

She seemed to fold under the weight of her own terrible words. There were tears in Mama's eyes and tears in Carol's eyes, and soon everyone in the damned room was crying.

We returned to the courtroom for the afternoon. Bruce Applegarth was called to the stand. His discomfort was obvious in his inability to keep his hands still. He played with the buttons on his shirt, twisting them nervously as Mr. Price approached.

"Mr. Applegarth, will you please tell the court your relationship to Leonard Fagot?"

"He's my ex–father-in-law; I was married to his daughter Carol."

"How long have you known the defendant?"

"About ten years."

"Were you acquainted with Mike Holland?"

"Yes, I knew him."

"What was your opinion of him?"

"Well, he had a lousy temper, and he drank a lot."

"Were you aware of any conflict between Mr. Fagot and Mike Holland?"

"Yes. Mr. Fagot was always complaining to me that Mike had stolen things from him."

"Did Mr. Fagot ever mention what was missing?"

"Yes. Once it was money, and once a gun was stolen from the house while Mike was there."

"Do you know what type of gun?"

"Yes. It was a thirty-eight automatic."

In three long strides Porteous reached the witness stand. "Mr. Applegarth, you've stated that you were acquainted with the deceased, Mike Holland, but isn't it a fact that you barely knew him personally?"

"I knew him well enough," Bruce protested.

"Your wife divorced you to marry Mike Holland. How did you feel about that?"

Bruce shrugged. "That was a long time ago."

"Then you're saying you bore no ill will toward Mike Holland?"

"Not really."

"Mr. Applegarth, you've stated that Mike drank a lot, haven't you?"

"Yes."

"Did you ever see him drunk?"

Bruce looked sheepish. "Well, no, not really. But I've heard it from several people."

"You've also stated Holland had a lousy temper. Did you ever witness an outburst of this temper?"

"No, but plenty of people did."

"So, you never witnessed Holland drunk, nor did you ever see him violent." Turning away, Porteous said, "I have no further questions for this witness."

I could not see how Bruce's testimony had proven useful to Daddy's case. In fact, it seemed to me that it had been damaging to him. For that matter, I wondered just what the defense's case really was. It seemed so far to have flip-flopped somewhere between self-defense and temporary amnesia. I wasn't able to see any clear-cut tactic of defense.

Roy Price asked for and was granted a ten-minute recess. Only a few people exited the courtroom; most were unwilling to risk losing their seats. Seats in this trial were a precious commodity.

I stretched my legs and rubbed the back of my neck to relieve all the tension that had settled there. I could hear people whispering in the row behind me. A man stated clearly that Daddy was a "goner." I didn't appreciate the comment, but I had to agree with him. Things were looking bad; that was for sure.

Court resumed. Roy Price said, "I call Mark Wright to the stand."

I was flabbergasted. What in the world could Mark possibly contribute to Daddy's defense?

I was even more taken aback when Mark entered the courtroom. He shuffled in, escorted by two deputies, manacles attached to a chain around his waist. He wore faded prison garb with his inmate number stenciled across the pocket of his shirt. I remembered then having heard through the grapevine that Mark was doing time for possession of marijuana.

Several of the jurors turned curious eyes on Mark, and the whispers started again among the spectators. Someone tittered loudly in the back of the courtroom, and Judge Carr banged his gavel with a stern look. The trial was turning into a three-ring circus.

Mark was sworn in. When the rustles and whispers died down, Mr. Price approached the stand. "Mr. Wright, you were a friend of Mike Holland's for a long time, is that correct?"

"That's right," Mark answered, nodding.

"Was Mike a heavy drinker?"

"Yes."

"Was he violent?"

"When he drank, he was violent."

"No further questions."

Porteous started his cross-examination in an affable manner.

"Mr. Wright, how long were you and Mike Holland friends?"

"I knew Mike for twenty years. We grew up together."

"Was Mike what you would call a good friend?"

Mark's dark eyes grew thoughtful. "Yes, he was a good friend."

Porteous moved closer to the witness stand. "Twenty years is a long time. I guess you and Mike had some pretty good times together."

"Yes, we did."

"Did you and Mike remain friends until the time of his death?"

"Yes."

"Then you must have taken his death very hard."

"I did."

Porteous cupped his chin in his right hand, as if he

were deep in thought. "You've stated under oath that Mike became violent when drinking. Did you ever see him drunk, or violent, Mark?"

"No." Mark raised his manacled hand to scratch his chin.

"What leads you to believe he was violent?"

"I've heard talk."

"Who did you hear this talk from, Mark?"

Mark looked down at his lap. "I can't recall, just around."

"Mr. Wright, you have stated under oath that your lifelong, good friend was a violent drunk, and yet you cannot recall ever having seen him that way. I wonder how you define the term *friend?*"

On the trial's tenth day Carol was in the courtroom as a spectator. Steve sat beside her, holding her hand. Mama was next to Joanne and Joe, her back straight as she surveyed the crowd gathered near the doorway. There was an air of excitement, the sense of an approaching climax, that made me anxious. Things would soon come to a close, and no matter what happened, I'd lose.

Roy Price began his closing argument to the court in a high, slightly shrill voice. He addressed the jury, but kept his eyes on Daddy, who lay on his litter.

"You have seen the evidence presented, and contrary to what Mr. Porteous will tell you, the state has not proven its case beyond a reasonable doubt."

Daddy gripped an oxygen mask with his right hand as if it were a lifeline.

Price went on to list the weaknesses in the state's case and claimed that Carol twisted the facts in her testimony. The defense contended that Mike had tried to rob Daddy, and Daddy had killed him in self-defense, suffering amnesia as a result of the ensuing car accident.

Mr. Price's voice lowered as he turned toward Ruth and Paul Holland. "All of us feel a deep sympathy for Mike's death and for his family, who have suffered and will continue to suffer. Mr. Porteous has suggested to you that the defense intends to play on the sympathy of the court, but it is not your sympathy I seek—it is your compassion. Leonard Fagot stands before you now, accused of a particularly heinous crime, but I say to you that Mr. Fagot is a victim of that crime, rather than the perpetrator the state would make him out to be. His fate lies in the verdict that this honorable court will decree, and I ask that that verdict be one of acquittal."

The defense was finished.

Tom Porteous's booming baritone described the events leading to Mike's death and Daddy's arrest in the days following the murder. The jury, he pointed out, had to be clear on the issue of reasonable doubt. It was not something to be taken lightly, and as such the jurors would have to sort through the evidence presented and rely upon their consciences to guide them. He went on to say that in spite of the defense's attempts to impugn the character of Carol Holland, she had spoken the truth, as was evident in the fact that she had not lied even to protect her own child. He pounced on the testimonies of Bruce Applegarth and Mark Wright, saying that these statements bordered on the absurd. They were shot full of holes, he said, gross exaggerations of pure hearsay. He reminded that jury that neither Bruce nor Mark had been able to cite a single incident of violence on Mike Holland's part. He then reached for the thirty-eight pistol on the evidence table and waved it in front of the jury. Most of the jurors sat straight in their chairs, suddenly alert.

"The defense would have you believe," he said, "that Mike Holland stole this gun from the defendant and then came back several months later to rob him with it. I say to you that Leonard Fagot is lying, for in spite of the attempts of the defense to shroud the ownership of this gun beneath a cloud of obscurity, we know from the testimony given by Mr. Marsolan that the gun belongs to none other than Leonard Fagot. I submit to you that on the night of September 11, 1976, Leonard Fagot waited outside his home with this gun in his possession. When Mike Holland pulled into the driveway, Fagot entered the car on the passenger side and shot him twice in the chest. As Mike was in the agonizing throes of death, his foot jammed on the accelerator, and the still-running car shot backward out of the driveway. During this mad rush backward Fagot panicked, because he couldn't be certain that Holland was dead."

Without warning Porteous whipped the gun to his head and held it poised there, his finger on the trigger. "So Mr. Fagot pumped two more bullets into Mike Holland's head to make certain that he died."

Two loud clicks echoed through the courtroom. The room buzzed. His voice, loud and mocking, continued above the noise.

"These were not the actions of a sick and dazed man, ladies and gentlemen of the jury. These were the actions of a vicious killer. The defense would have you believe that Mr. Fagot hid the most damaging evidence of all, the gun with Mike Holland's blood and hair still embedded in the cylinder, because he was suffering from amnesia. I say that Fagot hid the gun because he believed himself to be above the law, smarter than all of us, and accountable to no one for his actions. You may ask yourselves what motive Fagot had for killing his son-in-law, but bear in mind that it is not the state's responsibility to prove a motive in the case of second-degree murder. We can only surmise that Mr. Fagot took it upon himself to play God. He took upon himself the right to execute Mike Holland. The prosecution has done its share. We have proven beyond any reasonable doubt that murder was committed by Leonard Fagot. We have shouldered the burden of proof, and now it's up to you, the members of the jury, to hold him responsible for his actions and to bring in a verdict of guilty of second-degree murder."

CHAPTER 39

CAROL

There was nothing left to do but wait. We went with Tom Porteous and Mike's parents to Tom's office across the street from the courthouse to await the verdict.

Mike's mother sat on a chair between her husband and Mama. She clutched her purse to her bosom and fidgeted nervously in the chair. She had aged outwardly in the ten days the trial had dragged on. Her bright blue eyes, so like Mike's, had lost much of their previous luster, and her shoulders sagged as if she'd been forced to carry some heavy burden. But there was a strength in Ruth Holland, a strength that had been forged from generations of hardworking landowners. Endless chores had fallen on Ruth's shoulders over her years, but she had set herself to the task at hand and done an admirable job of it. She'd toiled and planted throughout the seasons, feeding her offspring with the fruits of her labor. She was a proud woman who relied on simple faith in God to carry her through the rough times.

After several minutes of sipping coffee and exchanging small talk, we all fell silent.

We were at the end. I, for one, was not happy with either possible outcome—win or lose. To win was to live with the knowledge that Daddy would spend the rest of his life in prison. To lose was to know that all I had lost on the road to truth had been in vain. Then I remembered the look on Mike's dead face. I vowed that Mike would not become what George Westerfield had—another trophy on Daddy's shelf.

Forty-five minutes into the jury's deliberations, the

phone on Tom's desk rang. My heartbeat quickened, and everyone came to attention.

Tom pulled nervously on a cigarette, nodding his head, and said "uh-huh" several times into the receiver. I wanted to scream.

He finally hung up the telephone and faced us. "The jury has asked Judge Carr to define the difference between second-degree murder and manslaughter." His features were composed, but you could see the worry in his eyes.

"What does that mean?" asked Ruth.

Tom cleared his throat. "Well, I think it's a positive sign, Mrs. Holland. It would indicate to me that the jury is not considering an acquittal at this time."

Joanne asked the question uppermost on my mind. "What if he is acquitted?"

Tom exhaled slowly, blowing out a thin stream of cigarette smoke. "It's unlikely. But"—he paused, his eyes on Joanne—"if he walks this time, I promise you I'll do everything within my power to arrest him for the murder of George Westerfield."

His expression hardened. "I'm going to bring him down, one way or another."

I had no doubt that he meant his words. He'd already spoken to Joanne about exhuming George's body, should it be necessary to do so. The arm of Tom Porteous's law was far-reaching. It would poke and pry into every sordid corner of our lives if need be. Tom demanded justice, and I was certain he would have it, no matter what the cost to us. I wasn't confident, though, that any of us could go through all of this again. Or would want to.

An uneasy silence settled over the room. Finally Ruth Holland spoke. Her voice was soft and sad. "I always had a bad feeling inside me that Michael would come to harm. He was always different, with a little bit of the wild in him. He teased his sisters unmercifully, changed the grades on his report cards, sneaked his Daddy's beer out of the fridge, and hot-rodded around town with his friends when he should have been in bed." She paused, gave a wistful smile of memory.

"Seems like I spent my life worrying about him. And I was always angry with him. Finally he joined the navy, and that was a relief, because I thought the service would keep him safe, maybe knock some of the wildness out of him. I should have known better." She sighed. "He got out of the navy more restless than ever. Seems like he was always searching for a way to make life fun. I tried to tell him there was more to life than having fun. He'd always tell me the same thing—'Mom, you live your life, and I'll live mine.' And he did. He lived his, and I lived mine, and we never did see eye to eye. He's gone now, and I miss him more than I can say. But I can never say that his dying young surprises me. I think for Michael it was just always meant to be."

Mama drew in a shuddering breath, on the verge of breaking down. Ruth Holland laid her hand on Mama's. "Don't cry for Michael, Shirley. His life is over. And don't blame yourself. Guilt is awful hard to live with; believe me, I know. Best we blame it on fate. What's meant to be will be."

I wished that I had her simple faith, her unquestioning acceptance of life's cruel blows. She was right in a way. Something had steered Daddy along the path that had eventually led to this moment. Maybe all of us were simply pawns destined to fulfill the whims of fate.

The telephone rang again. This time Tom was on the phone for less than a second before hanging up the receiver. He rose to his feet and stabbed his just-lit cigarette out in an ashtray already filled to overflowing.

"Time to go. The verdict is in," he announced brusquely. He was the prosecutor then—no more, no less.

The courtroom was tense and electric. I sat between Steve and Mama, with Joanne, Joe, Nancy, Shirley, and Ray pulling in the ranks on either side of us. Turning sideways, I caught Shirley's eye. Her eyes were filled with sorrow, beneath which lay a strength and wisdom beyond her nineteen years. I looked at Mama, Joanne, and Nancy, and was humbled to see that same courage in their faces.

The jury entered the room. Twelve faces showed that this hadn't been easy for them, either. Some seemed angered, others resigned. They all looked spent.

Judge Carr cleared his throat and addressed the jury. "Ladies and gentlemen, have you reached a verdict?"

"We have."

A uniformed officer of the court took the written verdict from the foreman of the jury and passed it solemnly to Judge Carr. The judge's face revealed nothing of what he read or how it affected him. He passed the verdict back to the uniformed officer and requested that he read it aloud.

I suddenly became aware of a stinging pain in my hands. Looking down, I saw they were curled into tight little balls, my long fingernails digging into the palm of each.

"State of Louisiana versus Leonard John Fagot, criminal docket number 762116," declared the officer of the court in a loud, clear voice.

I'd been living for this moment, and dreading it, for months, almost years. The little girl in me screamed for her Daddy. For someone to save him from what would happen next.

"We, the members of the jury, find the defendant guilty as charged for the crime of second-degree murder."

My heart sank to the floor. I couldn't move. Shirley was sobbing. Mama sat bent over. Nancy and Joanne were motionless, their faces pale. Getting to his feet, Roy Price requested a poll of the jury. The word *guilty* rang out across the courtroom twelve times. Daddy blanched, and Marty stood firm beside him. Then she turned toward me, her eyes shooting daggers into mine.

Price and Broussard ushered Daddy out through the side door. I watched him go, knowing that I would not see him again. I swallowed down that pain for the time being.

Tom Porteous approached me, his hand outstretched. I clasped his hand in mine only because it was expected of me. There was a look of pure triumph in his eyes. He couldn't possibly expect me to share his feeling.

"We won." His words were simple, but they said a lot. What in God's name had we won? Where was the joy of victory? My family was blown apart; the father I adored, who'd shaped who I was, would be going to prison.

A soft hand touched my arm, and I turned to face Ruth Holland. Her eyes were ravaged by grief. I saw none of the joy of victory there—only a sorrow that went too deep to contain.

"Bless you, Carol," she said, her voice breaking. "Bless all of you. Without you there would have been no justice for my son's death." She hugged me close to her before turning away.

Justice. A sorry substitute for George's and Mike's lives.

I was still standing there when Aunt Lacey appeared at my side from out of nowhere. She was shaking, and her blue eyes flashed. "Are you happy now? You've killed your father, you know. There's no way he'll survive this."

"Aunt Lacey, I don't know if I'll ever be happy again."

Her features twisted. I could feel her hatred as though it were a physical thing. It came at me with the force of a slap.

"Your father has done everything in the world for you. More than any other father would do! For all of you!" She whirled around to my sisters. "All you have ever done is take from him, and you've given nothing back! None of you! You've no loyalty, and I'm deeply ashamed for all of you!"

She was wrong if she thought I was going to take that quietly. "And you have no shame for what your brother did."

"Whatever he did or didn't do, he's my brother, flesh and blood."

Joanne had been holding herself back until then. "Mike Holland was somebody's flesh and blood."

Lacey sneered. "Since when did all of you become so self-righteous?"

"The day we realized we couldn't live with it anymore."

My aunt didn't bat an eye. "Believe me when I tell you that I speak for all of us. There are some things that can't be forgiven."

I nodded. "You're right about that. You are so right about that."

We stayed in the courtroom, waiting for the crowd to thin out before heading for the exit. Then I led us out, with Steve behind me, hand on my shoulder, guiding me through the crowd. I had barely gone through the doorway when I glanced up and saw my cousin Beth coming at me. Her teeth were bared in fury, and her fingers curled like talons over my face.

"You bitch!" she shrieked, and clawed wildly at me.

From behind me Steve lunged for Beth, almost dragging me down to the ground with the weight of his body. He caught her by the shoulder and shoved her backward. The crowd, already charged from the drama of the trial, surged forward, pushing to get a good view of the fracas.

Beth's husband, Mel, rushed Steve and yelled at the top of his lungs, "No one shoves my wife!" Steve put one arm forward and stopped Mel dead in his tracks before forcing him aside. Then Beth's father, my Uncle Ralph, a tall, strapping man in his late forties bore down on Steve from behind.

I was about to shout a warning to Steve when Joe charged Ralph and punched him right in the face. A uniformed man, perhaps a policeman or officer of the court, finally broke up the fracas.

The episode was embarrassing, childish, and dangerous. It also was the breaking point for all concerned in the family. The unspoken commitment that had once existed between us had become irrevocably null and void. Each side had taken its own stand, and no room remained for arbitration. The ties between us were severed forever.

CHAPTER 40

CAROL

Daddy had been released from jail on bond after his conviction to await his sentencing, scheduled for December 28. We had been through enough; we didn't attend. It was more than we could bear. On December 28th Daddy was sentenced to forty years in prison at hard labor without benefit of probation, parole, or suspension of sentence. Roy Price filed a notice of appeal, which was granted, with a deadline of March 1, 1978. Daddy remained free on bond pending the outcome of that appeal.

Our lives had been on hold for so long, it seemed almost incredible that we might once again resume our ordinary routines, that we could pick up a newspaper without seeing our names in it. When you live with the abnormal long enough, you begin to appreciate the serenity of normal day-to-day existence.

Even now, when I hear people complain that their lives have become boring, filled with the same things day in and day out, I want to say to them, "Be grateful for small kindnesses." Until you have lived in a constant state of upheaval, caught up in fear, anger, and grief, you can't appreciate things like contentment and peace of mind. Even boredom.

Still, having lived under such stress for seven years, I was left with an emptiness, as the victim of a hurricane is the day after. When you've been so caught up in the fierceness of that storm, so afraid that you won't survive, you're enormously grateful just to greet the miraculous calm that follows. Then you start to look around, and you see the terrible havoc the storm has left in its wake. That's when you become filled with this curious emptiness, because facing your fear of the storm was easier than facing the devastating loss the storm wrought. And we had lost so much.

Daddy was fond of the old cliché "There's nothing to fear but fear itself." Maybe he was right. Fear is such a powerful emotion that over time it begins to erode the spirit. I had lived on the razor's edge for so long, something vital inside me seemed close to dying. I felt depleted, not quite whole. I'd been losing something I'd always taken for granted, and I couldn't put a finger on what that something might be. I searched in my heart for a long time after those dark days until I came to know that what I'd lost along the way was a good measure of my human dignity, and with that knowledge came the pain that self-awareness often brings. Pain is a wonderful cleansing agent. It fills you with a profound desire to find a cure.

I took a good, hard look at myself and did not like what I saw. Fate had not been kind to me. And I had not been kind to myself. I had been wounded over and over again, but never mortally. I was still very much alive. There were people in my life whom I loved very much, and I had mistakenly placed every one of them second to Daddy.

For as long as I could remember, he'd consumed my world. It was as if someone had handed me a hunk of modeling clay when I was young and asked me to create the perfect father out of it. I kneaded it and fashioned it into my own conception of what a perfect father should be—a big, strong man full of things like honor, courage, and power. Then I somehow breathed life into the clay, and my perfect father magically came alive. It seemed as if I had created him myself, that he lived up to all my expectations and needs. The reality was that Daddy gave me the clay and guided my hands to make a model of him. My concept of a perfect Daddy came from what I was told and shown.

When, in later years, Daddy began to display qualities that I hadn't given him, that he hadn't wanted me to see before—such as selfishness, avarice, and cruelty—my perfect father lost his shape. I tried my best to remold him, to change my thinking to accept those things, but I failed, because I'd lost that childish innocence I once had. So I found a way to make him perfect again. I expounded his virtues and diminished his vices. Daddy had become unlovable, and I so needed to love him that I just took to loving my model and not the man himself.

In facing myself, I was also able to face my fears. I discovered that at the root of those fears lay a healthy dose of guilt. I'd believed in my heart that I'd wronged Daddy by going to the police. I'd believed that the worst thing a child can do is betray the parent who has given him life. In truth, my feelings of guilt were no more than a cop-out. A way to hide from the truth that Daddy had gotten his just deserts.

Mama was stunned by the severity of Daddy's sentence. Her reaction was understandable. Deep in her heart, despite everything, she'd believed—as all of us, including Daddy, had—that he was above the law. He'd trained us to think that, and we'd been very willing pupils.

One day shortly after the New Year I came across her leafing through a box of old photographs. I stood in the alcove of the dining room, not wanting to intrude on such a private moment. There was a sad, whimsical expression on her face as she gazed at one particular snapshot. I had to know what it was, so I crossed the room to her. She smiled gently.

"He had the world in the palm of his hand, Carol. He had such goals, such ambition; he wanted to set the world on fire."

She passed me the photograph she'd been holding. It was a picture of Daddy in cap and gown, taken on the day he'd graduated from Tulane Law School. The tassel on his cap hung cockily to one side, and the smile on his young face was a mile wide. In one arm he held Nancy, in the other arm me. I was three then. At his feet, clinging to his robe and gazing adoringly into his face, was five-year-old Joanne. It was the kind of picture you might find in any family's box of old photos, but at the same time it was unique. In a split second the photographer—Mama, no doubt—had captured the essence of all our family had been. The photo spoke of love, happiness, and oneness. It spoke of dreams to that point fulfilled, and dreams yet to be realized. More than anything, it spoke of hope, a virtue that had for so long been denied us.

As I gazed at that photo, a flurry of emotion stirred within me. There had been hope once; it was there in the faces of all of us in the photo. And what was hope, but the expectation of something desired, the promise of something yet to be achieved?

There was so much left to be fulfilled in our lives. "It seems incredible." Mama sighed. "A lifetime ago. And I can't help wondering why it all happened. Did we have too much? Was it some sort of punishment for having it too good?"

"Maybe. Maybe there's some terrible force that extracts payment in full for all the wrong that people do."

Mama shook her head sadly. "But it was your father who did wrong. Why are we having to pay for it?"

"Maybe we've been judged guilty by association. Maybe Daddy's guilt has become ours."

There was such bleakness in Mama's eyes. Such despair.

"You're right, Carol. You're right. His guilt has become mine. I mean, I blame myself for not seeing a long time ago the kind of man he really was. I loved him, I bore his children, and I thought I knew him. I admired his drive and his ambition. I thought they were signs of strength, and I still do; but when his strength was shot through with ruthlessness, I chose to look the other way. I convinced myself that he had to be ruthless to get ahead. It always frightened me. And now I understand that my looking the other way only made things worse for all of us."

I had been so blinded by my own guilt, I hadn't realized that Mama had shouldered her own. "Mama, please don't blame yourself. The things Daddy did have nothing to do with you."

"They have everything to do with me, Carol, because they have affected everyone I love. I've watched my girls suffer, seen your pain, and felt completely and utterly powerless to help you cope. I live daily with the fear that you girls might not come out of all this in one piece, emotionally. That we might not be able to survive together as a family. I worry. Have there been too many wounds, and too much sorrow? I really wonder if someday it'll be too hard to look at each other because we're all afraid of reopening the wounds."

Her fears were real. Could we always live together with this hanging over us?

She continued. "And Joanne. I know that she's being eaten up by her bitterness. She was always a precocious, headstrong child, always so full of life. Now look at her. She's unbending, unforgiving, and just too bitter for a woman only thirty. And then there's Nancy. I guess I'd have to say that Nancy was my happiest child. She was always so naive, and so dependent on me and your dad, that I was overprotective of her. I'm not sure now that I should have protected her so much. She doesn't seem able to comprehend all that's happened, or to accept even a small part of it. I wonder how she will go on without coming to terms with her life as it is now."

I had no answers for her. These were a mother's questions, born of a mother's deep love and concern. She was baring her heart to me, as I had bared my heart to her so many times before. She needed to do this, to share the pain so she could begin to heal.

When she spoke again, her voice was soft as a gentle breeze. "Carol, you were my sentimental dreamer. You always reminded me of when I was a child. Always needing to know what everything meant. Always looking at life through rose-colored glasses. I always wondered how a child so much like myself would come to be such a daddy's girl. Oh, all my girls adored their father, but you idolized him, put him way up high on a pedestal."

I suddenly felt ashamed, stupid. I stared down at the tabletop.

"Carol, all children need heroes. You're a romantic, an idealist. And with your father's incredible war record, and the way he always talked about the war to you girls, it's only natural that you would have felt the way you did about him. But how do you feel about him now?"

I looked up at her, surprised by her question. "I'm not sure how I feel about him, Mom. Part of me hates him. Part of me pities him. Another part of me loves him—not because he was my hero, but because he's my father. I'll have to learn to cope with my feelings the best I can. But I don't believe the day will ever come that I will turn away from all of you because remembering is too painful. I think the one who will suffer the most will be Shirley. She was only a child when everything started, and she's still just a kid."

Mama toyed with a cold cigarette. "Shirley was a joy to me when she was born. I'd had a couple of miscarriages during the seven years after Nancy. I was very sick while I was carrying Shirley and had to stay in bed most of the time. Do you remember that? Yes, but I didn't want to lose another baby, so it was worth it. Your dad was hoping for a boy, as he had with each of you, but once Shirley was born, he adored her, just as he'd adored the rest of you. Shirley was such a pleasant, well-behaved child. She's always been a loner. You girls were so much older than she was that she grew up by herself. She's gone through a lot, and I worry myself sick about her."

She paused, her fingertips lightly tracing the outline of her gold cigarette lighter on the table before her. When she finally started again, her voice was hoarse and raw with emotion. "You father has left a terrible legacy. Not only for you girls but for your children, too. When I look at those kids and see their innocent faces and think about what he has done to them, what he's taken from them . . . I could kill him with a glad heart."

Jarring words. She locked eyes with me.

"I think about it all the time, Carol. How easy it would be to simply walk up to him and shoot him right between the eyes. It would be worth any penalty I had to pay just to know that he was gone. Just to know that I didn't have to spend one more hour of my life fearing for the lives of all of you."

Harsh lines had appeared in her face, lines alien to her nature. In all my life I had never seen her look like that. "Mama, are you alright?"

Her face softened a bit as she squeezed my hand. "I guess you think what I said is horrible, and I know it is. But there you have it." She smiled at me. Just saying it seemed to have drained some of the tension out of her.

"How about a cup of tea?" I asked. Tea had always helped to relax her when she was upset.

She nodded. As I rose from my chair, she continued. "Carol, there's another reason I could do it with a glad heart."

"What other reason?"

"Because George Westerfield was the son I never had and always wanted."

On a late February night I sat alone in the den on St. Paul Avenue. Shirley and Ray weren't home, the children were sleeping, and so was Mama. It was one-thirty A.M., and I'd poured myself a shot of Drambuie, in the hope that the liquor might make me drowsy. I had been having difficulty getting to sleep the last few nights.

There was a knock on the door. I opened it, and there was Bruce Applegarth with a half-empty bottle of Heineken in hand. I was surprised. I hadn't seen Bruce since the trial and hadn't expected to. I invited him inside, and he took a seat on the sofa. He looked older than I'd remembered. His blond hair had begun to thin on top, and he'd gotten a little fat. His eyes, though, were still a clear, honest blue. He wore an odd half-smile on his face and seemed ill at ease.

"It's good to see you, Bruce."

"The same here," he said. "I've been to see L.J."

"Oh," I said lightly. No need to get all emotional with Bruce. "How is he?"

"He's in pretty bad shape, I guess."

"You look like you're feeling kind of down."

He shrugged his shoulders. "Yeah. He blames me for losing the trial." He looked away from me then, embarrassed for me to see the emotion in his eyes.

"You don't believe that, do you?" I asked, knowing he probably did.

"I guess not."

"Bruce, you know something? I blamed myself, too. I think all of us feel partly to blame."

"Do you know what he said to me Carol? He looked me right in the eye and said, 'You killed me, Bruce. You're the one that's put me in my grave.'"

I felt terrible for him. "You know Daddy; he's happiest when he's making someone else feel responsible for things. He's upset, and he's striking out at you because it makes him feel better."

"I guess so, but it isn't what he said that bothers me." He paused and took a long pull on the beer. "It's what I thought after he said it that upsets me."

"And what was that?"

He picked at the Heineken label for a second, then stopped. "I thought, Somebody had to, L.J., because you deserved it."

I hadn't known Bruce felt that way. A little respect for him crept back into me. "He's been deserving it for a long time."

"He won't go to prison. Prison's not his style. He'll kill himself first."

"I know."

Bruce finished off the beer. "I never believed the day

would come when they'd finally catch him. I always felt he was invincible. He was always too smart. Smarter than the law, I figured. Now I don't know.

"There's something about him," he continued. "I don't know just what it is. Something I always admired. It's sad, isn't it?" He smiled gently at me.

"Very sad."

"I wanted to help him. But he wanted me to lie on the stand and say that Mike always carried a gun. I couldn't do that."

"Face it, Bruce. You don't lie very well."

The beer and the memories had made him thoughtful, so I asked Bruce to tell me what really happened the day Daddy lost his hand.

"On the way to La Place I noticed his left arm. His watch was missing. I could tell because, you know, he always wore a watch with an elastic band. That morning the watch was gone, but there were marks on his arm, indentations left from the band. I didn't think about it until a few days later. Then it hit me that he'd taken the watch off shortly before we left. I kept wondering why he would have taken his watch off. It bothered me. Once I started thinking about it, I couldn't stop. Suddenly I remembered how he'd been the night before we left. He was having a sort of seance, I guess. I don't know what else to call it."

"A seance?" I asked. "With candles or something, you mean?"

"No, nothing like that. He just had some kind of weird music playing. But he sat in his chair in the library staring straight ahead, almost like he was in a trance, like he was psyching himself up for God only knows what. It gave me the willies, so I got the hell out of there.

"Anyway, the day of the hunting trip, when we left the truck, he insisted that I go in one direction and Marty go in the other. I swear to you that I hadn't been gone from sight more than a minute or two when I heard the gun go off. When I got to him, he was so in control, so *composed* about the whole thing. He'd shot his hand off, it was hanging by a string, and he was calm about it, totally in control. He gave me the runaround about slipping on a bottle and the dogs getting twisted around his leg. So help me God, there was a bottle on the ground, and I believed him, because how in the hell could I believe anything else?"

"I believed him for a long time, too, until I began piecing it together."

"I don't know," he said. "It just blows my mind. I'm going to tell you something, Carol, that I've never told anyone before. When I heard that gun go off, I hit the ground. I thought he was shooting at me."

So Bruce had been haunted by fears of his own. Even then. "Did you ever feel that you were in danger? I mean, over the trip to Colombia?"

His eyes were troubled. "Yes and no. A part of me was scared shitless, but another part of me wanted to believe that he . . ." His voice trailed off.

"That he cared about you?" I prompted.

"What can I say?" He smiled awkwardly.

"No need to say anything, Bruce. All any of us wanted was to believe he cared."

Joanne and Joe purchased a modern three-bedroom home along the banks of Lake Pontchartrain in Kenner, Louisiana. Joanne went to work as a sales consultant for an interior design corporation, and Joe continued the job in sales he'd had for several years. It was difficult to know exactly how Joanne was reacting to Daddy's conviction. Other than the darkened circles under her hazel eyes, there was no change in her appearance. She wrapped her feelings like a cloak around her, never showing the inner conflict I knew had to be there.

Nancy continued to go about her everyday life, dropping Kristen off at a day-care center in Metairie, coming home at night, and spending much of her time at the apartment she had recently moved to. Like Joanne, she hadn't said a word about Daddy's conviction or his sentencing. We knew she had her own conflicted feelings, so all of us respected her right to remain silent on the subject, but I worried that she was devastated inside. I sensed that she had never really come to terms with our involvement in Daddy's arrest. I didn't believe she condemned us for what we'd done—she loved us too much for that—but I didn't feel that she quite forgave us, either.

One evening I visited her at her apartment. She sat on the sofa, her back straight and stiff against the cushion, knees drawn up to meet her chest. I smiled at her, but she only faintly returned it. I didn't know what to say, but I had to start somewhere. "Nancy, I know how you feel," I began.

"Do you?" There were fine lines of sadness etched around her grim eyes, and her cheeks were sunken beneath her prominent cheekbones. She was twenty-five years, but she looked ten years older.

"You're right, Nancy. I probably don't know how you feel."

"It was so cut-and-dried for you and Joanne and Mama. You did what you had to do, and I don't begrudge you that. Matter of fact, I'm glad it wasn't me who had to make that choice. I don't know what I would have done if I'd been in your shoes. Maybe I'd have felt as strongly as you did if it had been Gary who died instead of Mike. All I know is that everything in my life has changed. I feel as though I have no roots, as if I've been dug up and planted in some foreign soil and I haven't adjusted to it yet."

She leaned her head back and closed her eyes. "I wish it were possible to go back in time, to fly right back to when I was happiest. I don't like this feeling I have. I'm not used to being sad."

Of all of us, Nancy had been born the happiest. All her life she'd been as happy-go-lucky as one possibly could be, and sadness and depression had been foreign to her before everything happened.

"I keep picturing Daddy the way he was," she continued. "You know, before he changed. I see him working in the yard, pulling weeds, planting shrubs, pushing that wheelbarrow around, sitting in his chair in the library, whatever. I can't relate that man to the one he is now, no matter how hard I try." She paused a moment, staring at me. "There was some good in him, don't you think?"

There was a pleading in her blue eyes, as if she needed to know that someone else had seen the good in Daddy. "In all honesty, Nancy, I could not have asked for a better father—during the times he was a father. But I'm not as lucky as you. I can't blind myself to the bad in Daddy. I've accepted the bad because I love him, but I can't pretend it doesn't exist."

"I guess that's what I'm doing, pretending. But it makes me feel better. The day I stop pretending, I have to face what I don't want to face."

"What is that?" I asked.

Nancy's expression never wavered. "That you crucified him. You nailed him to the cross."

Her words stung like the lashes of a whip. We all accept as best we can, and for Nancy, I think, acceptance lay on the shadow side of denial.

Steve asked me to marry him, and I accepted. He'd been a serene and constant friend during the worst days of my life; he had saved me. I loved him for that, but more, I loved him for who he was and how happy I knew we'd be. We moved to Baton Rouge together on February 25. We combined our money and bought a lovely house in Denham Springs on the outskirts of town. Before leaving, I drove past the house on Citrus Road. The boarded windows of the library looked menacing in contrast to the otherwise beautiful lines of the spacious home. The bushes and foliage, once so carefully maintained, had grown untended, the grass covered here and there by winter leaves. To the rear of the property I could see the tall, stately river birch that stood beside the stables, its skeletal branches lifted toward the wintry sky. I wondered if the tree had shed its leaves, as it did every winter without fail, upon the rooftop of the stables where George Westerfield had fallen in the last, brief moment of his life.

CHAPTER 41

SHIRLEY

March 1, the deadline for Daddy's appeal, was only a week away. I could not continue to live with my feelings of guilt. It was time to get on with my life. I told myself again and again that it was almost over, that he'd received life imprisonment because he'd deserved it, that the burden was now on someone else's shoulders, not mine. But I didn't quite believe that. I had never really given up on my father, not after Mike's death, or after Daddy's arrest, not even at the trial when I'd attempted to speak with him. I loved him—it was as simple as that—and my loyalty to him ran deep. I was drawn to him as if by a magnet, and the feeling was so intense that I didn't try to kid myself any longer. I had to see him one more time. I had known it even at that horrible scene at the trial. I had to say good-bye. I had no doubt that it would be the last time.

I wondered if the police would take him to jail immediately if his appeal was denied. If that was the case, Daddy wouldn't take the chance. If they tried to take him to prison, he would either commit suicide or arrange for somebody else to kill him. I believed what he'd told me the last time I'd seen him before the trial. *I'll have to die; there's no other way out for Marty.* And for a man like Daddy, death would be a more tender mercy than facing the embarrassment of prison.

So I drove to his house, determined to face him one more time. I stepped up on the brick porch and rang the bell. Fortunately, the gate on the right side of the driveway had been left open, so it had been easy to gain

entrance to the drive. I glanced over my shoulder uneasily at the overgrown bushes and shrubs lining the
drive, afraid that Marty might be lurking somewhere.

The house had a closed, neglected appearance. After
several minutes it became obvious that no one was going to answer the bell. As I drove away, I felt cheated,
and it angered me to realize that I was now an outcast
here, the enemy.

I was unable to put him out of my mind. I drove by
the house on Citrus Road often, in hope of catching a
glimpse of him in the front yard, but he was never
outside. I finally decided to call him on the telephone. I
dialed the number, very apprehensive. I knew I wanted
to talk to him. I wanted to say good-bye. I wanted one
last memory to cherish. Whether he actually killed himself or languished in prison for the rest of his life, I knew
this encounter would be the last private conversation
we would ever have. I desperately needed to tell him
that I loved him, that despite it all, I could forgive him. I
wasn't sure how to say all that. I was afraid.

Marty answered the phone and I almost hung up
without identifying myself.

"It's Shirley. Is my father there?"

There was a long silence. My palms started sweating.
Then she spoke, her voice cold. "Your father doesn't
want to speak to you."

"Let *him* tell me how he feels," I insisted. "I just want
to talk to him." If my father told me to go away, that he
never wanted to see me again, I would give up. But I
wasn't going to let Marty keep us apart. I had allowed
that to happen in the past, and I was determined it
wouldn't happen now.

"Haven't you done enough? There's nothing to say.
You've killed him; that says it all."

I had a sickening feeling of déjà vu. Something was
terribly wrong. I could tell by the tone of her voice; it
was almost challenging. Her words chilled me. *You've
killed him; that says it all.*

"Put him on the phone, just once, please." I pleaded

with her, but I was beyond caring about my own pride.
"Please, Marty—"

"Go to hell!"

I heard the phone slam on the other end of the line. I
didn't know what else to do, so I got in my car and drove
past the house on Citrus Road. Marty's Cougar was
parked in the driveway, but Daddy's blue Thunderbird
was gone. I supposed he wasn't home. I tried to remember if the Thunderbird had been parked there when I
had rung the bell a few days earlier, but I wasn't sure. At
the time I hadn't thought to look for it.

For a week I repeatedly tried calling, but either
Marty hung up the telephone when she heard my voice
or no one answered. I cruised by the house daily, but
there was no sign of Daddy. It wasn't long before I
realized that I would never be able to talk to him or see
him again.

Daddy's appeal date came and went. The newspapers
gave no information on the outcome of the appeal, and
I thought maybe Daddy had received an extension of
some sort. I hated knowing so little of what was happening; after all, we had done everything possible to help
the police and Tom Porteous win the case against
Daddy, and now we were left in the dark. I assumed
that Daddy was still in his self-imposed exile on Citrus
Road.

On March 18 my best friend, Sally Lincks, came over
to Mama's for a small get-together to celebrate her boyfriend's birthday. Andy Fath, who had been dating Sally
for years, was a likable guy with dark hair and soft
brown eyes. He had also been a friend of mine for many
years. Sally and Andy had remained steadfast throughout the trial. We sat in the living room, discussing old
times and catching up on the latest gossip.

At eight-thirty that evening the doorbell rang. I answered it and found myself face-to-face with Sergeant
Walter Gorman. Under the yellow porch light his features were unusually pale in contrast to his dark cloth-

ing. This couldn't be good. I studied him in silence for a moment before inviting him inside.

Sally and Andy rose to their feet when Sergeant Gorman and I came into the living room. There was an awkward, quiet moment as I waited for Gorman to speak. Ray stood up and offered Sergeant Gorman his hand.

Gorman asked me, "Is your mother home?"

I headed toward the den. "Follow me."

Mama had been watching television and looked every bit as surprised as I must have as she greeted Sergeant Gorman. We waited for Gorman to explain, but all he said was, "Mrs. Fagot, I'd like to talk to you in private, if you don't mind."

"Well, of course," said mama. She sent me away with an apologetic look.

I had been dreading this, but it had surely been coming. I knew what Sergeant Gorman was going to say. I joined the others in the living room. I returned the sympathy and questions in their faces with shrugs.

A few minutes later Mama called Ray into the den. I could hardly stay still. I got up and paced the wooden floor from one end of the room to the other, once every few trips stopping to gaze out of the bay window overlooking the front yard.

Ray finally came out from the den, with a sad, shocked expression. "Something's happened," I said.

He nodded and waved me into the den. Sergeant Gorman stood against the bar.

"What is it?" I asked.

"I'm sorry, Shirley, but I don't know any way to soften this. We found your father's body in the trunk of his Thunderbird at the Holiday Inn parking lot on the I-10 service road. Apparently it had been there for some time. We've identified the body; there's no doubt that it is your father."

"No!" I sobbed, "Please . . ." My worst fear and secret suspicion had become a reality. All I could say over and over again, was, "No, no, no . . ." Daddy was gone.

Gone forever. I refused to accept it. Then, quickly, the anger set in. The denial.

Mama, in a broken whisper, said, "What happened?"

"We're not really sure, but we do know that he's been missing since March third. I just don't know where he was between the time of his disappearance and the discovery of his body."

"I appreciate your consideration in telling us," Mama replied.

He nodded once to me then turned to leave.

I thought of Daddy's body lying in the trunk of his car, the familiar face I'd loved, frozen in death. I imagined the trunk closing on his limp form. I wondered how on earth he had managed to close the trunk without the aid of someone else. But most of all, I thought of Marty, alone now in the house that she had always coveted, that she had planned to one day make her own. I couldn't stop crying—loud, racking sounds from the center of my soul. Daddy, I thought, why? Why has it come to this?

My guests rose to their feet. Sally held me for a moment.

"We've got to tell your sisters," Mama said. "How can I tell them this?"

We both knew there was no way for us to ease the blow, no way to deflect the pain this would bring.

Sally and Andy offered to stay at the house with Holly while we went to tell the others. First Mama called Carol at her new home in Baton Rouge. There was no answer, so we decided to go to Nancy's apartment. Mama and I both cried so many tears on the ride, and poor Ray tried everything he could think of to comfort us. The simple truth was there could be no comfort. We had all been crying for months, nonstop it seemed, and this, I had to pray, was the end of it. We arrived at Nancy's building and knocked on her door. Ray tried to take control of the situation, greeting Nancy when she opened the door, leading the way inside. But it was obvious to her that something was wrong.

Nancy was alarmed. "What is it?"

"Something's happened, Nancy," Mama began. My heart was breaking. I knew what she would say next and how it would tear Nancy's world apart. "Your father is dead. They found his body in the trunk of his car at the Holiday Inn parking lot by Causeway Boulevard."

Nancy didn't look as if she understood. She made an abrupt about-face, leaving the room without a word. Mama followed her. Ray and I sat on the sofa, not sure how to react to Nancy. Mama returned to us a minute later, Nancy behind her with, oddly enough, a tray of beverages in her hand. She set the tray down on the coffee table and passed a glass of iced tea to each of us. She held her glass, stunned, immobile until she finally broke the strange silence. "Do Joanne and Carol know yet?"

"Not yet. We're going to Joanne's from here. Would you like to come with us?" Mama asked.

"No. I want to be alone right now."

We were afraid to leave Nancy in her condition, but we had to get to Joanne's house before the news came on the television. Mama got up, but hesitated. "Are you sure?"

"Yes. I'll be okay. Call me later."

Joanne had some old family friends over for the evening when we arrived. It would be hard to do this in front of others—so much of our lives had been public lately—but it had to be done, and, thank God, they were close to us.

Mama explained what had happened, and though Joanne did not cry, she seemed as shocked and unbelieving as the rest of us. Joe came to her side and held her close. How would Joanne cope with this new tragedy? Deep down, had she been expecting something like this, just as I had? When Joe released her, Joanne buried her face in her hands. It tortured me to see her grief so plainly displayed. Joanne had always been the strong one, and to see her in such obvious anguish was a shock to me. But I also knew she'd been holding back her emotions throughout this ordeal. In a way it was a relief to see her release her heart so. Mama approached her and held her, while Joe hovered over them both. My tears started afresh, and I turned to Ray, clutching him tightly as I sobbed uncontrollably. Joanne reached out her hand to me, and I held it in mine.

"I knew it would come to this," Joanne said, her voice muffled. "Just when we thought it was over, that we could finally start a new life. I thought I'd be glad if he ever died. I thought he deserved to die for what he did to George. But all I feel now is emptiness and pain, as if a part of me just died."

"I know, Joanne," Mama said. "Many times I wished he were dead myself." She paused. "Now I know better. I loved him for twenty-five years. There's no point in pretending I didn't care. What we have to do now is look toward the future. There is no other choice."

When we got back to Mama's, she tried Carol again. It was almost ten. The news would carry the story of Daddy's death within fifteen minutes. Steve answered, and Mama told him everything, asking that he be the one to tell Carol. Steve, a capable and kind person, would handle things better than she possibly could at this point.

Mama sat, the phone cradled to her ear, apparently holding to speak to Carol. I watched her cry, her hand pressed to her mouth in an attempt to stifle her emotions. "I don't know what to say, except that I'm sorry, Carol."

Listening to Mama's words, I realized that *sorry*, that useless word that gives no hope and changes nothing, would undoubtedly be the way we'd all feel for the rest of our lives. And I knew that Carol's guilt would be the hardest to bear.

Mama, Ray, and I sat in the den waiting for the ten P.M. news broadcast. None of us wanted to watch the program, but we simply couldn't turn our eyes away.

Daddy's blue Thunderbird appeared on the TV screen, surrounded by a swarm of police officers in the

Holiday Inn parking lot. A white van marked "Jefferson Parish Sheriff's Office" was parked near it, doors open. I shuddered at the sight of a dark body bag being lifted into the van. Was it truly Daddy's body in that bag, or was it maybe some other unfortunate victim who had been chosen to take his place? What secrets, along with his mortal remains, would go with Daddy to his grave?

The Jefferson Parish coroner appeared on camera. Daddy's death, he stated flatly, appeared to be an execution-style killing. He went on to say that the victim had been shot in the head with a large-caliber weapon, but that no gun had been recovered at the scene. He added that the absence of blood in the trunk indicated that the victim had been shot elsewhere and then placed in the trunk of the car. The coroner's office, he told the reporter, would be working in close conjunction with the Jefferson Parish sheriff's office in the investigation of the case.

The WLTV anchorman returned on the screen. "Thus ends the story of the marine war hero who returned home, took a law degree, amassed a fortune, and then became the storm center of one of the most bizarre criminal cases in memory."

I wondered how Daddy would have felt all those years ago, when his future had been bright with promise, to know that one day his whole life would be summed up in one sentence of television coverage.

CHAPTER 42

CAROL

I am floating on soft, billowy clouds. So peaceful, so serene. There is a face hovering just above the clouds. A face that glows with radiant light. A face that smiles at me. The smile is sweet and tender; it fills me with a warm glow. The face beckons to me. I yearn to touch that face. I long so badly to touch it that I reach out my hand. But as I do, the face begins to first dissolve, then change. I watch as the once benevolent face turns into a horrible parody of what it had been only seconds before. The smiling lips turn into a cruel sneer; the loving eyes turn cold and menacing. Then it speaks. "Look at me. Look what you've done to me. I'm dead. Daddy's dead because you killed me." I feel wetness on my face. Where did it come from? Rough hands shake me. Who is shaking me? Why? A second voice comes from nowhere. "Carol, Carol, wake up. You're dreaming." The voice is persistent. Why won't it leave me alone? "Carol, baby, please wake up." The voice is pulling me, tugging at me, sucking me from some dark vortex.

I opened bleary eyes to find there was another face before me. It was Steve's face. He gathered me in his arms. "Oh, Carol, baby. I'm sorry, so sorry. I promise you, everything will be alright."

But he was wrong. Daddy was dead, and so long as I lived, nothing would ever be right again.

It was Sunday, the day after Daddy had died, and I had not stopped crying. I wondered if I would ever stop. In the house on St. Paul Avenue, Nancy, too, was crying, as was Shirley. Even Mama cried. Joanne shed not a tear. Kelly and Lori cried, asking all about their Paw-Paw's death. Joanne answered their questions as best she could, but they were young and couldn't fully understand the truth. Bruce and Kim cried, as well. My children should have been a comfort to me, but they were not. My son sat beside me on the sofa, his beautiful, deep blue eyes filled with pain. He leaned his head against my shoulder, but I had no comfort to give him. When he spoke to me, saying, "When I grow up, I'm going to be a marine just like Paw-Paw," I could only remember Mama's words to me. *Carol, all children need heroes.* My daughter stood before me, blue eyes bright with tears, and asked, "Is Paw-Paw an angel now?" I nodded my head. I knew that if Daddy was anything at all now, he was not an angel.

Marty made all of Daddy's funeral arrangements. We were not told anything. Mama's friend George Whitlow called to say that he'd learned Daddy's wake would be held on Sunday night. A stampede of wild horses could not have driven me there.

We found out from a newspaper article that Daddy's funeral would be held on Monday morning at the Garden of Memories in Metairie. Nancy, Joanne, Shirley, and I decided to attend the funeral, but Mama declined. It was not her place to attend, or so she said. On our way out the door she hugged each of us in turn. "I love you," she said. "I'll be there with you in spirit. I'll be praying for you."

CHAPTER 43

CAROL

"There is nothing more final than death, Carol," my father once said to me. As I stood now before his flag-draped coffin, his words came back to haunt me. The raw, gaping hole in the earth ready to accept his mortal remains bore mute witness to the wisdom of his words.

He died a violent death, and his casket was sealed at the wake. Despite the reassurance of those in authority that there was positive identification of his body, I couldn't shake the irrational fear that it wasn't my father in the coffin, after all.

He was a man of many faces, an enigma, a clever mystery offering the subtlest of clues. A master of manipulation, he wielded control and instilled fear in all of us. Yet even now there are many who cannot believe he was anything other than the generous, intelligent achiever they thought they knew. Some will remember only the distinguished war hero, others the successful attorney, dutiful son, and doting father of four. They are the lucky ones, these nonbelievers who have insulated themselves from the brutal reality. We, his children, have not been afforded the comfort of such options. We have seen the face of our father stripped of its many disguises, and in seeing have been robbed of all illusion.

The obituary notice in the New Orleans *Times-Picayune* stated that my father, Leonard John Fagot, was survived by his mother, Ruby Fagot; his beloved wife, Marta Courtney Fagot; his brothers and sisters; and a host of nieces and nephews. There was no mention of the four children and seven grandchildren he left behind. But we do exist. There are ties that bind us more surely than the bonding of flesh and blood. The obituary was just one more falsehood in a tightly woven tapestry of untruths.

The young widow in blue was comforted by her parents. Her face had the best of all disguises, blandness. She was aloof, detached, and she seemed to revel in being center stage. She never glanced our way, but it seemed to me from the flush of anger in her cheeks that she was aware of our presence.

Although my mother understandably chose not to attend, there was consolation in the knowledge that her love was with my sisters and me. We took comfort, too, in the small circle of friends and loved ones who stood with us. Their unwavering support helped ease the pain. There is a need to lay the blame at someone's feet, and we were the likely choice.

In the background a priest droned words of comfort and solace, but they were empty words. He mentioned the word *forgiveness*. I hoped to one day feel it in my heart. Beyond him, a Marine Corps officer issued the command to fire. Seven marines in dress blues lifted rifles toward the gray winter sky and fired. The command to fire came again, then a third time, and the last of twenty-one volleys resounded in salute to the marine war hero deserving of the honor. The haunting strains of "Taps" echoed mournfully through the cemetery. With crisp precision the American flag was folded and placed into the waiting hands of the widow.

A friend offered each of us a red rose, pressing it gently into our hands. Together we took the few steps closer to the coffin. Beside me, Joanne, the firstborn, seemed stoic as ever, but the trembling of her body betrayed her emotions. No doubt she was remembering another funeral eight years earlier. I know that for Joanne, Daddy had died a long time ago.

Along with my father I buried a part of myself, the young girl inside of me who once loved and honored him above all others. Nancy, two years younger than me, stumbled, then righted herself. She seemed dazed. In her eyes was the look of one who has seen everything, but understands nothing.

Shirley, the youngest, clutched the rose in her hand, oblivious to the prick of thorns against her palm. A breeze touched her light brown hair. Hesitantly she approached the gleaming coffin, nearing the final truth she had not been able to face. I realized in that instant that she finally accepted what cannot be changed: Daddy was gone forever.

"Ashes to ashes, dust to dust . . ." intoned the priest as Shirley dropped the rose, watching it slip through her fingers before it landed on the sleek, glossy lid of the coffin below.

At the last there were only four roses resting upon steel gray.

EPILOGUE

CAROL

The autopsy performed on my father's body raised more questions than it ever resolved. The pathologist was able to determine that Daddy had been dead at least five or six days prior to the discovery of his body in the trunk of his car. He had been shot at close range in the right temple with a thirty-eight-caliber weapon, and the damage had been so extensive that it was virtually impossible to tell if the wound had been self-inflicted.

One interesting fact that did emerge during the postmortem examination was that although scar tissue indicative of an old heart attack was found, it pointed to a relatively mild attack, one not nearly as severe as he'd pretended all along. For years he'd faked those angina attacks, staging them at the most opportune moments. He'd used those attacks to ensure our sympathy and concern. I'd struggled with myself for years, not wanting to believe that he would use us that way, but suspecting that he was. In an odd way I was relieved to know that I had not suspected him unjustly. At the same time it hurt me to realize that Daddy had found it necessary to resort to such measures. It seems impossible that he would have been that uncertain of our love for him. Or maybe he'd simply relished the drama of an audience. He was undeniably a marvelous actor, the silver-tongued devil himself.

In the days following Daddy's death a search warrant was issued for the premises on Citrus Road. The objective of that warrant was to find a weapon, ammunition, household items or clothing containing bloodstains or soil, and insurance policies in Daddy's name. While neither a weapon nor bloodstained items were found, several insurance policies, totaling one-point-two million dollars, were. Two of the policies listed Marta Courtney Fagot as beneficiary. Daddy had left a will, in which he stipulated that Roy Price be left as executor of his estate and that Marty be coexecutrix. He also stipulated that two thirds of everything he'd possessed was to go to his children. It's impossible to say whether he would have left anything to us, much less two thirds of what he had, were it not for the fact that Louisiana law required that he do so. His will further stipulated that the remaining one third of his estate was to go to Marty, including the entire contents of the house on Citrus Road. He also bequeathed ten thousand dollars to his sister Lacey Bayard, and left a small rental home he owned on Banks Street in New Orleans to his sister Valerie Schanzbach. While I had expected that Daddy would leave Marty very well cared for, I hadn't expected that he'd leave her the contents of the house we had grown up in. When she eventually had to move, she took with her everything—boxes of precious family photographs, high school diplomas, children's books—things that couldn't have meant anything to her but meant everything to us. I feel certain that Daddy had left everything to her to hurt us, and he surely succeeded.

For months after Daddy died, I saw him in everything I did, and everywhere I went, even as I slept. I would suddenly spot a tall, lean man with glasses and a wayward lock of hair that fell across his forehead, and a feeling of complete and utter joy would pierce me: For a split second I believed that man to be Daddy; I believed it with all my heart. More often than not the stranger, apparently aware of me, would give me the odd look I deserved. Embarrassed, I'd turn away, feeling foolish, sad, and lost. By night I fell victim to horrifying nightmares in which I'd come across Daddy in an open meadow. My heart would fill with joy. Daddy's arms would open wide, and I'd run to him with arms outstretched. But my breath would catch in my throat as I'd draw near him and see the cold hatred in his eyes. His hand would go to the pocket of his windbreaker. A gun would appear, and he'd point it at me, his eyes like chips of ice, his lips curling in a sneer of hatred. In horror I'd whirl away from him, running across the meadow, waiting for the feel of the bullet as it entered my spine. Above the pounding of my heart and the rush of wind in my ears, I'd hear the sound of mocking laughter. I'd awaken to find the bed covers twisted around my legs, my body damp with perspiration.

I began to function like a robot; the simplest of daily chores became too much for me to cope with. I locked myself within my home, afraid to venture outside. I became paranoid, convinced that Daddy would seek revenge on me even from the grave. I was plagued by thoughts that maybe before he'd died, Daddy had hired a hit man.

I finally reached a point where, I feel certain, I lost my sanity. Things came to a head one day when Steve arrived home from work and found me, as usual, curled in a ball on my bed, staring blankly at the ceiling.

I sensed his presence and squeezed my eyes shut, willing him to disappear, just leave me alone. Instead, he crossed over to the bed and stroked my cheek. "He's dead, Carol. You have to bury him once and for all."

"People like Daddy don't die."

He gazed at me with serious green eyes. "All people die. He was just a man. You've turned him into something else."

"I'll never accept that he's gone. How can I, when he's always with me? Here, somewhere inside me."

"Of course he's still inside you, baby. He was too much a part of you to ever forget. I understand that. But try to remember the good. Try to remember that for a long time he did all he could for you, that he served his nation with honor and pride. That he loved you. Please, if you remember nothing else, at least remember this:

He gave you more than you know. He gave you qualities that make you what you are. You have a strength inside you, Carol, a conviction, and the courage to act on that conviction. You did the only thing you could have done. I believe that when all is said and done, your dad, in his heart, expected no less of you."

I guess I was ready to hear that, because that was the first step on my return to normal life. The rest of the family was having trouble, too. Joanne, who wore her denial of love for Daddy like a banner across her chest, suffered terribly from ulcers. Nancy, consumed by sorrow and grief, had found her own way of coping. She'd made Daddy her own personal martyr. Just as I had once done, she found comfort in expounding his virtues and ignoring his vices. Shirley seemed, on the surface, not to be affected at all. But in the middle of light-hearted conversation a look would enter her eyes, a look that went deeper than mere sadness.

Mama had lived for years under stress, and it had taken a heavy toll on her physical well-being. She suffered from high blood pressure and bouts of anxiety. She had a severe heart attack. While she was in the intensive care unit of the hospital, Joanne and I discussed Mama's health with her doctor. Once we had filled the doctor in on all that Mama had endured, he nodded solemnly and offered a plausible explanation for her heart attack. He felt that Mama, and most likely the rest of us as well, suffered from post-delayed stress syndrome, a malady that often strikes combat veterans. It seems that each individual has a certain limit to the stress he or she can endure. During the time that one actually experiences a stressful situation, the body seems not to be affected, but when the body passes the limit, it begins to suffer a form of burnout. Through the seven years of excruciating stress we all endured, each of us had reached our stress peak. We burned out.

Because of some problems in the execution of the will, Marty was forced out of the house three years later.

The house was eventually put up for sale, but not until after it had fallen into ruin. The grass had grown to monstrous proportions; Daddy's prized flowers wilted and turned brown for lack of water. Paint was peeling under the eaves of the house, and the swimming pool had become stagnant and green from algae. Even so, Marty made a bid to buy it, at a cost much lower than its appraised value. Since we were in control of the sale, we rejected her offer with great relish. Although she was disappointed, Marty turned around and purchased a new home on the street behind the house on Citrus Road, which gave her a perfect view of the backyard of Daddy's house. It would seem that she just couldn't let the house go easily.

No information of value ever came to light that would aid in determining the circumstances of Daddy's death. How and where he died remains as much a mystery today as it was then. At the time he died, because he had been found in a locked car trunk in which there was no gun and little blood, the possibility that he had been murdered was obviously considered. Investigators were soon telling the press, however, that they had not ruled out the possibility of a suicide made to look like murder. Most of the Jefferson Parish police who were involved in the investigation eventually came to believe that Daddy killed himself, making his death appear a homicide. I have to admit that the drama surrounding his death has all the earmarks of a Leonard Fagot scam. The fact that he'd been missing for an indeterminate number of days, then was found in the trunk of his car; the inability of the medical examiner to pinpoint the time of death or whether or not the bullet wound had been self-inflicted; the unusual circumstances surrounding the discovery of his body—all of this added up to the kind of baffling mystery Daddy would have loved.

Undoubtedly, he was caught between a rock and a hard place. As an attorney he had to have realized that the odds were against his murder conviction getting reversed on appeal. Of one thing I am certain: He was not about to spend the rest of his life in prison, nor was he the type of man who would flee the country. He needed an out, and death is, if nothing else, a definite out. It's not hard for me to understand what a man of Daddy's caliber might do if faced with no acceptable alternative. He might hold a gun to his head and pull the trigger. In any event, if Daddy did commit suicide, he accomplished the goal he had recounted to Shirley: He died, and Marty went free. Because his appeal was still pending when Daddy died, the state supreme court vacated his conviction, and the charges against Marty were later dismissed. Now a jury will never get to decide whether or not she helped Daddy to change his clothes and shower after Mike was shot, thereby becoming an accessory after the fact in Mike's death.

As I look forward to the rest of my life, I've tried to make sense out of all that happened. I believe that the capacity for violence was always present in Daddy and the war just brought that capacity to the surface. Somewhere on a bloody battlefield, where human beings die with no more dignity than a dog on the side of the road, that taste for violence within Daddy reared its ugly head and stared him right in the face. His personal satisfaction came from the thrill of the hunt, and the closing in for the kill. He emerged from that war not only alive, but a hero, with a finely honed instinct for self-preservation. In decorating a hero, the military had also spawned a killer.

At the war's end he'd wanted nothing so much as to recapture the tastes of triumph and power he'd had. He was hooked on them, I think. So he sought another challenge, a challenge of enormous proportions. He set his goals on a law degree. It was a long battle of a new kind, and Daddy won again. He became a successful lawyer. But at the pinnacle of his success, at the age of forty-seven, he gave up his practice. The challenge was gone; there was no opposition to overcome.

Then Joanne married George Westerfield. George Westerfield was opposition, and the plotting and carrying out of a perfect murder was most definitely a challenge. Next he'd shot off his hand and ripped out his eye, filing an insurance claim for both accidents. He'd flaunted a challenge to the insurance companies. "Catch me, if you can," he seemed to be saying. They hadn't been able to, of course; there had been no proof. While he'd had to settle for only a portion of the insurance money, once again he'd come out on top. He'd pitted himself against the system and had walked away with another notch in his belt.

Perhaps the greatest challenge of his life had been Mike Holland. There was a young man who could not be manipulated, who could not be taken in, despite Daddy's attempts. Unfortunately for Daddy, he had not taken into consideration that he and Mike had one thing in common. Neither could stand to be bested. Each had used common ground, me, as leverage in a game called winning. The game had ended in a tie. Daddy had succeeded in drawing first blood, but if the dead are able to laugh, Mike definitely had the last laugh. Mike had been as much the undoing of Daddy as Daddy had been the undoing of Mike. The prize for both had been the grave.

Those of us who survived are not the only ones who have been left with scars. When my daughter Kim turned fifteen, I felt the time had come to tell her the truth about her parentage. I'd wrestled with myself for so long, wondering if I should always keep it to myself. The Applegarths, who'd learned the truth years earlier, had refused to acknowledge the news. They considered Kim their own, and loved her accordingly. It would have been easy to let things stay that way, but I had taken the easy way out too many times in the past. I loved Kim, and honesty had always played an integral part in our relationship. One day she might discover the truth on her own. It seemed best that the truth come from me.

She was in her bedroom studying when I approached her. She'd grown into a lanky, long-legged teenager, with thick, wavy hair and bright blue eyes the same shade as Mike's. "Kim," I began. "So many things have happened over the years, things that I've tried to protect you from. I think the time has come for you to know and try to understand some of those things."

"Did you love my father?" she asked softly.

I was floored. "Yes. Of course I did."

I thought she was talking about Bruce.

"I've known about Mike for a long time."

I felt suddenly flustered, as if she were the mother and I the child.

"I remember a lot about Mike," she said. "And I remember that I loved him. I guess I'm luckier than some kids: I have two Dads. Bruce and Mike. I only wish that Mike were alive. That Paw-Paw hadn't killed him."

My heart heavy with sorrow, I had to look at her, my own dear child, and say, "Me, too. And I would give anything in the world if only it weren't so."

I held her in my arms and rocked her as I had so many times when she'd been a small child, knowing that nothing would ever right the wrong that had been done her.

In the spring of 1987 my son graduated from high school and announced his decision to join the Marine Corps. I begged him to reconsider, to attend college instead. He agreed to try it. That first semester of school he did surprisingly well, but then he failed his second semester. I sat him down and told him all of the things my dad had said to me—that he should try to make something of himself, try to succeed; that without a college education his opportunities for employment would be limited. Then he hit me with what I'd known all along would come one day. "Mom, I'm going to join the Marine Corps. I'm a man now, and I have to do what's right for me."

I gazed at him and saw that he was right. My son had grown into an incredibly handsome young man, strong, proud, and independent. I wouldn't stand in his way, but I needed to know why he had made his decision.

"Why the Marine Corps, Bruce?"

He rose from his chair and left the room, returning a moment later with a battered, black photo album. He sat down beside me and opened the album. Glued to the pages were dozens of newspaper clippings, all yellow with age. An old, familiar sadness rose in me as I gazed at that old album. Bruce pointed to one of the clippings. Emblazoned across the top of the clipping in black type were the words "Fagot Awarded the Silver Star."

"Paw-Paw won that for running a gauntlet not once, but six times. He was wounded from shrapnel, but he kept on going. He saved those men's lives. Paw-Paw did a lot of bad things, Mom, but he also did a lot of good ones. I'm doing this in memory of the good things. In memory of the marine he was. And if I have a son of my own, I hope he'll grow up wanting to keep that memory alive, wanting to keep the Marine Corps a family tradition."

Two weeks later Bruce became a soldier in the United States Marine Corps. He returned twelve weeks after that from basic training, wearing his dress blues. He stood tall and proud, and my heart swelled with pride. I felt a catch in my throat as I observed how very much he resembled Daddy. Though Bruce's features were softer and more refined than Daddy's had been, my son had the same proud bearing, the same leanly muscled frame and strong jawline of his grandfather. In my heart I knew that Daddy would have been very proud of his grandson.

Of the three men in my life who have died, there seems little left but memories. Memories and three graves—one in Gretna, where George is buried; one in Natchez, where Mike is buried; and one on Airline Highway in the Garden of Memories, where Daddy lies. Though I have visited George's grave on occasion, I have never been to Mike's. I mean no disrespect. I just can't bring myself to lay my burden of sorrow and guilt at his feet, when I know it is the last thing Mike would want of me.

For the longest time I would not visit Daddy's grave. I could not overcome the irrational feeling that he might reach out from that grave and strike me to the ground. It has only been in recent years that I've mustered the courage to go. And even those infrequent visits on Father's Day leave me drained.

Nancy, who goes often, has noticed, as I have, the absence of flowers on Daddy's grave. It seems obvious that those who professed to love him most and who defended him to the bitter end have come to the conclusion that some things *are* best forgotten.

Thick saint augustine grass covers his grave. His gravestone is set flush into the ground. It is made of black marble, embossed with gold lettering that reads:

Leonard J. Fagot
April 24, 1923–March 18, 1978
World War II
U.S.M.C.
SEMPER FI

As I stand before Daddy's grave, I feel humble and exposed, much as I did in his presence when he was alive. There are so many things I never said to him, and I pray God that he is somehow able to understand that I loved him, as I always will, with a purity and passion. That I am deeply sorry his life turned out so badly, and that I would gladly give my own life if it would change all that has been. That I have finally learned how to forgive. And that if he was wrong, then so was I—because I never had the courage to tell him that he'd left me no choice but to do what I did. I pray that he knows he has two new grandsons, Shane and Stevie, as well as a great-grandson, Spencer, Kelly's child, and how much a part of each of us he will always be. Mostly I pray that he has found peace, the one thing that eluded him all of his life.

The gravesite ritual is always the same for me. I lay flowers at his feet—an offering, a small token of respect, and the only thing left I can give. Upon leaving the cemetery, I invariably head for Citrus Road. It seems a part of my odyssey, somehow.

The house remains unchanged, a reality born of dreams, tall, stately, proud—much like the man who built it. Across the sweeping expanse of green lawn I see a man. A lean, handsome man with sunlight gleaming on his bronzed shoulders. The man is surrounded by four blond-haired little girls, his daughters, whom he adores. Ghost visions. Maybe one day those visions will disappear, and I will be able to look upon that house as only a structure made of wood, and brick, and glass. For now it's Paradise Lost, and too much a part of me still.